Using Money Wisely

Gladwin B. Williams BSc. (Economics),
MA (Banking & Finance)

Front cover designed by Raule A. Williams, MD.

Second Edition Printed and published in 2015 by CreateSpace, 1200 12th Ave South, Suite 1200, Seattle, WA 98144, USA

Front cover photograph downloaded from Microsoft Clip Gallery

ISBN-13: 978-1515047919

ISBN-10: 1515047911
Title ID: 5614293

To order additional copies, please contact us.

CreateSpace, 1200 12th Ave South, Suite 1200, Seattle, WA 98144, USA www.createspace.com

1-866-6308-6235

To order additional copies, please contact us.

www.createspace.com

Table of Contents

Caps were used to begin words such as His and You as far as possible, when referring to Jehovah, the Holy Spirit and Jesus, while common letter were used for satan and the devil.

DEDICATION

Dedicated to our son, Mr. James B. Williams – *'son of my right hand,' I love you guy – continue to fan the flame of excellence, we are proud of you.*

ACKNOWLEDGEMENT

Sincere appreciation is expressed to my precious children, Raule, Paul, James and Candace; my mom, Uranie; brothers, Frank and Oliver; in-laws and their families and the numerous other persons who have contributed in some way to the completion and publication of this book. This includes Sisters Patricia Crichlow, Susana Grant and Michael Ifill who have spent valuable time and energy in proof reading the manuscripts of this book. Most importantly, all praise and glory belong to my Provider, Jehovah-Jireh.

INTRODUCTION

This book reviews many of the prudent Biblical financial, managerial and other principles which have been successfully used by millions of persons to liberate themselves from the oppression of living a sub-optimum life of their full potential. It must be stated from the onset that the Bible does not offer a quick fix strategy to become rich financially, morally, spiritually or in any other way. This issue has caused one of the greatest divisions within Christianity and between Christianity and other religions. Among Christianity, one school contends that the Lord has not provided any guarantee that all of His followers will attain abundant material wealth. Other Christians contend that the poorer we are on earth, the greater will be our reward in Heaven. Another debate is that Christianity has not stood out as a religion where there is a high percentage of very wealthy persons who claim that they acquired material wealth as a result of applying Christian principles to their personal and/or other sources of wealth.

Chapter 1 reviews some of the primary financial management principles which are highlighted in the Bible. Prudent financial strategies which we should follow are detailed extensively in the Bible. A review is also conducted on some of the reasons why money plays such a primary role in our lives as individuals, the economy of a country and internationally. Money is identified as a primary asset which influences the standard of living that we enjoy 'from the cradle to the grave.' The financial strength of a family will, for example determine the nutritional start which a baby enjoys and also the environment in which he grows, which will in turn influence his intellectual ability, the school he attends, the financial and economic conditions under which he lives. It is also true that one's genetic and other inmate disposition, and the social environment to which a person is exposed also has a profound influence on his future. However, there are several examples in the Bible and throughout the ages, where it can identify that the intervention of the Lord changed the direction of the lives of a large number of persons.

Chapter 1 also reviews issues surrounding the principles of tithing and offering. Here again, there is much controversy surrounding these principles, where some Christians advocate that these principles are only practiced rigidly during the Old Testament era, hence, we should not be dogmatic in their practiced today. Other Christians contends that these practices were not abolished but are also observed during the New Testament. A review is also conducted on some of the popular doctrines which are common in Christian circles. They include the 'Prosperity doctrine' which has been popularized by preachers such as Kenneth Copland and Creflo Dollar, who advocate, among other doctrines, that Christians have a right to be rich, since our Heavenly Father owns the world and everything that is in it. Conversely, there are the more moderate preachers who advocate that Christians are not guaranteed wealth, instead our emphasis should be on spreading the gospel, being aware that we will face prosecution. Therefore, we should be prepared to forsake earthly wealth, if necessary, to spread the Word of God.

Chapter 2 reviews some of the methods which persons employ to acquire and manage material resources. Many persons devote much time and attention to acquiring as much wealth as they can, very often exploiting others and sacrificing their health, family life and other important relationships and assets, merely to be wealthy. Even though they may perform good deeds such as helping the poor, many of these persons die without a feeling of fulfillment since their wealth did not bring them much happiness and more importantly, they did not fulfill their spiritual obligations. This chapter also reviews the importance of allocating our time and other assets in a manner which maximizes their use.

Chapter 3 discusses the subject of debt management which is topical from the poorest to the richest societies. It is very important that Christians are the masters of debt, rather than its servants. Failure to manage debt has resulted in the enslavement of the debtor by the creditor even today. As a matter of fact, a BBC documentary recently focused on the lives of an entire African tribe which was enslaved by another tribe since the fore-parents of the slaves were unable to pay the debt owed to the other tribe. The slaves are hoping to raise enough money to be able to repay this debt and secure their freedom. Even though debt does not result in physical slavery to persons in most societies, it is still a fulfillment of the Biblical pronouncement of the debtor being a 'slave' to the creditor because of the struggles which most debtors experience as they attempt to secure the credit facilities.

Chapter 4 reviews fundamental principles of saving and investing which are important in most society to enable persons as they seek to improve their standard of living and cater to their short, medium and long term needs. It is true that some persons become 'rich overnight' by receiving an inheritance, a huge promotion, highly successful business and, for the non-Christian, from winning a large lottery or bingo jackpot, the sale of narcotics and/or illegal weapons. However, for most Christians the process of acquiring and expanding wealth is usually achieved over a number of years of saving and investing prudently. Therefore, the content of this chapter is vital.

Chapter 5 presents a micro perspective of financial management as it relates to budgeting and the management of personal and family budget. The failure to manage personal finances and family budget are primary factors which contribute to the disintegration of many families. Many persons do not have the financial discipline to formulate a well structured budget and to live within the confines of the budget. Failure to manage the budget adversely impacts on our ability to save and invest, hence, millions of persons live in poverty or have to depend on the assistance of the state, relatives and charitable organizations for their maintenance after retirement. It is true that very often even the best human plan fails, however, the following maxim is also true: 'failure to prepare is to prepare for failure'.

Chapter 6 reviews issues surrounding important area of choosing and pursuing a beneficial career path. Far too many persons are forced into a career by one or both parents and/or other persons to fulfill the dreams and aspirations. There are also many persons who peruse a given career primarily because of the financial rewards and/or other benefits which are associated with it. As Christians, our primary choice of a career should be in conformity with the perfect will of the Lord for our lives. Therefore it is important that parents, relatives other persons and the church as a corporate body assist our children and other persons to identify and pursue the career which they were created to fulfill.

Chapter 7 presents a summary of some of the important factors which must be considered when a Christian embarks on a business venture. This is a continuation from the issues discussed in Chapter 6, since unless a person is called to be intimately involved in managing or even financing one or several business ventures, it is better to stay away from this activity. Increasingly, many Christians are becoming involved in business ventures, however, unless one is adequately prepared to manage the inevitable challenges which are confronted in managing a business, there is a high probability of failure of the business. We are reminded of the maxim which states that 'failure to prepare, is to prepare for failure.'

NOTES

****

Chapter 1: *ESTABLISHING AND MAINTAINING A GODLY FOUNDATION*

INTRODUCTION

There are several fundamental differences between a born again believer and the unsaved; the most basic of which is that the former is born of the Spirit of the Lord while the others are not. Being born again does not mean that we would not be confronted with most of the same challenges as the unsaved. As a matter of fact, we are not called into a life comfort in this world; instead, we are called into a life of war against the devil and his demons. The devil has unleashed his fiery darts which are aimed at destroying our faith in the Lord and win us back to himself. A Christian who does not experience any difficulty, who has found life to be 'easy sailing' has to be careful that he is really in right standing with the Lord. One sure test of our standing in the Lord which has been repeatedly pronounced on in the Bible is the fact that we will experience trials and testing. It is true that the Lord has promised us rest when we serve Him, but this is not a rest from testing, trials and temptation. This rest is more in the area of being more than conquerors and being able to withstand all the fiery darts of the devil, since we are trained to master the art of using the weapons of our warfare which He has given to us.

Some of the areas which the devil attacks us are in the area of our mind, where if we are not strong enough, we can experience problems in areas such as our mental and physical health, difficulties in our relationship with others and financial difficulties. Since this book is focused on financial management, the emphasis is on identifying the attacks of the devil in the area of financial management and the strategies which the Lord has given us to overcome these problems. It is noteworthy to state that even though the strategies to overcoming these difficulties may be different in specialized areas, the basic principles are that we have to spend quality time with the Lord, studying His Word and applying the relevant principles to our lives. We also have at our disposal prayer, praise and intercession, waiting on Him. We should also spend time listening to the instruction and teachings of persons who have the necessary experience and expertise in various aspects of financial management and apply prudent financial management principles in our personal and family life, businesses and further afield to achieve success in our financial and other undertakings.

| The importance of money |

"Is the love of money really the root of ALL evil?"

1 Timothy 6:10 states: **"¹⁰For the love of money is a root of all kinds of evil, and in their eagerness to be rich, some have wandered away from the faith and pierced themselves with many pains."** *(underline mine)*

The Kings James version states that: "The love of money is **the** root of all evil." This has caused some controversy since the former quote infers that the love of money is one of several evils, while the latter states that it is the only cause of evil. A compromise is usually presented that the principle of sin is one and the same in that the foundation is the disobedience to the teachings of Jehovah.

The Bible identifies three primary types of sin from which the others falls into, they are, **the pride of life**, the **lust of the eye** and the **lust of the flesh.**

Satan used this strategy when he deceived Eve and Adam to disobey Jehovah and eat the 'forbidden fruit'. In Genesis 3:4-6 Satan stated: **"⁴But the serpent said to the woman, "You will not die; ⁵for God knows that when you eat of it your eyes will be opened, and you will be like God, knowing good and evil." ⁶So when the woman saw that the tree was good for food, and that it was a delight to the eyes, and that the tree was to be desired to make one wise, she took of its fruit and ate; and she also gave some to her husband, who was wither and he eat."**

The three concepts of sins are illustrated by:

Type of Sin	Deception
Pride of life	• You will not die • You will be like God
Lust of the eye	• Your eyes will be opened • The tree was to be desired to make one wise
Lust of the flesh	• The tree was good for food

These three areas were illustrated in Satan's temptation of Jesus when he emerged from His forty days and forty nights of fasting in the wilderness. Matthew 4:3-4 states: **"³The tempter came and said to Him, "If you are the Son of God, command these stones to become loaves of bread." ⁴But He answered, "It is written, 'One does not live by bread alone, but by every word that comes from the mouth of God."**

This was Satan's attempt to cause Jesus to commit the sin of the **lust of the flesh**. Satan was appealing to the fact that Jesus was hungry in an attempt for him to produce bread in order to satisfy his natural desire to eat. It would have been easy for the average person to fall prey to the ploy of the Devil. Jesus saw through Satan's deception and shut him up with 'the Word'.

In the second temptation satan tried to persuade Jesus to throw Himself from a pinnacle of the temple of Jerusalem where Satan had taken Him, by quoting that Jehovah would send His angels to protect Jesus from hurting Himself. Even though Jesus was aware of this fact, Jesus rebuked satan and quoted that the Scriptures also instructs that no one, even the fallen angels should put Jesus to the test. This was a demonstration of the principle of the **pride of life**.

In the third temptation satan took Jesus to a high mountain and showed Him all of the kingdoms of the world. Satan told Jesus that he give Him all of the kingdoms of the world if Jesus would worship him. Jesus reminded satan that Jehovah was the only One to be worshipped. This was the temptation of the **pride of the eye**. Even though Jesus knew that satan had the authority over the kingdoms of the earth, His authority was superior to that of satan's.

Some of the categories of these three types of sin are as follows:

Lust of the Flesh	Pride of Life	Pride of the Eye
Sexual sins	Blasphemy	Envy
Gluttony	Idolatry	Hatred
Stealing	Boastfulness	Lust
Drunkenness	Arrogance	
Drug addiction	Selfishness	

Even though we may not be able to trace every sin to a monetary phenomenon, there is no doubt that the love of money can cause a person to exhibit all of the above sins.

> **Existing without money**

"Can we exist in this world without money?"

There are several items which are philosophized as being beyond the purchasing power of money. They include:

1. A baby's smile,
2. True happiness and contentment,
3. A home where love, peace and joy abound,

If we were to analyze the first example, several interesting observations can be made. The most likely conclusion would be that liquid money (such as notes, coins and checks) would not induce a baby's smile, unless someone playfully dangles it before the child's face, for example. Money is an essential requirement to purchase the necessities which will enable the child to be healthy and happy. Inducing a smile from a healthy child is usually easier than from a child who is dehydrated due to sickness or an acute shortage of water due to a drought, or from a child crying from hunger or sickness.

The Bible highlights several problems associated with managing money. They include 1Timothy 6:10, which states: **"¹⁰For the love of money is a root of all kinds of evil, and in their eagerness to be rich, some have wandered away from the faith and pierced themselves with many pains."**(underline mine)

This verse is often misinterpreted to infer that Christians should abandon all desire to accumulate material wealth, since it ultimately leads a person to focus so much on material possessions. They were afraid that they may become obsessed with acquiring and seeking to increase it, or that person's god, and would eventually force him to stop serving Jehovah. The verse rather decries the sin of **lusting** after wealth, which will cause persons to sell their very souls, in some instances, in an attempt to acquire wealth. In their **eagerness** to become wealthy, many persons have committed several sinful acts. The Lord does not dwell in the lives of such persons. It is rather healthy to have a **desire** to be wealth and seek to achieve this end by engaging in honest acts. Christians are not expected to be misers, as is portrayed in the life of the legendary Charles Dickens' character Mr. Scrooge. Neither are we to love money for the joy of having it, merely for the power that can be exerted over others when we have it. We should not indulge in sinful acts to obtain money, or to maintain and expand the amount which we have. Jesus himself admonished us in Matthew 22:21(b) that we should: **"²¹⁽ᵇ⁾..."Give therefore to the emperor the things that are the emperor's, and to God the** *things that are God's."*

From this verse we can infer that we should pay our taxes, contribute towards the development of society and be involved in other legitimate activities.

Unless we live in a society where barter (the exchange of goods and services without the use of money) is in operation, we need money (or at least a replica of money such as credit or debit card) to purchase the necessities of life. One can reflect on the lives of Monks, Yogi and Sages, for example, who often relinquish 'worldly' attachments to live a life of seclusion. However, for most of us, money plays an important part in our lives. We are reminded of Ecclesiastes 10:19[b] which states: *"19(b)......and money meets every need."*

The usage of money

"What are some of the reasons why we need money?"

There are several reasons why money is held:
1. Defraying everyday expenditures such as purchasing food and the payment of utility bills (*transactional*),
2. Financing emergencies such as sickness and bereavements (*precautionary*),
3. Savings for future needs such as the education of the children and to purchase a house (*store of value*),
4. Engaging in investments that have the potential to increase one's earning power in business ventures and investing on the stock market, for example (*for speculation*),
5. Conducting spiritual duties such as paying tithes and giving offering and helping the poor (**'Kingdom' business**). When preachers emphasize on the need for Christians to tithe and to give generous offering toward the proclamation of the gospel, many persons would make comments such as he is merely 'trying to full his own pocket.' This include construction of the church building and its upkeep, the payment of pastor and other staff in many ministries, support to missionaries and missions, purchase Bibles and other Christian literature and the support of social and other programs. Even though this might be a reality, in extreme examples, there is no doubt that the effective spreading of the gospel is expensive. The Lord has given us the mandate to finance the spreading of the gospel so that we can derive the rewards of giving to

the Lord's work.

A person who takes out an endowment life insurance policy, for example, may be more interested in catering for the financial needs of his/her family in the event of the serious incapacitation or death of the policyholder. Conversely, an investor on the stock exchange might be more interested in increasing wealth, although it is often used as a long-term investment. A common practice among many wealthy persons is to hold one or more bank accounts and investing in securities while they hold liquid cash, credit cards and/or check books to meet their daily expenditure.

A story is told of a woman who at was home alone when she saw three elderly strangers sitting outside of her home. Being a hospitable person, she went outside and invited them into the house so that she can offer them a meal. The men refused, stating that they could not enter the home of a married woman when she was at home by herself. When her husband returned from work he also invited them in and they refused. Feeling very offended at the refusal of his kindness he inquired from them what was the basis for their refusal. Before giving an explanation, of their action, the men told him that they usually do not enter a home together, and would only do this in the odd circumstance when the occupants of a home make what they have come to recognize as a most unpopular choice.

The strangers told the man of the house that their names were **Love, Wealth** and **Happiness,** and that the three of them would only enter the home of a family together if they chose the correct person to lead the way. Since he was a wise man, he requested that **Love** should come into the home first. With his choice, all three men got up and went into the home. They explained that it it if he had chosen **Wealth** in front of the others, then **Love** and **Happiness** would seldom follow since most couples who make this choice have their priorities mixed up, thus, the Lord would not be the centre of their lives. The men also explained that they did come into a home when the wife or the husband is at home alone, it usually causes dishonesty in a family. The contention is that if one spouse alone acquires **Wealth** without the other knowing the source, or if one is selfish and is not willing to share the wealth among loved ones and others, it usually causes enmity in the home. They also stated that many families choose **Wealth** first and the other two cannot enter the home since much strife would occur in a family which is disunited.

As Christians, we have several financial responsibilities:
1. **Spiritual Obligations** such as tithes and offering, helping the poor and needy as unto the Lord.
2. **Statutory Requirements to the government** such as income, corporate and property taxes, National Insurance and other government contributions from individuals and institutions.
3. **Personal and Family Obligations** such as budgeting wisely and spending accordingly, saving and investing for short, medium and long-terms goals.
4. **Contributing to the development of our society** such as being good corporate citizens.

Laying money at the apostle's feet

"Why did the believers place money at the apostles' feet?"

Many persons are of the opinion that money and material possessions should not be prominent in the lives of believers. For most of us money is very important in facilitating many of our daily transactions such as purchasing food, paying our utility bills and meeting medical and other expenses. As a part of the curse which Adam received from the Lord was that by the sweat of his brow, he would eat food. The 'sweat' in modern day is to earn a wage or salary, which is measured in monetary terms. There is also overwhelming evidence that money played an important role in the service of God. Acts 4:34-37, for example states: **"³⁴There was not a needy person among them, for as many as owned lands or houses sold them and brought the proceeds of what was sold. ³⁵They laid it at the apostles' feet, and it was distributed to each as any have need. ³⁶There was a Levite, a native of Cyprus, Joseph, to whom the apostles give the name Barnabas (which means son of 'encouragement'). ³⁷He sold a field that belonged to him, then brought the money, and laid it at the apostles' feet."**

Twice in this passage, it is stated that the money was placed at the feet of the apostles. Many persons find this practice offensive when it is done today. The question is why the money was not placed in an offering basket or in the pockets of the apostles. The explanation which is usually presented for this practice is that this was symbolizing that money to them was a tool and not their master. It does not mean that we should necessarily physically walk on the money, rather it enunciates the principle that we are not servants of money but rather that we are using it to take care of our needs and to bless others. Once we are faithful to the Lord with money, then it is often an indication that He will be able to trust us as channels into which He can pour more finance and other resources into our lives so that our needs can be met and we can be a source of blessings to others.

I have been to several church services where members of the congregation would put money on the altar during the preaching of what they perceive to be an anointed message and present an offering to the preacher or to contribute to a worthy cause. The pastors of many churches would give the money collected from this practice to the preacher as a love offering, which he may choose to accept or reject. The leadership of some churches discourages this practice, claiming that it distracts persons who are listening to the preaching. Others contend that this is a Biblical practice, as highlighted in the above passage. There is also a special anointing which is received from giving to the prophet.

> *Money should not be our master; where we literally and figuratively 'kill' ourselves to get it. Rather, it should be our servant, where we use it to secure the things which we need, invest it to generate additional income, give freely to the Lord and to be a source of blessing to others.*

There is a popular belief among persons who prospect for gold, pearls and other precious metals that their colleagues who come into the job with the good intentions that when they 'strike it rich' they will purchase a home, invest in some business venture and have other favorable projections, usually do not find much of these metals. Conversely, many miners who are carefree, and who do not seem to have any concrete plans are often the ones who find many minerals. Such persons often spend most of the proceeds from the find lavishly until they are broke, and would then return to the mine and work until the 'strike it rich once again, or sadly, many of them die practically broke. This belief is not absolutely Biblically correct, in the light that the spending which many minors engage in is indulging in prostitution, alcoholism and other non-scriptural activities and they would continue to 'strike it rich' until they can no longer work in the minors and very often die as paupers. This obviously is not God's plan for us. However, even though budgeting and wise spending are essential, it is also important that we do not allow the accumulation of money and other material things to be the centre of our lives. We should always give God pre-eminence in every area of our lives.

God 'testing' our faith

"Is it true that God sometimes tests the faith of believers by causing at least some of us to be poor?"

In Psalm 37:25, King David related his experience that although he was old, he had never seen the righteous forsaken, or his offspring begging for bread (food). We are reminded that for the forty years that the Children of Israel wandered through the wilderness, God continually provided for their material needs, including the fact that their shoes grew as the size of their feet increased. This was done although they murmured that the manna did not include the many delicacies that they were accustomed to eating in Egypt. On one occasion when they murmured, God provided them with a meal of quail. Of course, the Creator of the universe was well able to provide delicacies in greater abundance than they could have imagined. This was possibly so because He wanted them to focus more on spiritual matters, He did not give them extravagance. It should also be remembered that the children of Israel left Egypt with their cattle and other animals. In addition, hunters may have been securing game as they traveled. Therefore, there would have been meals of meat on occasions.

Matthew 7:9-11 states: ***"⁹Is there anyone among you who, if your child asks for bread, will give a stone? ¹⁰Or if your child asks for a fish, will give a snake? ¹¹If you then, who are evil, know how to give good gifts to your children, how much more will your Father in Heaven give good things to those who ask Him?"***

A popular explanation to this passage is that Christians should not be materially poor. A common example used in explaining this characteristic is in the review of the life of the legendary sufferer - Job. It was highlighted that poverty and disaster are curses from the devil (Job 1:12). Because of God's protection on his life and his faith, Job overcame the test and was blessed more abundantly than before.

> *God never tests His children's faith by inflicting them with poverty, sickness or other adversities. He may, however:*
> - *Harden the hearts of the 'Pharaohs' who stand in the way of our victory, to show His glory to His people.*
> - *Allow Satan to inflict adversities on His People, as occurred with Job.*
> *Jesus also told His disciples that they must be prepared to suffer persecution and other adversities on account of following Him. Examples of this statement are reflected in the lives of Stephen, John the Baptist, Apostle Paul and Jesus himself, who were all killed by persons who opposed their faith.*

The Importance of Money

"Are there spiritual principles which can be derived from the management of money?"

There are several challenges which the management of material assets presents. They include the fact that they can be:

1. **Tools;** which will challenge us to optimize our returns from them when they are used effectively for the purpose for which they were created. Failure to manage our resources results in these assets being used against us, resulting in debt and other financial difficulties which contribute to poverty and other undesirable financial difficulties.

2. **Test;** in that unless we are able to manage our material resources, we will experience financial difficulties. Jehovah has established several principles such as tithing, offering and other forms of giving so that we can reap the benefits which can be derived from managing our material resources.

3. **Testimony;** in that we can rejoice over the fact that the financial and other blessings which we receive are from Jehovah. This fact should challenge others to trust in the Lord to meet our financial and other needs also.

There are so many references in the Bible to money management principles such as saving, investing and leaving an inheritance which should enable Christians to be the best financial managers. A good example of these guidelines is presented in Ecclesiastes 5:13-17 which states: *"¹³There is a grievous ill that I have seen under the sun; riches will keep their owners to their hurt, ¹⁴and those rich were lost in a bad venture; though they are parents of children, they have nothing in their hands. ¹⁵As they came from their mother's womb, so they shall go again, naked as they came, they shall take nothing for their toil, which they may carry in their hands. ¹⁶This also is grievous ill, just as they came, so shall they go; and what gain do they have from toiling for the wind? ¹⁷Besides, all these days they eat in darkness, in much vexation and sickness and resentment."*

This passage should challenge us to budget, save and invest prudently, give wisely and abundantly and engage in other healthy practices to ensure that the Lord blesses our financial and other resources so that our lives can truly be a blessing to the Lord and those around us. Another scripture verse which should challenge us to budget wisely is Proverbs 16:9 which states: *"⁹The human mind plans the way, but the Lord directs the steps."*

We have to do our part and allow Him to do His. If we do not do our part, then He is prevented from doing His. He does not force Himself on anyone; we have to willingly submit to His ways. If we do not seek, we will not find; if we do not knock, the door will not be opened; if we do not sow, we will not reap. However, He grants the abundance beyond our human capabilities as we obey Him.

Non-Christians benefiting from Biblical principles

"Is it possible that non-Christians who use their material and other resources in accordance with Biblical principles will benefit from the blessing of the Lord?"

We have established in Chapter 1 that the Lord is the source of wealth. So, how do we explain the massive amount of wealth which is enjoyed by so many persons who are not serving Jehovah? Many of the richest persons in the world are Muslims, Hindus, heathens and of other religions and other persuasions which are not in keeping with Biblical principles. We are reminded that when Satan tempted Jesus, he showed Jesus the kingdoms of the world and told Jesus that he would give Him all of them once Jesus worshipped him. This episode suggests that Satan has acquired control over some of the resources of the world.

Jehovah has established several universal principles which, once they are satisfied, we will benefit or suffer from the consequences associated with the action. Once a farmer plants, the rain falls on the seeds planted by the godly and the ungodly and they flourish. Therefore, both crops will flourish, even though the Lord has demonstrated in several examples in the Bible that His favor and blessings go beyond human and natural laws. The mere fact that persons who are not serving Jehovah are also wealthy infers that they are receiving a blessing. It is noteworthy that once they are not walking in accordance with the Bible, their blessings will not be eternal in nature. They may enjoy abundance in this life, but they will live in poverty in hell, as illustrated in the lives of the beggar Lazarus and the rich man.

A popular definition of blessings is *the empowerment to prosper in the area of your calling or ministry from the Lord*. The mere fact that a person prospers infers that he has been blessed. Sadly, even if a person's blessing enables him to become wealthy, once they are not serving the Lord, the blessing is not eternal. Even a person's good works, charity and financial and other forms of assistance to others will not be eternal unless the giver establishes and maintain a personal relationship with the Lord. In Jesus' encounters with the Pharisees, for example, He often rebuked them on the hypocrisy of their actions, yet, they were wealthy since they followed many of the statutes of the Law, including giving of alms.

Psalm 145:9 states: **"⁹The Lord is good to all, and His compassion is over all that He has made."** It should be noted, however, that even though He is good to all persons, He extends special blessings to His children. Some of the special blessings which the Lord has reserved for His children are highlighted in Deuteronomy 28.

> **As Christians, our primary objectives for accumulating material and other resources should not be to only enable us to live affluently. Instead, we should seek to use our financial and other resources to fulfil the plan of the Lord for our lives, that of our family, the church and the wider community. Integral in this scenario are financial principles such as giving to the work of the Lord and assisting the poor and needy.**

Living by faith, not by work?

"Does 'living by faith' infer that Christians can stop working and just depend on 'manna to fall from the sky'?"

Some persons are of the opinion that the phrase 'living by faith' implies that a Christian should not hold a secular job but depend on the contribution of believers to support them and their family. Many pastors and other believers who serve in a ministry are supported by the tithes and offering of the church and/or the support from other believers or churches. This is not being idle and their function is usually to spread the gospel while they are being supported by the contribution of persons who attend the church. Other believers work in an economic arm of a ministry which is designed to generate revenue and pay the staff and assist in the upkeep of the ministry. Several other sections of the book discussed the importance of Christians being gainfully employed.

Hebrew 11:6 states: **"⁶And without faith it is impossible to please God, for whoever would approach Him must believe that He exists and that He rewards those who seek Him."**

Our relationship with Christ commences with us having faith in Who He is and accepting that He is willing and able to forgive our sins, even as we confess them to Him and accept His offer of eternal life. Our relationship with Him is also dependant on having continuous faith in Him. James 2:17 states: **"¹⁷So faith by itself, if it has no works, is dead."**

This verse informs us that the manifestation of our faith is illustrated in practical ways such as having a right relationship with the Lord, the renewal of our minds and the implementation of the principles of the Bible. 2:4(b) states: **"4(b)....but the righteous shall live by their faith."**

This passage implies that Christians should rely on God to directly and indirectly supply their physical, material and spiritual needs. This principle is also repeated in Romans 1:17(b). The Bible has several references where miracles were performed to satisfy a particular need. They include:

1. The Children of Israel wandered in the wilderness for forty years and God sent them manna (food) which fell from the sky. Water was also provided when Moses struck a rock with his staff.

2. A prophet had died and his creditors threatened to enslave his sons if his widow did not repay the outstanding balance of his debt. She consulted the prophet Elisha who instructed her to borrow oil jars from her neighbors and to fill them with oil from the one jar of oil that she had. She obeyed this instruction, and as she poured the oil into the borrowed jars, the oil from the original jar was continually replenished until all the jars were filled. Therefore, she sold the oil and accumulated enough money to repay the creditors.

3. Jesus changed water into wine at the marriage feast in Cana (John 2:1-11).

4. Jesus prayed and five loaves of bread and two fishes were miraculously multiplied so that there was enough food to feed 5,000 persons. There were twelve baskets of crumbs collected from the meal (John 6:1-14).

There are also many examples of modern day miracles. Many Christians have taken the Scriptures literally when Jesus instructed his disciples in Luke 9:3 that they should not take anything for their journey when they go to proclaim the Gospel, not even a change of clothes or money. He was teaching them a level of faith where if they labored for God, He is obligated to provide for them. We are also reminded of Paul's admonishment in 1 Corinthians 9:11 as follows: ***"¹¹If we have sown spiritual good among you, is it too much if we reap your material benefits?"***

Some believers have also left secular jobs and careers to pursue the call of the Lord on their lives and to serve in the ministry. These believers usually claim that they have received a personal revelation from God, via methods such as a prophecy, a specific text from the Bible and/or a vision, confirming that God has called them into a life set apart for His service.

> **Even though many persons are specially called to leave their secular jobs and pursue a life of full-time ministry such as being a pastor or missionary, the majority of us are called to be ministers in the profession in which we are serving and to the persons with whom we come into close contact with.**

There is much controversy among some believers on the concept of a full-time ministry. Each believer is in fact called into full-time ministry. We are all called to bear testimony of the work the Lord has done in us every moment of the day. The difference is that some person's primary area of ministry in on their secular job while others may be 'called' to serve as a Pastor, missionary or other offices and in a location which may require that they do not hold a secular job and are supported wholly or partially by the ministry. Like Paul and Barnabas, many Christians have confessed to receiving a special call from the Lord to dedicate their lives exclusively to serving in specific areas of the ministry.

When a person is called by the Lord to serve full-time in a ministry, it is often associated with several piercing questions. The first of which is usually on the issue of financial support, particularly if one has a family to support. The answer to this question is found in scripture verses such as John 15:7 which states: ***"⁷If you abide in me, and My word abide in you, ask for whatever you wish, and it will be done for you."***

There are several examples where the spouse of a person who enters into a full-time ministry still maintains a secular job and can provide the financial support to the family while the other partner seeks to fulfill the particular calling. Several conflicts can result from this arrangement unless the couple is fully conversant with, and accept the demands that such a commitment would make on their personal lives and that of the family. This is another example that emphasizes the importance of being 'equally yoked,' not only from the perspective of being Christians but also in being single in their vision and faith to trust the Lord to accomplish His will in their lives as individuals and as a couple. Disagreements in such areas have resulted in many couples divorcing or a believer being unable to fulfill his/her calling. We can be assured that once we are walking in the will of the Lord, He will supply our every need, even as we trust in Him.

I can reflect on the life of a wonderful missionary from Jamaica, whose wife was initially content to continue working to support their two children while he went around the world preaching. They also traveled with him occasionally. It was evident that there were difficult moments for them, but the important factor was that they recognized and accepted that fulfilling the calling of the Lord on the life of a person was the most important reasons for living. This does not mean that the wife was playing a subservient role, for her ministry, as the 'caretaker of the children' must have received special grace and blessing. Sadly, after over twenty years of marriage the couple was recently divorced. Possibly because of the grief of separation, he died shortly after the divorce.

As Christians we have an obligation and duty to understand and apply the Word of God to our lives. Once we fulfill our part of the covenant, the Lord has given us His commitment to fulfill His promises that He will provide for His children. We are to believe that God will fulfill His promises, contend for it and 'walk' in the fulfillment of these promises. Without faith it is impossible to please God. If we expect to serve God without rewards, that is what will happen. As a man thinks, so is he.

After we have asked, knocked, and sought, we may still be financially poor. We must have the discernment, capacity and wisdom to use wisely that which the Lord gives to us directly and through others and in terms of our health, material and other blessings.

The 'right' of Christians to be materially wealthy

"Since man was created to have dominion over everything on the earth, surely, the regenerated man, the Christian, should be materially wealthy?"

To fully appreciate what Jesus was saying, we have to refer to the first purpose for which man was created as explained in Genesis 1:26: *"26And God said, "Let us make humankind in our image, according to our likeness; and let them have dominion over the fish of the sea, and over the birds of the air, and over the cattle, and over all the wild animals of the earth, and over every creeping thing that creeps upon the earth."*

Man was created to have dominion over the elements, animals, plants and everything other than each other and of course, he was to be submitted to the sovereignty of the Lord. After the first Adam sinned, Jesus, who was also referred to as the Second Adam (1 Corinthians 15:45) came to demonstrate the authority which man was created to employ over the elements and adverse situations. When we review the miracles, teaching and general lifestyle of Jesus, we will see that He was demonstrating the authority which God has given us. The authority of Jesus is seen in miracles such as His dominance over:

1. **The elements** – Jesus, for example, turned water into wine, commanded the waves to be calm, walked on water, and winds and the waves obeyed Him,
2. **Material lack** – Jesus performed several miracles which demonstrated His ability to meet the material needs of persons. This included the multiplication of two fishes and five loaves of bread to feed thousands of persons, changing water into the best quality wine and causing a fish to provide the money for the tax for He and His disciples.
3. **Plants** – He cursed the fig tree which was not bearing and it died,
4. **Animals** – He instructed the fishermen to cast their nets into the Jordon River during the day, even though they had toiled for hours during the night (when it was customary even today to fish during the night) and did not catch any fish. So many fish came into the nets that they had to seek the assistance of other fishermen to place the fish into their boats.

5. **Sickness** – He healed several persons,

6. **Satan, death and hell** – He overcome the temptations of satan, laid His body down, died for our sins, went to hell and took the keys of death and hell from satan, rose from the dead and ascended to His Father to reign forever.

7. **Injustice** – He confronted the unjust judicial system of His day and informed Pilate that he does not have any authority over Him, but instead He was laying down His body and would take it up again,

8. **Demons** – Jesus cast out demons from several persons,

9. **Sexual inadequacies** – Jesus gave the woman at the well the truth of the Word, which indicates that she does not have to be a slave to the sexual demands of men, possible because she could not find gainful employment or they were controlling her sexually. The water which He gave her was liberating, in that she recognized that Her Heavenly Father was more than able to provide for her every need.

10. **Confounded misconceptions which were imbedded in the teachings of men who were only educated with human knowledge which may be inconsistent with the principles of the Bible.** At age twelve Jesus was demonstrating His superior knowledge with the learned men in the synagogue. Many persons were also at awe at the wisdom of His teachings which captivated the intellectual, yet, simplistic enough that the uneducated man could be saved through them.

The 'seed' of material wealth is planted in each Christian, since we have a heavenly Father who has promised to give us the desires of our hearts. **The extent to which we use the various gifts which the Lord has endowed us will determine the degree of our material and other resources.** We have examples of persons who have amassed much material wealth when they were very young and have expanded it over the years. There are persons who suffer severe challenges such as blindness who are world renowned singers and players of musical instruments, for example. We also have persons who are dyslexic who have achieved success in acting and other professions. There are also persons who are deaf who are also famous painters, entrepreneurs and excel in other career paths. Jesus presented the example of the servants with the various talents to among other things illustrate that unless we use that which the Lord has given to us, we will also be counted as unwise servants. Each one of us should seek to identify what the Lord has placed 'in our hands' and to use it for our good, that of others and for the Lord.

> **Can we succeed without the Lord?**
> *Irrespective of how good a financial manager a person is or an investor, he would never be able to accomplish the level of success which God intended him to achieve unless he relies on the Lord to take him to the level which He wants him to achieve. God's intention in creation was to forge a partnership with man which would have enabled us to prosper in all of our ways by applying Heavenly principles on earth.*

> **'Some persons followed Jesus because of the 'fish and bread'**

"Isn't it true that the disciples followed Jesus primarily because of material benefits?"

Many persons wonder why the disciples followed Him. Fishermen were highly paid in those days. There were also at least one doctor, several tax collectors, wealthy women and other persons who follow Him. Yet many of them were willing to leave their highly paid occupation and follow a Man who demonstrated to them the level of authority which God intended them to implement. They were making an investment since they wanted to be near Him to understand and apply the level of authority which He demonstrated.

The central theme of Matthew 6 is that as citizens of the Kingdom, we should not worry about the mundane things of life; as a matter of fact, we should not be worrying at all. Once we seek first the Kingdom of God and His righteousness, then **all** these things will be added unto us. Many persons limit the magnitude of what **all** entails in this context. Is it that we should not be living in the best house, eating the best food, wearing the best clothing and enjoying all the other material blessings, even as our soul prospers? Some persons would view this statement as heresy.

Once a person becomes a citizen of the Kingdom of God, he becomes endowed with the authority to become wealthy materially, since he now has the authority of the King of Kings living in his being and his mind is being renewed to understand and practice Kingdom business. As an ambassador of the Kingdom, we have the right and authority to have dominion over mammon. However, it should be noted that:

1. Not all of us may know of, have the opportunity or choose to exercise this authority,
2. Others choose to die as martyrs, forsaking earthly possessions because of the gospel,
3. There are also persons who have turned to the Lord when they were very old or died shortly after accepting the Lord. They therefore did not have the opportunity to fully exercise their rights,
4. Many Christians attain much personal, family and/or corporate material property honestly. Therefore, those of us who can, should.

It would be erroneous to suggest that once a person becomes a Christian he immediately becomes materially wealthy or that there is a guarantee that he will be materially wealthy in this life. Jesus told His disciples repeatedly that as His followers they were called into His suffering, and for many of them this included not only rebuke from the religious leaders but martyrdom. Mark 8:34-35 states: **"34He called the crowd with the disciples, and said to them, "If anyone wants to become my followers, let them deny themselves and take up their cross and follow me. 35For those who want to save their lives will lose it, and those who lose their lives for my sake, and for the sake of the gospel, will save it."**

When we review the lives of past and present-day martyrs, we see that we are indeed called into a life of self-denial and we have to be willing to forsake everything for the sake of the gospel. Our number one priority must be to serve the Lord, irrespective of the personal and other sacrifices which we have to make.

Many Christians are as' poor as a church mice'

"What are the factors which contribute to so many Christians being materially poor, even though we serve Jehovah, who owns the world and all that is in it?"

The question which has baffled Christians and non-Christian alike is what is the possible explanation to the fact that so many Christians remain as poor as a 'church mouse' throughout their lives? Possible answers could be:
1. The low level of their faith, in that they cannot trust the Lord to see His promises materializing.
2. They may ask for things which are inconsistent with the word of God and/or their motive may be wrong.
3. They do not ask, as is highlighted in the life of the brother of the 'Prodigal Son' (Luke Chapter 15).

4. *Some Christians consciously shun material wealth because they fear that they might be distracted from their faith in God if they have to manage such wealth.* This is disappointing since it indicates that they have no trust in the integrity of their ability to manage wealth. Are we really God's workmanship, His likeness and other characteristics?

5. *Some of us are just too lazy to pursue or prudently manage wealth and/or we are not making adequate use of opportunities which will enable us to significantly increase our material and other resources.*

6. *They are not cheerful givers or even not giving at all.* Since God loves a cheerful giver, what would be His relationship with such persons? If you don't give, men cannot pour into your bosom and the Lord cannot open the windows of Heaven to bless you.

7. *They do not delight in the Lord.* Psalm 37:4-5 state: *"⁴Take delight in the Lord, and He will give you the desires of your heart. ⁵Commit your ways to the Lord; trust in Him, and He will act."*

It is the desire of most persons to have an enjoyable life on earth, that the other members of the family and wider community also enjoy a satisfactorily standard of living. A large number of persons also desire to establish and expand their relationship with Jehovah. We will only be able to take delight in the Lord if we first have a relationship with Him and our ways are pleasing to Him. The relationship must be reciprocated since if our ways are not pleasing to Him, then we will be corrected and even rebuked by Him.

As we spend quality time studying His word, in prayer and praise, spreading His word and engaging in other activities which please Him, we will enjoy a pleasant relationship with Him. As we graduate to the level where we can see the Lord as our Friend, then our relationship with Him will graduate to the point where we will experience delight in serving Him, spending time in His presence being obedient to His word. As we take delight in the Lord, then our desires would be for things which are consistent with His will for our lives.

For reasons such as the above, many preachers present the pros-and-cons of attaining material wealth to their congregation and allow each person to find balance in their lives.

> The embodiment of salvation is a total liberation of our spirit, soul and body from the control of Satan, self, generational and other bondages. This includes the establishment of a free communication link between us and the Father, through Jesus, healing for our body (by His stripes) and financial and other material blessings. It does not mean, however, that we will all be millionaires while we are on earth, even though we have the 'seed' in us which can generate that capacity. Sadly, many persons do not know about their financial and other privileges, others choose not to exercise this right, while others give up this right because of the gospel. Please note that these are all personal choices and not prerequisites to salvation or following the Lord.

The difference between 'enough' and' too much'

"Is there a way of determining how much material possessions is enough for us to have in order to live comfortably?"

Many persons would prefer to have enough money so that they can 'shop until they drop.' The more they have; the more they want. They would prefer to be in a position where they would have to build 'bigger barns' and increase their affluence. Thankfully, many Christians have come to the realization that our lives on earth have a bigger responsibility than merely eating and drinking, even though financial management has its place of importance in our lives. Other important considerations include:

1. **Being able to satisfy the short-term needs of the family** such as provision of food, clothing, shelter, education, leisure and other necessities of life.

2. **Accumulate enough savings to cater for emergencies.** Some provision should be made to provide medical and other forms of insurance to protect the assets of the family or at least provide some support for financial expenditure which is beyond our ability to support one's financial resources.

3. Many persons are comfortable with short-term savings of at least six times the total income of the family. Amounts beyond this would be invested in medium and long-term savings and investment programs.

4. **Investment generating activities which complement our income, pension plan and other sources of income to adequately cater for old age and catastrophes which may occur later in life and to cater for retirement.**

Most persons would prefer to live at a standard where they would not have to worry about meeting their financial needs and that of at least their loved ones and extend this state to the wider community and beyond. Sadly, this utopia is not possible on earth for most persons in view of the attraction to accumulate more and more material wealth and to have financial security. There is an innate craving in the minds of unregenerate man to accumulate more and more wealth until we literally and figuratively 'drop dead.' This can be summed up as 'a lustful quest to satisfy an unquenchable desire.' The more we have, the more we want, and we crave to 'build bigger barns' and increase our affluence. Thankfully, many Christians have come to the realization that our lives on earth are worth far more than perpetually dwelling on the material realm, and instead we focus more on the spiritual, eternal and other aspects our lives.

Irrespective of how financially secure we may feel we are, we may only be able to prolong life and make the suffering less painful as we age. All of us have to die from one cause or another irrespective of how financially secure we are. We will never have enough money to prevent the inevitability of death occurring. In addition, when Christ comes, money will be irrelevant.

Christians benefiting from the 'spoils' of the unrighteous

"Are there scriptural references to the doctrine propagated by some preachers which states that Christians will benefit from the possessions of the unrighteous?" Ecclesiastes 2:26[a] states: *"26(a)For to the one who pleases Him God gives wisdom and knowledge and joy; but to the sinner He gives the work of gathering and heaping only to give to who pleases God."*

It should be stated that not every person who has a good business idea, who is successful at business and/or who is wealthy, pleases God. Many unrighteous persons achieve their wealth by cheating others and/or by making alliance to the devil by offering him sacrifices, for example. The above passage is referring to a special favor which the Lord endows to His followers. The wisdom, knowledge and joy being referred to are beyond the level which we can achieve on our own. These are special endowments presented by the Lord. *In order to derive the benefits of this covenant, our lives have to first please the Lord.*

Several scripture passages admonish us that a person

who reaps what he/she did not sow is a thief, even though widows, orphans and other needy persons were allowed to glean the fields where the remnant of crops were specifically left for them. As alluded to earlier, many Christians who felt that they had enough faith, 'laid their hands' on a car which belonged to another person, walked around a building and conducted other feats in an effort to induce a miracle so that they will receive the item/s. Many such persons prayed and fasted, and possibly had others backing them up in prayer, yet they did not receive 'the desires of their hearts'. However, there are so many testimonies of other believers whose prayers were answered in a miraculous way. We have to be very careful in attempting to 'tie the Lord down' into doing things in only one way. The Bible is full of examples of the diverse ways in which the Lord operates. An important guideline which we should follow in assessing the accuracy of miracles is that the event/action was in conformity with the Word of God.

There are several instances in the Old Testament where Jehovah allowed the Children of Israel to plunder the property of the heathen nations after a victory in battle. There are also examples where heathen nations merely surrendered their sovereignty to the Israelites which included their possessions of animals, crops and precious minerals. Conversely, the theme of the New Testament era was the promotion of peace among Jews and Gentiles and the inclusion of the heathen into the Kingdom of God. A very interesting concept is highlighted in Psalm 49:10: "**10When we look at the wise, they die; fool and dolt perish together and leave their wealth to others.**"

Christians are therefore expected to benefit from the wealth of the unrighteous. How are we to derive this special grace of the Lord? This may occur in ways such as:

1. Persons who are terminally ill or even before this stage of their lives, may bequest a percentage of their assets to their Christian relative, friend, doctor, nurse or other persons,

2. Being offered lucrative business opportunities by business associates and other persons who may be impressed with the management style and/or lifestyle of the believer.

3. One is offered significant discounts when purchasing items which other persons may not be deriving,

4. The experience of miraculous debt write-off from agencies with whom they are indebted and to whom they may not be in a position to repay,

5. Being promoted to very senior positions in organizations

not only because of one's outstanding performance but primarily because of the special grace which is on our lives as a result of our walk with the Lord. We are a chosen people, a royal priesthood.

6. Special favors being received by the children and other relatives of Christians because persons in the society recognize the exemplary lives which their Christian parents lived and the fact that they made a significant contribution to the good of the society,

In Luke 16 Jesus presented some very important reasons why many Christians have not been successful in acquiring material wealth. In this parable Jesus related that the servant had squandered his master's money, and the master had called him to give an account of his stewardship. Fearing that he would be fired, the servant went to his creditors and agreed with them to reduce the amount which they would repay his master. He did this in anticipation that if he was fired he would possibly be hired by, or at least be able to continue doing business with them since they would recognize that he had saved them much money. Luke 16:8-12 states: *"⁸And the master commended the dishonest manager because he had acted shrewdly; for the children of this age are more shrewd in dealing with their own generation than are the children of the light. ⁹And I tell you, make friends for yourselves by means of dishonest wealth so that when it is gone, they may welcome you into the eternal home. ¹⁰Whoever is faithful in a very little is faithful also in much; and whoever is dishonest in very little is dishonest in much. ¹¹If you have not been faithful with the dishonest wealth, who will entrust you with true riches? ¹²And if you have not been faithful with what belongs to another, who will give you what is your own?"*

This is a very serious passage since at face glance one may arrive at misconceptions such as:

1. *It is okay to be dishonest, once it is for the purpose of 'saving one's own skin,' or to do something which will have some positive effect on others,*
2. *It is permissible to conduct business deals with dishonest persons,*
3. *The accumulation of wealth by dishonest practices is scriptural,*
4. *If a person loses his wealth which was acquired by dishonest practices, he will still have friends among the rogues whom he befriended in the dishonest deals which he conducted, who will assist him in times of difficulties,*

5. *Even if you accumulate wealth due to dishonest practices, you also have to take good care of it,*

The above issues are incorrect. The following statements are presented to address each of them:

1. *God does not expect us to indulge in any sinful act, irrespective of if our ultimate intention is for good.* We are expected to be one hundred percent honest in all of our activities and we are not to seek to 'assist' Him by committing a sin even in an attempt to convert someone, for example. We should not feel, for example, that by over-exaggerating a testimony, it would enhance the chances of a person being converted. If the testimony is what He is directing us to give to lead that person to Him, we can be assured that there is something about our true experience which would lead that person to Him. There are many testimonies in the Bible and also among modern day Christians who choose death rather than renounce their faith. These experiences have resulted in the conversion of millions of persons rather than the lives of persons who in cowardice renounced their faith. They prefer the reward in the Lord rather than nailing Him to the cross once again by denying Him.

2. *The Bible does not advocate that Christians should totally abstain from interacting with non-Christians even if they are involved in illegal business practices.* Tax collectors were viewed as dishonest persons. Luke 19 highlighted that Jesus dined with Zacchaeus who was the chief tax collector, even though tax collectors were usually dishonest men and they were viewed by the Jews as traitors who were in league with the Romans. However, there are several scriptures which rules against Christians being yoked to unbelievers, that is, they should not be partners in business and activities or partners in crime. Abraham and Lot, for example, even though there were uncle and nephew, had to be separated since Lot was not grounded in the Lord and his desires were different from that of Abraham.

3. *Genuine repentance entails the following at least the following stages:*
   I. *Recognizing that we have sinned,*
   II. *Being sorry for committing the sins,*
   III. *Confessing them to the Lord,*
   IV. *Repenting of the sins,*
   V. *Accepting the forgiveness of the Lord,*

VI.   *Turning from one's former sinful ways,*

Using the example of Zacchaeus, we see that when he came to Christ, he was prepared go beyond these stages to give half of his possessions to the poor and also make restitution of four times the value of whatever he had taken fraudulently from anyone (that is, restitution). He also expresses the commitment to live a life of honesty.

4.   *While we live on earth we are expected to live a life which is separated from 'worldly' standards but instead follow the principles of the Bible.* This does not mean that we should not interact with non-Christians but rather that our lives should reflect His righteousness. Many persons, upon becoming a Christian would relinquish a close business association with persons who are not Christians. This is so because their business ethics may now be vastly different.

Jesus was not condoning unrighteousness, per sé, rather, he was lamenting the fact that as Christians we very often do not tap into the wisdom and other gifts which He has vested in us. We are often willing to give up when we are confronted with even minor difficulties. An illustration of this attitude was displayed by the Prophet Elijha who after performing extraordinary miracles, went and hid himself under a juniper tree in fear for his life because of the threat of Jezebel.

It was very likely that Elijha could have called the fire of God's wrath down from heaven to kill her, if he so desired. Instead he hid from her. In the same way, we are often willing to accept poverty, rather than finding some useful things to do and see God use our obedience to provide the right type of job for which we are looking, the business venture through which He will pour His blessings to us, accentuate a talent which we have and take opportunities which are available to us. When we are in difficult situations which we cannot manage, we have recourse to seek counsel from persons with any of the five fold ministries operating in their lives for the appropriate advice, prayer, the Word and other spiritual tools at our disposal.

5.   *Some of our methods of dealing with problems are unorthodox and contrary to practices of non-Christians, yet, we have the necessary tools which are needed to*

enable us to succeed in all of our undertakings.

In conclusion, it can be stated that the Bible supports the issue that believers will benefit from the assets of the unbeliever. The Lord often uses this method as a demonstration of His infinite power and also His love for His children.

A popular example of God's people benefiting from the wealth of the unrighteous is illustrated when the children of Israel were about to leave Egypt. Apart from allowing the Israelites to take their flocks and herd with them. Exodus 12: 35-36 states: *"35The Israelites had done as Moses told them, they had asked the Egyptians for jewellery of silver and gold, and for clothing, 36and the Lord had given the people favor in the sight of the Egyptians, so that they let them have what they asked. And so they plundered the Egyptians."*

The question is how can someone plunder another for whom they asked a favor? This must have been the Lord intervening on behalf of the Israelites, causing the Egyptians to give an excessive amount of jewellery to the Israelites. The Egyptians were possibly giving so much since they were happy to get rid of the Israelites out of Egypt when they reflect on the calamity which befell them as the plagues ravished Egypt. There must have been jewellery in abundance, when we note that in disobedience they forced Aaron to make a golden calf which they worshipped. When Moses returned with the tablets on which the Ten Commandments were written by the Lord, and saw the abomination of the people, he broke the tablets and burnt the golden calf, scattered the ashes on water and ordered the people to drink the water.

The Lord also instructed Moses to request that the people bring an offering of gold, silver, and other items and present them to be used in decorating vessels and other items in the tabernacle of the Lord. These are but two examples of how vast was the amount of jewellery and other items which the children of Israel received, resulting of their plunder of the Egyptians. There was no record of them mining for these minerals on their way to the Promised Land.

Isaiah 60 describes some of the benefits which the righteous shall derive when the glory of the Lord comes upon us. Isaiah 60:5, 8-10 states: *"5Then you shall see and be radiant: because the abundance of the sea shall be brought to you, the wealth of the nations shall come to you.... 8Who are these that fly like a cloud, and like doves to their windows? 9For the coastlands shall wait for me, the ships of Tarshish first, to bring your children from far away, their silver and gold with them, for the name of the Lord your God, and for the Holy One of Israel, because He has glorified you. ¹⁰Foreigners shall build up your walls, and their kings shall minister to you; for in my wrath I struck you down, but in my favor I have mercy on you."*

In this passage the prophet was expounding on some of the blessings which the Israelites will receive as they faithfully follow the Lord. Even so, as we can visualize the blessings which will be derived by individuals who faithfully follow the Lord, we must be cognizant of the fact that most of the blessings which the Lord has in store for us go beyond what we are able to achieve on our own. For this reason, in our planning we should not restrict our projections to what we can achieve on our own. Ephesians 3:20 states: *"²⁰Now to Him who by the power at work within us is able to accomplish abundantly far more than we can ask or imagine."*

The Lord often provides the measure which is beyond our capabilities by channeling the resources of other to us. This may be in the forms such as giving of their expertise, financial and other material resources, making the right contact for us and even giving good advice.

| Christianity and bribery |

"Is it okay for Christians to give and/or accept a bribe?"

There are two scripture verses which are often viewed as contradictory. Exodus 23:8 states: "⁸*You shall take no bribe, for a bribe blinds the officials, and subverts the cause of justice.*"

This scripture clearly outlaws a person presenting a gift to another with the deliberate intentions of perpetuating a dishonest deed. Yet, Proverbs 18:16 states: "¹⁶*A gift opens doors: it gives access to the great.*"

This scripture is very dear to one of my friends, a businessman who has a principle of presenting gifts to persons who have assisted him in facilitating the successful completion of a business deal. He is genuinely showing appreciation for favors granted to him, even if it was within the terms of reference of a person's job for which he/she is being paid. He stated that he does not make it a point of publicly displaying the gift, nor does he leave without informing the recipient that the gift is a genuine show of his appreciation and he does not expect any special favors from the person in the future.

There are many persons who would refuse to accept a gift from a client in this way particularly if they may have to come into contact with him in the future. This is so because there may be a feeling of expectation that they would have to extend favors in the future even at the expense of other customers who possibly should have been given preference. They may feel pressured to facilitate that person even if it entails 'bending a few rules'. Some persons will also be afraid that it might be circulated that they are on the 'payroll' of the giver, which could result in disciplinary actions from the management of the organization.

It is important to be able to differentiate between a bribe and a genuine gift. A bribe is offered with an ulterior motive such as the subversion of justice or in anticipation of the return of some favor. A gift on the other hand is usually extended:
1. **In appreciation of a kind gesture expressed by another person,**
2. **In appreciation of someone, and even with the intention of challenging the receiver to excel in a particular area,**
3. **In commemoration of a special event,**

The above focus is but one of several interpretations of Proverbs 18:16. Another issue which can be related to this verse is the fact that each of us is endowed with gifts or talents, which, if carefully nurtured and developed can open doors for us which we may not have imagined could have become a reality. For this reason it is important that a person learn from an early age and early in one's Christian life what is God's specific calling on their life. Knowing this and being able to consistently 'tap' into the resources which He has placed at our disposal to facilitate the fulfillment of that calling is enough to ensure that we are successful in fulfilling God's agenda for our lives. It should be recognized that the 'door' may not always be the way to enormous material wealth. However, this goal is often achieved after the person recognizes that financial blessings are not to be used for selfish or sinful purposes, but for the furtherance of the gospel.

A scripture verse which has evoked controversy in some circles is Proverbs 21:14 which states: **"¹⁴A gift in secrete averts anger; and a concealed bribe in the bosom, strong wrath."**

This could be misleading since it would appear that this passage is propagating that we should engage in bribing. However, there are so many other verses which states that the Lord prohibits persons engaging in bribes since it pervert justice. The original Kings James version uses the word **reward instead of bribe** which is consistent with other passages in the Bible. There is no scripture verse which supports Christians taking a bribe.

Non-Christians benefiting from Biblical principles

"What are some of the material and other benefits which are available to Christians?"

There are several privileges which Christians enjoy from the Lord which are highlighted in scripture verses such as Genesis 14:20, Exodus 22:29, Malachi 3:8-12 and Hebrew 7:1-2. They include:

1. Granting a harvest to the sewer and persons who tithe and give of their offerings,
2. Whatever we put our hands to is blessed,
3. Eternal life where we can enjoy the treasures which we have laid up for us in heaven,
4. He repays those who 'lend' to Him and support His cause,
5. He protects and blesses the work of our hands,
6. He directs our paths,
7. We have weapons at our disposal to protect us from the attacks of the devil,

Mark 10:2-30 states: *"²⁹Jesus said, "Truly I tell you, there is no one who has left house or brother or sister or mother or father or children or fields, for my sake and for the sake of the good news, ³⁰who will not receive a hundredfold now in this age – houses, brothers and sisters, mother and children, and fields with persecutions – and in the age to come eternal life."*

So does it mean that we have to give away our possessions and forsake our relatives in order to achieve material possessions on earth? The general interpretation of this passage is that we should not make anything an idol or treat anything with more importance than Jehovah. For we should be able to enjoy material and other blessings on earth and still enjoy eternal life with the Lord. It is interesting to note, however, that the earthly blessings come 'with persecutions' (not due to dishonest practices but because satan will not allow us to enjoy financial and other forms of freedom, without 'giving us a run for our money.') We are also reminded in Matthew 5:5, where Jesus stated that the meek will inherit the earth.

It would be useful to likewise reflect on the fact that God created humans in His image and for us to establish His Kingdom of **righteousness** and **justice** on earth. Righteousness can be defined simply as being in right standing with God. Righteousness is not attained, it is accepting by faith. **We are justified (made in right standing with God) firstly, by the grace of God. Secondly, we must be willing by faith to accept His gift of righteousness – Romans 3:21,22.** When some persons hear the word justice in reference to God, they conjures up the misguided perception of a God who is merely looking down on us with a 'big stick in His hand' to inflict punishment on us when we sin. This obviously is not the image which the Bible presents of Yahweh, Who is a loving Father. The justice of God is important in that once we know our benefits; we can approach the Father, not as beggars but to receive what He has already decreed that we should have. For this reason, in Christ we are not slaves but sons and daughters.

When we approach God, we can come in boldness, for once we know our rights and fulfill the requirements of the **constitution of God, that is, salvation,** then we can claim what is rightfully ours, without fear or timidity. God does not give us anything because He likes or dislikes us *per sé*; He rather does this because it is our right since we have fulfilled the requirements in order to receive them. In other words, once we fulfill the requirements, there is nothing which will prevent Him from granting it to us.

The failure of many Christians to understand and implement the principles of this fundamental truth is responsible for many of us living in perpetual poverty, or at least way below realizing the optimum standard which God has provided for us. We should be aware that a benefit of salvation is that we become righteous immediately upon becoming saved. This truth is identified in scripture verses such as Romans 4:3-6, which states: "³**For what does the scripture say? "Abraham believed God, and it was reckoned to him as righteousness. ⁴Now to one who works, wages are not reckoned as a gift but as something due. ⁵But to one who without works trusts Him who justifies the ungodly, such faith is reckoned as righteousness. ⁶So also David speaks of the blessedness of those to whom God reckons righteousness apart from works."**

Romans 10:4 also states: "⁴**For Christ is the end of the law so that there may be righteousness for everyone who believes**."

Once we are righteous, then we can enjoy the benefits which are inherent in serving Him.

Poverty will never be eradicated on earth

"Why did Jesus say that the poor will always be with us? Is this inferring that poverty will never be eradicated?"

A similar quotation by Jesus was recorded in Matthew 26:11, Mark 14:7 and John 12:8. In Matthew 26:11 Jesus stated: "¹¹**For you will always have the poor with you, but you will not always have me."**

It should be noted that being **poor in spirit** is actually a positive attribute. Matthew 5:3 highlights that such persons will inherit the kingdom of Heaven. In addition, Jesus did not regard the issue of the poor only from a financial or material perspective. There are other categories of persons who are referred as being poor and who are in need of some form of assistance. They include:

1. **Poor health;** that is persons who are physically and/or mentally ill,
2. **Poor sense of hearing, taste, sight and touch,**
3. **Poor sense of understanding or, perception,**

Jesus came to liberate persons who are held captives to the bondages of poverty. He was aware that not every person would follow Him. Those who choose to reject Him remained in their poverty. Similarly, many persons who come to the Lord do not walk in the complete liberty which He offers. Some persons do not embrace the total deliverance of the Lord, thus, they remain as captives to various sins in their lives.

TITHES AND OFFERING

The relevance of tithing in the New Testament

"Is tithing still relevant today?"

God introduced tithing and offering in the Old Testament. The proceeds from the tithes were primarily to support the priests and their families and to finance other activities pertaining to the temple. The offering was presented for reasons such as in appreciation of the loving kindness of God, as atonement for the sins a person, one's family and the nation of Israel. It was also presented to the Lord as a thanksgiving offering at the end of a period of uncleanness, for example. This principle was continued in the New Testament. In Genesis 14:20 Abram gave one-tenth of his possession to King Melchizedek. After this incident, Abram received the promise of God that his descendants were to be as numerous as the stars. Other references of tithing, and First Fruit, include Numbers 18:26, 2 Chronicle 31:5-6 and Hebrews 7:4-9.

We, along with everything that we own are His. However, there is a mandatory 10% of our income and other forms of earning which is classified as the tithe. A person may choose to pay more than the mandatory 10% tithe. Offering on the other hand, the offering constitutes amounts beyond the percentage that is paid as tithe. A common activity for which the offering is used is to contribute to the building and expansion of the work of the Lord in the local church and other congregations, as a gift to individual believers, pastors and missionaries and to help the poor and needy. Much blessing will be received by a person, family or other bodies who give an offering, particularly, when it is given from a heart of love and to a worthy cause.

> **Ten (10) is the number for redemption. When you give the first tenth, you redeem the other ninetieth.**

Malachi 3:8 states that a person who does not pay the **full tithes** into the house of God is in fact robbing Him. Each household was obligated to present the produce of their first harvest from their farm, and the first born of their cattle, and other animals to the priest. Therefore, tithing is a very important requirement of the believer, so that God can also fulfill His covenant of protection, provision and other blessings to us.

In many Christian communities there is a heated debate surrounding the issue of whether or not Christians should tithe. There is controversy in some Christian circles pertaining to the relevance of tithing in the New Testament. Some of the arguements against the continuation of tithing are:

1. Christ has fulfilled the 'Old Covenant', hence; we should not practice 'Old Covenant' principles such as tithing and offering burnt offering, 'an eye for an eye and a tooth for a tooth' and abstaining from eating the meat of animals such as pigs, shrimps and crabs which were classified as unclean. It is noted, however, that **tithing was not abolished by Jesus.** In Matthew 23:23 and Luke 11:42 Jesus rebuked the scribes and Pharisees for observing some practices while neglecting others. In Matthew 23:23 Jesus stated: "**23Whoe to you, scribes and Pharisees, hypocrites! For you tithe mint, dill, and cumin, and have neglected the weightier matters of the law; justice and mercy and faith. It is these you ought to have practiced <u>without neglecting the others</u>.**" (underline, mine – see also Luke 11:42) Would it therefore be incorrect to conclude that in this passage Jesus stated that the Scribes and Pharisees should emphasize more on observing justice and mercy and faith, without neglecting practices such as the

contribution of tithing and offering?

2. Another argument which has been presented against tithing is that the tithe in the Old Testament was presented to the Priest. In the New Testament, the office of the Priest was primarily replaced by the ministerial gifts and the five-fold ministry. Nevertheless, most churches which practices tithes, would contribute the tithes towards financial administration of the ministry and to assist with other expenses, outreach and other activities of the ministry.

The Apostle Paul stated in 2 Corinthians 8:3 and 4:"³*For as I can testify, they voluntarily give according to their means, and even beyond their means, ⁴begging us earnestly for the privilege of sharing in this ministry to the saints – and this, not merely as we expected they give themselves first to the Lord and, by the will of God, to us..."*

3. The ministry of Jesus and the New Testament Pastors, Apostles and other ministers were financed primarily from the contributions of other believers and the Apostle Paul, for example, worked as a tent maker to support himself.

The following are eleven important principles which have to be followed when offering a tithe:

1. *The tithe should be the first item which is deducted from our salary.* A person should give from their gross income (before taxes, National Insurance deduction, loan deduction (if any), and the payment of medical insurance. Hence, it can be concluded that if the tithe is made after these deductions, what we are giving to the Lord is an offering from our net income, and not the full extent of the tithe. It is true that deductions such as income tax, national insurance, group medical insurance and a loan payment, for example, may be deducted before a salary earner receives his net income or what is commonly referred to as one's 'take-home-pay'. Even so, *the tithe represents one tenth of the gross, or salary payable before any deduction is made*. A Christian who is self-employed or is an entrepreneur, may decide to tithe from his net income, since he recognize that he does not have control over the taxation policy of the government. Many such businesses have become highly profitable because the owner tithes from the gross instead of the net income.

2. *We should give as an expression of our love for the Lord and is an act of worship.* This principle is highlighted in the fact that we, and everything which we have are His. Therefore, we are merely giving back to Him a percentage of what belongs to Him in gratitude of what He has enabled us to achieve. The Apostle Paul stated in 2 Corinthians 8:3-5: *"3For, as I can testify, they voluntarily give according to their means, and even beyond their means, 4begging us earnestly for the privilege of sharing in this ministry to the saints – 5and this, not merely as we expected: they give themselves first to the Lord and, by the will of God, to us."*

3. *We should give cheerfully*; that is, our attitude should not be one where we are not tithing merely because we are obligated to, for there is an abundance of blessings allocated to a cheerful giver. 2 Corinthians 9:6 states: *"6The point is this: the one who sows sparingly will also reap sparingly, and the one who sows bountifully will also reap bountifully."*

4. *The amount that we give as an offering is an individual decision and no other person should impose or compel us to give a prescribed amount. Nevertheless, even though parents, for example, should encourage children to tithe and give an offering from their allowance or other amounts of money which they receive.* 2 Corinthians 9:7 states: *"7Each of you must give as you have made up your mind, not reluctantly or under compulsion, for God loves a cheerful giver."*

5. *We must give with the correct attitude.* A popular representation of this truth is the parable of the 'widow's mite.' Among the principles highlighted in this parable is that our heart should be right with God and we must be humble as we give, or our giving would be like 'sounding brass' where it is a curse rather than a blessing to us.

6. *Our giving should be generous.* When we reflect on how much He has done for us, no amount should be too big for us to give to Him. Can we measure our life by the standard of 10% of our salary, for example?

7. *If we sow on barren ground our harvest will be minimal, if any at all.* Thus, it is important that we tithe at a church where the full gospel of Christ is preached and practiced, where believers are in unity and there is a dynamic evangelism outreach program, for example. Nevertheless, we must take cognizance of our financial

obligations such as to pay our utilities and other bills, savings and taking care of the financial needs of the family.

8. ***Claim the promises of God*** as found in Malachi 3:10-12, which states that God will bless the produce of our land and all the blessings that we can conceive as 'overflowing.' This includes good health, financial prosperity and spiritual blessings.

9. ***We should give expectantly.*** As alluded to earlier, He is no man's debtor and when we give to the poor, we lend to the Lord.

10. ***Our giving should be with the full understanding that we are not giving to a person.*** Our giving should not, for example, be a means of 'buying favor' among the leadership of the church and we should not stop giving when we cannot have our 'own way' which is not consistent with the word of God.

11. ***Our giving should be consistent***; there must be a commitment to pay our tithes and give of our offering on a regular basis in order to enjoy God's full blessing. The devourer, for example, must be stayed on a perpetually for us to enjoy continuous blessing. Many persons experience 'good days' and 'bad days' because of their inconsistency in giving their all to the Lord each day of their lives.

> **Proverbs 3:9, 10 states: "Honour the Lord with your substance and with the first fruits of all your produce; then your barns will be filled with plenty, and your vats will be brimming with wine."**

Tithing is a very important aspect of budgeting in the Christian family. ***It is advisable that, as far as possible, that the tithe is the first item that is taken out of our salary and expenditure is deducted from the remainder.*** Unless the family tithes in the correct way, they cannot enjoy the full benefits of the promises covenanted by God to this principle. The tithe is usually paid to the church where a believer is a member. In circumstances where one is not a member of a church but is fellowshipping there regularly, tithes can be paid to that church. In a situation where there are no Bible believing churches in close proximity to where one resides, some believers pay their tithes to a ministry that they feel is fulfilling Biblical principles such as an international evangelism organizations.

> **When we sow financial seeds by giving to the poor, giving towards evangelism and to support missionaries, we reap financial, spiritual and other forms of returns from the Lord directly and also through other persons.**

Tithing versus offering

"Where does tithing end and the offering begin? Secondly, what should we do with our tithes and offerings?"

The **tithe** is the first 10% of our income, profit, increase or other sources of revenue. This is compulsory giving. The **offering** is the amount beyond the tithe which we choose to give. The tithe goes to the church where we fellowship, whereas the offering can be given to the church along with the tithe or can be used as a special gift to the pastor or other Christians, to the poor, to support other ministries and other programs as the Lord directs us (see Genesis 14:20, Exodus 22:29, Malachi 3:8-12, and Hebrew 7:1, 2).

A simple example to illustrate the difference between tithes and offering is shown when reference is made of a person dining in a restaurant. The tithe is tantamount to paying for one's meal (one, two or three course, appetizer, drinks and dessert, as one prefers or can afford to pay for), the payment goes to the restaurant (an illustration of the local church). The offering is viewed as the tip given to the waiter for the satisfactory level of service rendered. In the same way as a person cannot eat at one restaurant and pay the bill at another, it is unethical to fellowship at one church and tithe at another. The tip is given to the waiter in appreciation of the courteous service which was extended. A waiter would usually seek to ensure that a good tipper is given the best service. Can we really fathom the outpouring of blessing which we will receive from the hands of the Lord as we give; to His work, to the poor and other areas of the ministry beyond the obligatory tithe. Therefore, in appreciation of Who He is and what He has done, continues to do and will do in the future for us? Jehovah is no man's debtor and He will give out of His abundance, which is far beyond what we can ever think or imagine.

When a person moves to a location where one does not have access to one's local church, the tendency is usually to maintain the relationship with the former church by sending one's tithes to that church. Care should be taken when applying this principle, for we should 'pay where we eat'; figuratively speaking, or we may be classified as a thief.

As we 'cast our bread on the water' it will be returned to us in abundance, pressed down, shaken together and running over (Luke 6:38). As we bless others, we, the members of our families, our descendants and other persons will receive blessings in abundance in return. God appreciates it more when we give, even when we are in need, rather than when we give merely because we have in abundance. Our giving should be out of a heart of love and gratitude for who He is, what He has done for us and for our love for others. A typical example of this principle is illustrated in the parable that Jesus related of the widow's mite (Mark 12:41-44 and Luke 21:1-4).

The issue of tithing has received much criticism from members of 'traditional' churches where this system is not emphasized as much as in many of the Pentecostal and Charismatic churches. The view is often that the leadership of the churches who emphasize on tithing does this primarily to 'fill their own pockets.' Many of these leaders enjoy a standard of living which even some Christians criticize. This may including traveling to several international conferences, visiting several countries with an entourage, drive fancy motor vehicles, live in 'fancy houses' in an upper-class neighborhoods. Even though the source of the affluence of senior officials of the church may be from personal investments, they will still be viewed as deriving it from the coffers of the church.

There are, of course some dishonest church officials, who have brought disrepute to the name of the Lord. However, this is not usually in the majority. The sad reality is that regardless of degree of the high standard which the leaders and other members of a church live, there will always be critics of their lifestyle. Nevertheless, most persons would feel more comfortable attending a 'church' where the building is attractive, the pews are comfortable, air conditioned or at least fans and other amenities are in place which projects comfort. It is also important that the Spirit of the Lord is doing mighty work in the lives of believers and persons are being saved, through sound doctrines being preached and other scriptural practices are adhered to.

We have to pray for our leaders, and indeed fellow believers, that they will consistently maintain their focus on the Lord and not divert the tithes and offering for activities which are not consistent with the will of the Lord. However, a leader whose life reflects success is usually better able to challenge and inspire others to improve their lives and the standard of development in their community. (The word 'usually' is used since it is also true that there are persons who are challenged to seek to avoid the pitfalls of others who exhibit negative behavior, and in so doing, achieve success in their lives).

> I have found out, from painful personal experiences and that of others who attempt to, figuratively speaking, 'put the cart before the horse' by endeavoring to pay the Lord's tithes after fulfilling other obligations, that it simply does not work. In giving, even out of our need, the Lord rewards us bountifully for our faithfulness.

Many persons contend that Jesus did not support tithing since it was under the old covenant. This is not so. We can refer to Jesus' comments in Luke 11:42 when He was dining with the Pharisee who was surprised that Jesus did not wash His hands before He ate, as was customary. *"42But woe to you Pharisees! For you tithe mint and rue and herbs of all kinds, and neglect justice and the love of God; it is these you ought to have practiced, without neglecting the others."* (see also Matthew 23:23)

Jesus rebuked the Pharisees for their emphasis on the outward appearance while they were neglecting the important commands such as observing justice and loving God. At the same time they were to continue the practice of tithing. There is a famous Christian cliché which states: *"The Lord said it, I believe it, and it is done."*

Do we need to entertain any further dialogue on this issue?

> God does not need 'our' money in order to accomplish His will. When we give to Him, it is among other things, an investment into receiving an abundance of blessings in return.

We are also reminded in 2 Corinthians 9:6 states: *"6The point is this: the one who sows sparingly will also reap sparingly, and the one who sows bountifully will also reap bountifully. 7Each of you must give as you have made up your mind, not reluctantly or under compulsion, for God loves a cheerful giver."*

Tithe or go to hell?

"Will I go to hell if I cannot or do not tithe?"

There are many persons who do not tithe since they do not earn enough to meet their materials needs and that of their family. There are for example Christians who begin some poor countries and those who are on Social Security benefit in welfare states. This obviously is not God's best for our lives. One of the ways to get out of such impoverishment is to begin to tithe with the correct attitude. Even so, I have not seen any scripture verse which stated that our tithes should be premised on whether or not we have enough for ourselves and/or family. As a matter of fact, the reason why many Christians are poor is because we disobey the commandment of God in areas such as tithing. Malachi 3:8-18, identifies several of the benefits which will be derived when we obey the Lord with our finance and in other areas of our lives. The moment we begin to rationalize using human knowledge, like Peter who was walking on the water in obedience to Jesus' command, we will begin to 'sink' and eventually 'drown.' There is some element of radicalism in faith. Unless we can stand on the promises of the Lord, come what may, we will be walking in disobedience.

A person who earns an income, may receive a pay increase and/or other sources of material blessings, and does not tithe the requisite increase, is classified as robbing God – Malachi 3:8. In addition, if we do not give to the Lord as we commit to give to the Lord directed in 2 Corinthians 9 and to the poor, we will not receive the blessings associated with these acts of obedience. There are situations, when we are in such an adverse financial situation, where it is either the tithe or meeting a serious financial expense such as a medical bill or even to purchase food. Once we are faithful to the Lord, He will be faithful and provide the things which we need. We hear numerous testimonies of the Lord multiplying the returns of persons who take Him at His word and would tithe and give their offering even during adverse circumstances. Even though the scripture is usually rigid on tithing, the commandment for the offering is usually 'as one determined in his heart to give.' Many persons see tithing as an option and not as a responsibility, primarily because the view tithing as an Old Testament Principle and/or that it is applicable only to the Jews (even though many such persons would agree that Christians are 'spiritual Jews.) Robbing God is a serious offence. Even though a person can be forgiven if he repents of this sin, there are likely to be many persons who may not have had a chance to repent of this sin before they die, and their sin may have prevented them from getting to heaven, since sin cannot enter heaven.

I have not met a Christian who cannot tithe or at least give of an offering. Even if one is so poor that like the widow, all one has is the last coin, the act of giving financially *would result in* financial and /or other blessings. The word 'usually' is used advisedly since many preachers major on the teaching that 'you cannot sow the seed of one plant and reap the fruit of another plant,' literally inferring that if you sow finance in the form of tithes and/or offering then you will only reap financial blessings. It should be noted, however, that the blessing which we receive may not necessary be financial in nature, and/or we may not be able to measure it strictly in financial terms. In addition, we may benefit from the blessings of our parents and even grandparents and others. Similarly, our children, grandchildren and even other persons may benefit from the blessings which we receive.

The act of the poor widow who prepared the meal for Elijah, for example, can be likened to an offering. Her immediate reward was a material miracle which was converted into money when she sold the oil. Therefore, we can infer that many persons remain poor not because they did not have anything to offer to the Lord, instead they eat their 'seed,' that is, they did not use their time, talent and/or treasury to bless the lives of others and to give to the work of the Lord in conformity with the Biblical guidance on giving. Many persons can testify to having 'sowed' their way out of debt, poverty and other states of financial difficulties by observing the **'3 – T'** (that is time, treasury and talent). Similar to the fact that one seed could produce millions of fruits and indeed a forest of trees, even so our investment in the Lord is not limited to returns which are limited by inflation, the law of average or other human standards. The more we give, the more we will receive in return.

Benefits of offering

"What are some of the benefits of giving an offering?"

The Bible highlights several **types of offering**. Two of them are:
1. **Thanksgiving** – in appreciation of the goodness of God in general, or for some specific blessing which we, or someone else received. Psalm 50:14 states: *"**14Offer to God a sacrifice of thanksgiving, and pay your vows to the Most High.**"*
2. **Sin offering** – in repentance for a sin committed. Numbers 15:24 identified that the priest would present a sin offering on

behalf of the people. Verse 27 also highlighted the offering of individuals who sin unintentionally.

Questions often arise as to whether we should use our tithes for purposes such as; making a contribution to a charitable organization, to assist a relative in need, or to purchase essential medication for a relative who is ill, for example. The scripture passages which were quoted above highlighted that the tithes should be brought to the house of the Lord. There are instances in the Bible where the Lord was firm on His word such as when he struck down Uzzah even though he did what many person would consider to be a just act in trying to prevent the ark from falling (2 Samuel 6:6-11). Ananias and Sapphira were also killed by the Lord when they lied to the Lord and to the Peter about how much money they had sold their house for.

Even though there is no record of anyone being killed for not bringing their tithes to the Lord, there are consequences for not following this command. For this reason we should not deviate from following the principle of giving directly to the Lord, unless it is an emergency, and we should endeavor to replace the shortage as soon as possible. When we fail to be obedient to Him, we should not expect His financial and other blessings, unless of course, He extends His mercy in this area. This should not be a consistent defect since He blesses sacrificial giving. Some of the benefits of tithing correctly are described in Malachi 3:8-12.

Faith Pledge

"Is it scriptural to give a faith pledge?"

When some churches raise funds for the construction or expansion of the church building and other major projects, they may request that members commit to contributing an amount, which they can afford or which they feel led to contribute, by signing a **pledge certificate**. This is usually a legally binding contract to contribute a fixed amount towards the project. Some churches discount the pledge with a financial institution and receive the money in advance of the fulfillment of the pledge by members. Persons who signed the pledges are expected to honor their obligations and make the payment at the church or deposit it in an account with the financial institution. Failure to do this can have consequences such as a representation from the financial institution calling upon the church, who would in turn call upon delinquent members to honor their commitment. Most churches would not penalize a member who provides genuine reasons why they could not honor their pledge. We should not make a pledge. However, unless we are sure that the funds are available, or will become available shortly.

A **faith promise**, on the other hand is a commitment to contribute a given amount, once the funds become available. This is not a legally binding commitment, but it is expected that the amount quoted will be honored once the funds become available.

Some churches would not pass an offering plate or another receptacle around to, collect the offering since they teach principles such as that giving should be in secret and persons should not feel pressured to give. Instead they may have one or several receptacles at strategic locations where persons would deposit their tithes and offering. This practice may avoid the delay by persons taking their tithes and offering to the altar as practiced by some churches. Nevertheless, the practice of giving in the New Testament included believers laying their gifts at the feet of the apostles joyfully. For this reason some churches have a period of worship, where persons dance and praise the Lord as they place their gifts in a receptacle at the altar. It should be noted that Matthew 6:2-3, commands that when we give alms and assist the poor, we should do so in secrete.

It is true that **persons should not be pressured into giving** and a person should pray about how much offering they will give. However, there are times when a need may arise in the church which the pastor would make known to the congregation and request that persons who can give should do so. There may even be a second or special offering collected specifically for that purpose.

Giving to charitable organisations

"Should giving to a charitable organization be from our tithes and/or offering?"

Several large charitable organizations are known for their involvement in the distribution of aid and other programs to assist the poor and destitute and other needy groups locally and internationally. Some of these organizations are the Christian Aid, Save the Children Fund of the UK and USA, and the Catholic Relief Service. These bodies are known to provide relief and aid, particularly to developing countries. Some programs that they undertake include the construction and furnishing of schools, providing medical services, the provision of pure water supply and the introduction of new and improved technology in farming, industrial and other projects.

> **What we spend money on and how we arrive at** financial and other **decisions** displays the level **of our spirituality.**

Voluntary contributions from Christians support many aid organizations and the poor in several countries. Many Churches have a council involved in raising funds particularly to purchase medical supplies, food items, clothing and other items to contribute to the needy in their community, to disaster relief programs and to provide financial and other forms of assistance to impoverished countries. Such contributions may be over an extended period or when a particular need arises, and/or when enough funds are available.

There are missionaries in several countries who are assisting communities in areas such as teaching literacy and numeracy programs, providing health care and other services. A common view in Christian circles is that we will only have a significant impact on the community if our focus is concentrated on preaching the gospel by word and deed. We are to be doers of the Word, which implies that as the light of the world, we must be good examples in giving of our time, money, professional skills, talents and other abilities in winning the lost to the Lord. These principles demonstrate the extent of our love to the Lord and for our fellow man. They are popularly summarized as *the '3-Ts' – treasury, time and talent*.

> The three principles of giving to God:
> * *Treasury* - giving to God His tithes, offering and also adequately supporting our family, giving to the poor and needy and other areas of financing the promotion of the gospel.
> * *Time* - quality time should be spent each day, as far as is possible, studying the Bible, in prayer and praise to God, spreading the gospel and helping the poor in community activities, for example.
> * *Talent* - most persons have some from of talent which they can use to enhance their standard of living as well as those around them and even further a-field. This include writing and publishing of Christian literature, singing gospel songs, teaching literacy and numeracy programs and being kind and loving to others.

Support of Christian Ministers

"Is it scriptural that we should support Pastors, missionaries and other persons in 'full-time ministry'?"

1 Corinthians 9:14 states: *"14In the same way, the Lord commanded that those who proclaim the gospel should get their living by the gospel."*

Galatians 6:6 also states: *"6Those who are taught the word must share in all good things with their teacher."*

These verses should be an impetus for ministers of the gospel to recognize that their ministries should be dynamic enough so that other persons would invest in their ministries. Some believers are professional singers, musicians, actors and use their profession not only to spread the Word, per sé but also as a commercial venture. The Levites in the Old Testament were instructed by the Lord not to hold secular jobs; instead they received support from the other tribes.

Some Christians feel the special call of the Lord on their lives to enter full-time ministry as a Pastor or missionary, for example, where they may be dependent on financial support from their local church and/or are sponsored by national and/or international Christian organizations. It is usually easier if one is serving under the administration of one's local church or other bodies since some established churches provide their full-time workers with amenities such as a salary and allowances, a furnished house, some means of transportation, a pension and other material benefits. There are, however, some persons who are called to serve in a particular geographical location or area of the ministry that their local church may not be willing to, or cannot provide the necessary financial and other forms of support.

There are instances where a person's vision is different from that of the Pastor or vision of the church. The Lord may also lead a person to start their own ministry. Even in such circumstances, it is important that such persons are supervised, report to, or are 'covered' by some ministry, if not from the inception, as early as possible. This is because Christians should not operate as 'headless bodies'. Very often a person who chooses to be 'non-aligned' eventually forms or joins a cult and/or preaches false doctrines. Care must be taken that one is not being rebellious or is being mislead by the Devil out of a spirit of pride, for example.

> Many Christians prefer to sacrifice earthly wealth in order to enjoy the riches of our heavenly kingdom. Sadly, many unsaved persons prefer to enjoy the wealth of this world to the detriment of the eternal wealth. Thankfully, Christians can choose to enjoy the best of both worlds.

CONCLUSION

This chapter reviewed several fundamental Biblical principles which will enable Christians to acquire, maintain and expand our material resources in according with the will of the Lord for our lives. Even though many unsaved persons become extremely wealthy by using methods which are not scriptural and they enjoy a high level of success in their achievements, they will never be able to enjoy the 'peace which passes all understanding' which the Bible speaks about. They also will not enjoy the favor of the Lord on this earth nor inherit eternity with Jehovah, His angels and His people.

Christians have the solemn responsibility to show the world that even though life is far more than the material things which we possess, yet we have the right to enjoy our life on earth, even 'with persecution'. How can we be poor and sad when we are the salt of the earth and the light of the world? If we are not in a position to cater for the material needs of our family, assist the poor and needy and also assist in the financing of the gospel; then we are a poor example of the manifestation of the provision of our Heavenly Father.

It is true that Jesus identified that there will always be poor people in the world. However, there is no evidence that He was inferring that Christians should be perpetually poor. It is also a fact that there are Christians who are refugees, living on welfare, and in other conditions which display their poverty. This should not be our permanent state and we have to trust Him and use the principles of the Bible to enable us to emerge from poverty. It is important that Christians follow the principles of the Bible which would enable us to acquire, maintain and expand our material resources, even as we grow in our spiritual lives. Once we build on the solid foundation, Christ Jesus, God will ensure that we have more than we need so that we are able to bless the lives of those around us, leave an inheritance for our children's children and engage in other activities which characterize the blessings which the Lord has bestowed on His children.

NOTES

****

Chapter 2: THE APPLICATION OF BIBLICAL PRINCIPLES IN MANAGING MATERIAL RESOURCES

INTRODUCTION

This Chapter continues to build on the foundation which was established in Chapter One by applying many of these principles to financial management practices which are topical today. Many Christians have become receptive in recent years to the fact that we have to present the Gospel in its holistic perspective; ministering to the spirit, soul and bodies of persons. Each of these aspects of our lives is important and even though issues pertaining to our spirit are given pre-eminence on many occasions, neglecting the other two spheres has led to an unbalanced life. This deficiency is increasingly being overcome as Christians apply Bible principles of financial management in our lives as individuals, the family and to the wider society.

We are called to be good stewards in all of our undertakings. Being good examples in spirituality alone has led many believers to neglect other important areas of our lives which should also glorify the Lord. We will thus focus on the application of Biblical principles in our daily financial dealings.

The Acquisition and management of wealth

"Who/what is the source of wealth, is it the Lord, the Devil and/or our common sense?"

Deuteronomy 8: 18 states: "¹⁸**But remember the Lord your God, for it is He who gives you power to get wealth, so that He may confirm his covenant that He swore to your ancestors, as He is doing today.**"

The first issue to note is that this passage only applies to followers of Jehovah. It is therefore possible for a non-Christian to acquire wealth but the source, even though they may acquire it honestly, is not Jehovah. This was an admonition to the Children of Israel which can also be applied to the lives of individuals even today. This scripture confirms that God does not pour wealth in one's pocket, per sé; rather He empowers His people to acquire wealth. This principle of the wisdom of God empowering persons to become wealthy is highlighted in most of the followers of Jehovah who are identified in the Bible. Examples of righteous persons who were wealthy include Abraham, Jacob Joseph, Job, Kings David and Solomon. In these examples we are told that they used the wisdom which God imputed in them or they received specific revelations of principles which they applied to enable them to amass much wealth. Even though the methods may differ, the application of His wisdom enabled these men to become wealthy.

Psalm 1:1-6 states: *"¹Happy are those who do not follow the advice of the wicked, or take the path that sinners tread, or sit in the seat of scoffers; ²but their delight is in the law of the Lord, and on His law they meditate day and night. ³They are like trees planted by streams of water, which yield their fruits in its season, and their leaves do not wither. In all they do, they prosper. ⁴The wicked are not so, but are like chaff that the wind drives away. ⁵Therefore the wicked will not stand in judgment, nor sinners in the congregation of the righteous; ⁶for the Lord watches over the way of the righteous, but the way of the wicked will perish."*

These verses identify that apart from the fact that the Lord gives us wealth, He is the one who is able to sustain us to the end of our days on earth and we will enjoy eternal life with Him. Among the blessings of the righteous which are highlighted in verse three is that they bring forth their fruits in season and their leaves will not wither. We are also told in verse five that the Lord watches over the way of the righteous. Surely, if the Lord is on the side of the righteous, then we are a victorious people.

The principle of God giving us the power to become wealthy is still applicable today, for there are numerous Christians who are rich materially as well as in wisdom, hospitality and other aspects of their lives. Many of these persons are involved in giving in abundance to charities, to various foundations, financing the spreading of the gospel, creating employment for hundreds of persons through their business, churches and other organizations.

It is true that the devil counterfeits many things which Jehovah has done. Many persons make sacrifices to Satan and serve him and they derive riches. An example of this is found in Acts 16where a slave girl who had a spirit of divination, was used by her owners by foretelling to future of persons who had to pay her owners for her services. She followed Paul and the other believers who were with him for a number of days and publically proclaimed them as being "slaves (servants) of the Most High God." This attest to the fact that satan and his demons are subject to the command of believers. After Paul cast the evil spirit out of her, her owners were angry since their source of income was taken away. They seized Paul and Silas and they were imprisoned. (The Lord miraculously delivered Paul and Silas from prison). The source of the wealth of the owners of the slave girl was not Jehovah since demonic forces influenced her practice.

> **Loving money, or anything else more than God is idolatry.**

Wealth versus materialism

"Is the wealth of Christians confined to material possessions?"

We are reminded of 2 Corinthians 8:9 which states: ***"⁹For you know the generous act of our Lord Jesus Christ, that though He was rich, yet for your sakes He became poor, so that by His poverty you might become rich."***

Riches are not confined to material things. However, when we examine the life of Jesus it is evident that He chose to live a materially humble life, yet He was not 'poverty stricken.' Even though Jesus' ministry was financed by persons who contributed to the material wellbeing of himself and disciples, this was by His choice, since He could have received 'riches untold' from His Father, if he desired that. It should be noted, however, that Jesus' ministry had well supported, since Judas was the Treasurer for the group. So, why is there need for a Treasurer if they were a bunch of poor men? Nevertheless, there were times when they did not have adequate amount of money to pay taxes and to feed the multitude of followers, for example. However, His robe was so valuable, that after He was crucified, the Roman Soldiers wagered for the possession of the robe. In addition, Mark 2:1 state: "'When He had returned to Capernaum after some days, it was reported that He was at home." Verse 4 relates that after it was discovered that Jesus was in the house, so many persons came to see him, that the house was crowded. The friends of a sick man who could not get through the crowd, removed a part of the roof of the house and let their friend down in front of Jesus. Jesus healed the sick man.

The question is often debated on what was implied in his response to the scribe who offered to follow Him. Matthew 8:20: "20And Jesus said to him, "Foxes have holes, and birds of the air have nests; but the Son of Man has nowhere to lay His head." This answer may have been in response to Jesus' perception that the scribe was not sincere and seeking to follow Him because he perceived that he would have derived material wealth if he followed Jesus.

The Biblical interpretation of wealth or riches is not confined to material possessions but also include:

1. Our abundance of spiritual authority such as the weapons of our spiritual warfare,
2. Protection of our health – by His stripes we were healed (inferring that the healing has already occurred and all we have to do is to claim it. Some translations use the word 'are' - inferring this is a continuous process).
3. He would not see His children begging bread,
4. Abundance of blessings in our home and other aspects of our lives, place of employment, community and nation,
5. The blessing of having the Holy Spirit guiding us, Jesus making intercessions for us, angels protecting us from danger and other benefits,
6. The blessing of the spiritual gifts operating in our lives and other forms of support from believers,
7. We have an eternal inheritance with the Father, the angels and the other saints when we die,

It is a fact that the riches which 2 Corinthians 8:9 promises does include the material riches which have been decreed on Christians. The reality is that many Christians are like the Prodigal Son No. 2, who has the wealth of Our Father at our disposal but refuse to pursue and/or to use.

Acquisition and management of wealth

"Are there fundamental differences between the ways the average Christian and non-Christian view wealth?"

There are so many fundamental differences in the way Christian and non-Christian view and manage money and other material possessions. The following are some of the general differences between Christians and non-Christians in the management of money and other assets.

The famous 'Jabez Prayer' in 1 Chronicle 4:10 identifies several fundamental principles which should guide the attitude of Christians as they seek to acquire and manage material wealth and other blessings. The verse states: "¹⁰***Jabez called on the God of Israel, saying, "Oh that you would bless me and enlarge my border, and that your hand might be with me, and that you would keep me from hurt and harm!" And God granted what he asked.***"

There are several aspects of this verse which are important to us. They include:

1. Jabez recognized that the source of all blessing was Jehovah. He did not rely on his own strength, wisdom, influence over others or other attributes which are under his control or that of others on whom he could depend for the necessary support. It is a fact that the Lord often uses several resources which we may have at our disposal to enable us to receive our material and other blessings. However, we should never lose sight of the fact that He is the source of all blessings.

2. We should not seek material and other blessings merely to satisfy our selfish ambitions and motives. It is true that in the blessings we should derive some of the benefits. Nevertheless, we should ensure that the majority of the benefits go to bless the lives of others. This truth is reiterated in King Solomon's request that the Lord would grant him wisdom to execute his duties as King, instead of desiring selfish gratifications.

3. We should always endeavor to stay within the control and anointing of the Lord, even as we fulfill His calling on our lives. A sad reality is that when many Christians begin to receive the blessings of the Lord and/or the influence which often comes with the blessings, they often misuse it by using it to their own detriment and/or that of others. Many of us become too greedy and are so engrossed in acquiring more wealth that we spend less time fellowshipping with the Lord and with other believers and doing the work of the Lord. Hence, our relationship with the Lord declines dramatically. We no longer wait for His direction, but in our own wisdom walk into our own destruction and very often the lives of others also. The life of Sampson is a good example of this principle.

4. We have to consistently rely on the Lords to keep us out of danger, seen and unseen.

5. This distinction is made since a person may be enjoying much financial and other forms of success but this is counted as a failure by the Lord if one is not living in

accordance with the principles of the Bible. As a matter of fact, Matthew 16:26 states: "²⁶*For what will it profit them if they gain the whole world but forfeit their life? Or what will they give in return for their life.*"

- **From a natural perspective**: One of the manifestations that a person has began to achieve financial freedom is when he moves beyond living from 'pay-check-to-pay-check' and instead enjoys large returns from the profitable returns from his investments.
- **From a spiritual perspective**: Financial freedom entails using one's financial and other resources in accordance with the direction of the Holy Spirit.

Some of the fundamental differences in the management of material resources between Christians and non-Christians are highlighted in the following table:

No.	Subject	Christian	Non-Christian
1	Source of wealth	Jehovah (Deuteronomy 8: 18)	Personal achievement, luck and chance, the devil.
2	Method by which wealth is acquired	Working smart, inheritance, from the unrighteous and other blessings from the Lord.	Working smart, inheritance, dishonest practices, gambling and other unscriptural methods.
3	Who owns it	The Lord (Matthew 6: 33).	Personal, family, corporate and other agencies.
4	Attitude toward material things	The more we give the more we get.	It is horded and often used for selfish and dishonest practices.
5	The use of money	To meet daily expenditure, helping others, for the spreading of the gospel and other things which glorifies to the Lord.	Many non-Christians obtain money and other assets honestly and use it for to finance daily expenditure, helping others. However, many others use their wealth to secure political power dishonestly, for selfish motives, to oppress others. It is true that many non-Christians use some of their money for humanitarian and other good causes. However, they do not derive the full blessings which such acts produce since the Lord does not accept the gift if the giver is not serving Him and/or his attitude is not pleasing to Him.

No.	Subject	Christian	Non-Christian
5	The use of money	To meet daily expenditure, helping others, for the spreading of the gospel and other things which glorifies to the Lord.	Many non-Christians obtain money and other assets honestly and use it for to finance daily expenditure, helping others. However, many others use their wealth to secure political power dishonestly, for selfish motives, to oppress others. It is true that many non-Christians use some of their money for humanitarian and other good causes. However, they do not derive the full blessings which are imputed in such acts, since the Lord does not accept the gift if the giver is not serving Him and/or his attitude is not pleasing to Him.
6	Primary quest in life	To pursuing God	To pursue material and/or other forms of success,
7	Importance of money	Christ is the center of our lives (Deuteronomy 8: 3)	Money is the center of life,
8	Recovering from loss of assets	Loss of assets for the sake of the gospel will receive one hundred fold in this life and eternal life (Mark 10: 29 to 31)	No guarantee of recovering assets once it is lost,

Table 2.1 Comparison Between Christians and Non-Christians the Acquisition and Management of Material Resources

In summary, we can conclude that we can be wealthy and still be Christians, once we follow the principles of the Bible in the acquisition and management of wealth.

Wealth Acquisition

Methods of accumulating wealth

"What are some of the scriptural and unscriptural methods which some persons use to become materially wealthy?"

Scriptural methods of acquiring material resources are:

1. **Pursuing lucrative career opportunities** such as owning and/or managing a well established business entity, a successful career as a musician, actor/actress, established farmers, holding senior management

offices and also careers such as a surgeon, judge, senior government official and other offices at the national level.

2. **Making prudent business decisions and investing their money wisely**,

3. **Years of consistent savings**,

4. **Earn it** by working at home, on a farm, factory, office and/or other places, from one's involvement in a business venture, or from a professional sport, for example.

5. **Receive an inheritance, gift/s and other forms of material blessings** from a relative or some other benevolent person. This is prevalent where the children and other relatives of wealthy persons would be included in the will of the deceased. Even the unrighteous gives to the saints. This should not be chorused dishonestly, but given willingly.

6. **Work smart** – this is still the most common method where a person works consciously and consistently to earn a salary and spend it wisely. It is common to hear that working smart is more profitable than merely working hard. Most persons would cherish something that they have acquired by planning, working and making sacrifices to achieve, rather than if it was acquired by a 'quick rich' scheme such as a large winning on the lottery. The beautiful principle is that while a person is accumulating resources, it would usually increase his capacity to manage it and plan meticulously to see it expand. The building process is usually the period where the Lord will interject His wisdom to enable us to expand our vision.

There are of course examples in the Bible where the Lord had to perform a miracle and provided financial and other resources instantly. However, generally, He works diligently on us to take us to the place where He can trust us with an abundance of earthly treasures when we have mastered the principle of giving all to Him so that He can bless it and return it to us in abundance.

7. **Investing wisely** – this includes acquiring the necessary skills in order to secure a high paying job, being involved in corporate activities and investing one's resources privately or purchasing shares, for example.

8. **Saving prudently** – this includes discipline methods of

saving consciously over a number of years in at least one high interest yielding account.

9. **Spending wisely** – this allows more money to be available for saving and investing.

10. Enjoy the **abundance of 'goodness and mercies' from the Lord.**

There are many ministers of the gospel who have acquired much wealth as a result of the significant growth of their church and the fact that members are faithful in their giving of finances and other resources to the church organizations *per sé* and also specifically to pastors and other officials. Some ministries also have a team of aggressive sales personnel who market tapes, CDs, literature and other products of the organization. Some ministries also have a private school, university or other training centers which students have to pay to attend.

Christians should not indulge in methods such as robbing and drug trafficking since these activities destroy the body and condemns the souls of the perpetuator and persons who partake in these activities. In addition, Christian should not seek after wealth for selfish reasons and to manipulate others because of the influence which the wealthy can exhort over the poor. Rather, the wealthy should use their resources as a means of improving the standard of living of their family, the community as a whole, and to spread the Gospel.

There are also several unscriptural practices from which material wealth can be acquired. They include:

1. **Cheating workers** – these methods include practices such as underpaying them, making deductions for income tax, medical and other funds and not paying them. These practices are unscriptural and also illegal.

2. **False representation** – including committing fraud, confidence tricksters who swindle the gullible of their hard earned money and other resources.

3. **Stealing** – this includes stealing from relatives and friends, from one's place of employment, breaking and entering homes and other places and carjacking.

4. **Gambling** – even though the percentage of players verses the outstanding winners is small, there is nevertheless a number of persons who have become rich after winning a large amount of money by playing the lottery, betting on horses or other forms of gambling.

5. **Usury** – a fundamental principle of most commercial activities involves some form of usury, where a

commodity is sold for more than it is worth, thus generating a huge profit to the seller. The notion of usury goes beyond merely making a profit. It also entails deliberately overvaluing an item in order to realize a huge profit.

6. **Cheating the Lord** – this feature includes not paying of one's tithes, not giving an offering which is commensurate of one's ability to give the increase profit and other forms of blessings, not helping the poor and not using one's time, talent and/or treasury for activities which bring glory to God, but instead is concentrating on personal and/or corporate wealth.

7. **Trafficking in narcotics, arms and ammunition and other prohibited items.**

8. **Prostitution including male and female prostitution, gigolos, gays, lesbians, pedophiles and persons who profit from the sex trade.**

In summary, there are three basic ways in which a Christian can acquire wealth. They are to:

1. **Earn it** from one's salary, income from a business venture, or from a professional sport (such as professional athletes, cricketers, footballers, baseball and basketball players), for example,

2. *Consistently* saved and invested prudently over a number of years,

3. **Receive an inheritance and other forms of blessings** from a relative or some other benevolent person. This is prevalent where the children and other relatives are included in the will of a deceased person.

4. **Imputed** means such as from the unmerited blessings from the Lord. It is true that as joint hairs with Jesus and the fact that we are in a covenant relationship with the Lord, there are several blessings which are inherent with this relationship. However, the Lord often blesses us merely as a demonstration of His loves for us and also to use us to 'show off' His mercies. 'We do not deserve it, yet we are blessed.' This is often in the demonstrated in activities such 'men giving to us', the Holy Spirit often birth and develop investments and other revelations which enable us to acquire financial and other blessings.

Methods of acquiring wealth:
• Work
• Inherit
• Returns from investments
• Imputed blessings from the Lord.

Basic necessities

"What are some of the material possessions which can be classified as 'basic necessities?"

Many families aspire to have basic necessities, depending on the society in which they live. In an affluent society this may include items such as:

1. A well-furnished and comfortable home with enough room to adequately accommodate the family and visitors,
2. One or several motor vehicles,
3. Having enough money for their education, to educate the children and to save for a 'rainy-day,'
4. Being able to have enough money to spend on food, clothing, leisure, sporting and other activities,
5. Engaging in investment programs which would significantly increase their income and provide them with the future financial security which they desire,
6. Having enough money accumulated for their pension, to take care of the family after the retirement of one or both partners, and to be able to maintain their home and live comfortably,
7. Having enough money for the medical, funeral and other expenses of loved ones and to sustain the family after the death of the breadwinner/s,
8. To be able to leave tangible items such as a house, jewelry and other assets for their survivors,

Nevertheless, there are millions of families who are extremely poor and are living in abject poverty, and one of their primary prayers for the day may be that they survive for another day. For the middle income family, even though their aspirations may not be as extensive, sadly, many such families may not achieve most of the above targets since they are living above their means. The rich and the famous may have a mansion in a luxurious location, villas in several countries and other luxuries, yet inwardly, they are unfulfilled in this life and will remain separated from Jehovah for all eternity. Whatever our material status in this life, it is important that we enthrone the Lord as the center of our lives – for what profit is there if we live in this world, irrespective of our material and other status and lose our soul and live separated from Jehovah in eternity when we die.

> God has never promised us, according to the paradox, a 'bed of roses' in this life. As a matter of fact, Jesus told His disciples that His true followers must be prepared to suffer afflictions and adversities as a result of following Him. As we choose to shun dishonest practices, such as stealing, gambling and other unscriptural activities for the sake of the gospel, we will be rewarded on earth and in the life after death.

Christians and Financial *Management*

"What are some of the financial management principles which are important to Christians?"

Prudent financial management principles which should be observed by Christian families include:

1. **Where possible, we should consistently invest at least ten percent (10%) of our income on prudent future income generating activities.** Since **the Lord blesses the work of our hands**, persons who are employed by an organization should ensure that some of the blessings 'of our hands' come directly to us, rather than to allow all of it to go directly to the owners of the organization. The blessing of promotion given by one's employer is not all that God has in store for us.

2. **Avoid getting into debt as far as possible,** primarily for consumer items which we can forgo and purchase when we have accumulated the cash price. Very often what is advertised as a bargain, pay later plan, gifts to accompany a purchase and/or other attractions have some hidden costs such as high interest rates and high penalties for defaulting on payments.

3. **It is unwise to seek to follow the 'Joneses' and purchase consumer items merely to keep up with the lavish life style of other persons.** This does not infer that a family should not strive to 'move up the social ladder' and improve their standard of living. Rather, the family must stay committed to:

   I. **Budgeting wisely,**
   II. **Living as much as possible within our means,**

III. *Ensuring that they engage in rigorous saving and investment programs,*

IV. *Encouraging their children to start saving at an early age. They also have to be groomed to make prudent, independent financial and other decisions,*

V. *Saving for future expenditure* such as for the higher education of the children, commencing early in the marriage,

VI. *Children should be encouraged to tithe from their allowance as well as to forgo the purchase of nonessential items for a good book and other items which will have a more profound influence on their lives in the future,*

VII. *Parents should also provide financial and other forms of support when the child shows an inclination to engage in an investment that may generate substantial returns in the future.* Preparation for life is not only emphasizing academic excellence but also the development of a well-rounded personality.

VIII. *Parents should, where possible, secure adequate medical and life insurance coverage for each member of the family to cater particularly for any emergencies which may occur, that is beyond the financial ability of the family.*

IX. *Investments in shares and other securities* in the name of the children are also practices of the more affluent families,

As far as possible, priority should be given to the fulfillment of long term goals particularly when it is possible to forego some short-term, less important pleasures.

The way we shop has a profound influence on the management of the family budget. Important considerations which are observed by several families who have been able to manage their budget include:

1. It is important that a grocery list is made of all of the important, and particularly the expensive items which have to be purchased. It may be necessary to include the price of the larger items so that an approximate cost can be allocated to the items to be purchased from particular stores or the market. It is not uncommon to find persons going to the cashier only to

find that the cost of the items presented to the cashier is more than the amount of money which they took with them. The embarrassment is usually in deciding which items to return while there is a line of other customers who are impatient. For this reason some persons would take a pocket calculator with them to avoid such embarrassing situations.

Adhering to purchasing only items on the list can be a mammoth task, particularly if there are small children who are demanding items which they may have been lured to by television advertisements. Of course there will be items which may have been omitted from the grocery list which may have to be purchased. However, this should be limited based on the budgetary constraint. Some families choose to leave their small children at home to avoid the temptation of patronizing them to the disadvantage of adhering to the budget, particularly if the child/children are liable to misbehave in the store. They may be taken to the store on occasions when there is excess money budgeted for them. Some wives extend this principle of leaving their husbands at home or in the car, particularly if he is prone to purchase items which may not be absolutely necessary at that time. Many husbands would 'go-over-board' to purchase items which they feel that their family deserves to have, even though it may not be on the budget. Of course there are also wives who are compulsive spenders and who would not adhere to the discipline of a budget.

2. It is important when purchasing vegetables, fruits and other perishable items that careful consideration is given to purchasing those which are in season and are therefore fresh and cheap. Very often locally produced items are also cheaper than imported items even though the imported items may be better packaged.

3. Principles such as purchasing items at a sale and storing them until they are needed also prove to be cost effective. This is particularly useful when purchasing items when stores are having a clearance sale in preparation for a new season, new stocks, as a sales promotion, or which are going out of business. Purchasing items at jumble and garage sales or on auction often prove to be great cost savers. Many persons purchase items such as a car and house at an

auction by making prior arrangement with a bank or mortgage company to inspect them prior to the date of the sale. These items may have been put on sale due to the inability of the previous owner to meet their mortgage payment.

4. Purchasing items in bulk at whole sale depots has proven to be a huge cost advantage for persons with adequate storage facilities and of course, the financial resources to engage the purchase without placing unnecessary pressure on their budget. Some persons indulge in group purchases to enjoy the cost advantage, and subdivide the items according to their individual contribution.

When we can keep our focus on the achievement of long-term goals, the more likely we are to forsake less important short-term objectives.

How much material assets are 'enough'?

"Is there a point at which the average individual becomes satisfied with their financial and other material resources?"

There is an insatiable desire for persons to consume more and more as their affluence increases. Very often we are deceived into believing that if we only are able to acquire a few basic necessities we will be satisfied and begin to enjoy life. However, most persons realize that as our income increases we will be able to 'live in comfort' with the material possessions which we envisioned would have been 'enough.' We also find that our vision becomes expanded and we aspire to achieve more material possessions. Very often this is so similar to the parable of the farmer who desired to build larger barns and enjoy his materially secured lifestyle and neglect the importance of the Lord in this equation.

Very often, as a person's income increases, his taste and lifestyle increases at a level which is beyond the scope of his immediate income. As an employee is promoted from a supervisor to a manager, for example, his associates often change as he is 'rubbing shoulders with the 'suits,' that is, persons in senior management positions who enjoy high income and a lavish lifestyle. The demands of the position may entail entertaining senior managers at one's home, or at least be associated with persons who live in an 'upscale' neighborhood, drive the latest and most expensive models of vehicles, and dress in a fashionable way. This additional pressure causes some persons to seek to live at a higher, or at least comparable, lifestyle to their peers. The result is often that they end up overextending their financial capabilities. The weak natured person may even engage in illegal practices to support his 'uplifted' lifestyle.

History has so many examples of persons who engaged in an extravagant lifestyle as their status in life increased. Notable examples are found among pop stars, actors and other celebrities, royalties, government officials and other persons. Emelda Marcus, the former First Lady of the Philippines, for example, is remembered for her extravagance in the collection of shoes. For the more wealthy persons it may be the collection of vintage sports cars and/or purchase a mansion or villa.

It is only a person who has truly committed all of his ways to the Lord who would be satisfied with what one has and not seek to accumulate more and more wealth as one's affluence increases. For the unregenerate man, the principle of 'the more one gets the more one wants' is applicable. The mature Christian would recognize that if one seeks to horde all of one's resources, it would eventually run dry; but that the more one gives, the more the Lord will pour into our lives. Nevertheless, there comes a time in the life of a believer, when one must recognize that like Moses and Apostle Paul, one has completed one's course and that it is time to pass the mantle on to one's successor/s.

> There is a famous Economics jargon which states: **The propensity to consume is a function of one's income.** The simple explanation to this phenomenon is that for most persons as their income increases, their consumption expenditure also increases to match the new income level. In actual fact, this is more applicable to persons who are poor, since for the average wealthy person, as his income increases, he seeks to increase his level of savings, and particularly investments.

The 'name and claim doctrine'

"Is it scriptural to indulge in the 'name and claim' practice which is common among some Christian congregations?"

Three important principles in our relationship with the Lord are:

1. Without faith it is impossible to please God. We have to believe that He will meet our needs, according to His mercies and love for us.
2. We have to confess or speak what we need,
3. We must learn to wait on Him for the manifestation of His promises,

For these and other reasons, it is important that Christians indulge in the practice of '**naming and claiming**' the things which we need or desire to see accomplished, and trust the Lord that it will be so. There are things which the Lord has placed within our abilities to do, for which we do not have to pray, but just do. There are other things, particularly spiritual gifts, which we have to trust the Lord to provide. However, there are other things, particularly those which are material in nature, which we have to trust the Lord to impress upon others to do for us. It is very important that we recognize that we have to name or confess what we desire from the Lord and claim it, or have the level of faith to see it come to fruition.

In summary, the three areas of 'having the desires of our heart' are:

1. The Lord strengthening or otherwise endowing us to accomplish it,
2. He provides it for us, particularly, spiritual gifts,
3. He uses others and/or circumstances to bless our lives,

The origin of the practice of the 'naming and claiming' principle was based on the necessity of identifying what one desired the Lord to do and believing that He would fulfill His promise to hear and answer our prayers, of course, once it is in conformity to His will for our lives. It is true that what we ask for and even fast and pray and trust the Lord to provide, we do not receive immediately, or sometimes not at all. However, once we pray in accordance to His will, He would grant us the desires of our heart.

Many persons have added a 'twisted' version of the practice of 'naming and claiming'. They are of the view that by simply confessing their desires to the Lord and believing that He will provide it, they will receive it. This belief has given rise to many persons refusing to work and 'claim' that the Lord would provide money for them, a house which someone worked hard to acquire, a 'fancy' car and other material things.

The contentious issue is usually where does Biblical faith end and disobedience begin? We are reminded that we are to 'decree a thing' and to 'command Him' is not limited to spiritual things since the Lord knows that we have need for material things which we may not have the means to acquire on our own at a particular time. Examples of the principle of 'naming and claiming' are manifested in areas such as revival and national transformation. God may not move unless His people call on Him and believe Him for the fulfillment of the desires of our heart. We have to reveal to Him the desires of our heart and have the faith for their fulfillment.

Some of the misconceptions which cause a distortion of this fundamental principle are:

1. We pray for things which are unscriptural. This may include things which would harm rather than bless the lives of others.

2. Our motive is sinful. This may include the fact that our motive is selfish and/or out of greed.

3. We do not knock, seek and have the patience to wait on the Lord for the fulfillment of our needs,

It is important that we are living in accordance to the will of the Lord for our lives and that what we name and claim is in conformity with His will for our lives, and that we are patient, obedient and persistent as we wait for the manifestation of His promise to grant us the desires of our heart.

We are reminded of Hebrew 11:6 which states that: "**6And without faith it is impossible to please God, for whoever would approach Him must believe that He exists and that He rewards those who seek Him.**"

We have to be careful that our 'faith' is not misdirected into the sin of coveting what belongs to our neighbor instead of working to achieve our own, when it is within our ability to do so. We are reminded that greed is tantamount to the sin of idolatry.

Hire purchase

"Why are items purchased on hire purchase so much more expensive than the cash price?"

When purchasing expensive furniture, a car, and other expensive assets, many couples choose the option of hire purchase, where this facility is available, rather than a cash payment. The hire purchase is usually more expensive because of factors such as:

1. The store has to add the extra cost associated with bearing the cost of the loss of immediate income since only a deposit is paid by the customer,

2. A risk premium is added onto the cost of the item as a reflection of the possibility that the customer may defaults on the payment on the facility,

3. The customer usually has to pay for the cost of insuring the item against fire, theft and other contingency as stated in the contract,

4. Hire purchase gives the customer the privilege of using the item immediately while depositing only a fraction of the actual cost of the item,

Lease finance

"Is leasing a prudent investment decision, particularly for middle and lower income earners?"

Some persons prefer the luxury of purchasing a new car every three years or so on hire purchase and trade in the old one. There are several advantages associated with this practice. They include:

1. They are afforded the opportunity of always having a trouble free vehicle, since most new cars will not normally experience major mechanical difficulties, unless it was involved in a major accident and there was gross neglect, for example,

2. It may add to their flamboyant lifestyle of always being in the fashion, since this practice enables them to lease vehicles which are fashionable at that time,

3. They avoid the problem of spending much money on repair and maintenance due to major wear and tear,

Unless one is very wealthy, this option is often not the best since if one is the owner of the car, with good care it will run for more than five years before major problems, such as the need to overhaul the engine and to re-spray it, occur. Savings from an owner driven vehicle can be channeled into other areas of the family budget. In many instances, a senior executive enjoys the privilege of being given a company vehicle to drive, thus one does not have to worry about maintenance or even purchasing petrol from one's salary. This privilege may be extended where a senior executive may be chauffeur-driven, which adds to the comfort of working hard at one's career.

Blessing others with our wealth

"What are some of the ways that Christians can use their wealth to be a source of blessing to themselves and others?"

There are several tangible ways which the wealthy can assist their community. They include:

1. **Establishing legitimate business ventures** which would create secured jobs for members of the society,
2. **Funding needy causes** such as orphanages, homes for the elderly and destitute, and contributing generously to other charitable events,
3. **Establishing scholarships and other programs** which would assist poorer persons to improve their standard of living,
4. **Contributing towards the establishment and maintenance of libraries, sports complexes, and other services which would benefit the community**,
5. **Paying their taxes and contributing to other funds** which will provide the revenue necessary to facilitate infrastructure activities such as health, education and other social services,

---

Methods of acquiring material resources include:

- **Earn it** through methods such as working at home, on the farm, factory, office and/or other places, from one's involvement in a business venture, or from a professional sport, for example,
- **Receive an inheritance, gift/s and other forms of material blessings,**
- **Obtain it through illegal practices** or the unrighteous it would include stealing, defrauding, blackmail others, and other unscriptural methods. These methods are not in keeping with Biblical principles.
- **Returns from savings and investments** such as dividends, interest and net income from business ventures,

---

'Enjoyment' by wealthy non-Christians

"Does a wealthy person who is not a Christian really enjoy life?"

An interesting passage to meditate on in this area is Proverbs 10:15, which states: **"¹⁵The wealth of the rich is their fortress; the poverty of the poor is their ruin."**

It is no secret that the majority of wealthy persons who are not Christians use their wealth to exploit the poor. This reality is vividly demonstrated in so many historical events and is prevalent in most societies today. The exploitation of the poor by the wealthy and the weak of the strong, was evident in slavery which existed and still exists in several societies in the world today. The exploitation of domestic servants, children and women in 'sweat shops' and other occurrences, is ample evidence of this practice. Many persons have transferred their material wealth into political and other power because of the influence which wealth wheels in most societies, sadly, even among Christians. This influence has been often used to pervert the course of justice, where the rich commit crimes and they are able to bribe the jury, judge and other officials and have verdicts made in their favor.

There are many examples which can attest to the literal truth of the former part of Proverbs 10:15. The home of the wealthy are usually constructed with the best building materials which they can secure. This is not only to make their home fashionable and comfortable but also to protect them from intruders. Some of the features of such homes may include:

1. Sturdy walls, doors, windows and other protective devices,
2. Iron grills to reinforce the protection of the occupants,
3. Very high concrete, chain-link and other types of fencing which may be supported by special material at the top which will seriously injure persons who attempt to climb over,
4. There may be electronically controlled gates and garage doors,
5. Security personnel may be employed to provide twenty-four hours protection. They may also be surveillance cameras where activities in various areas are constantly monitored by security personnel.
6. The house may be surrounded by a wide lawn, where intruders can be easily identified if they were able to enter the estate and approach the house,
7. The home is usually staffed by servants who would defend the household in the event that an intruder was able to enter the premises,
8. The wealthy may also be protected by security guards wherever they go,
9. The mansions of the wealthy are often located in exclusive neighborhoods where one would need special security clearance before entering,

The story is often so contrasting for the poor that one often wonders if the two groups are living in the same world and even the same society. It is common to find slums in close proximity to luxury homes and commercial centers. This is a common sight even in affluent countries.

Many wealthy persons enjoy several privileges such as:

1. Living in a 'fancy' house, which is lavishly furnished,
2. They may also be able to eat the quality and quantity of foods that they desire,
3. They may be able to wear the type of clothing which they desire and enjoy vacationing, driving the types of

cars (and/or other modes of transportation such as a private jet and several yachts) they desire and generally enjoy a high standard of living,

4. The children may be able to enjoy the standard of education and secure the type of career they desire,

If the average persons were given the choice of being rich or poor, most persons would prefer to be rich. They would however, be several qualifications such as they would prefer to be rich and still enjoy a happy family life, maintain a good relationship with other persons and not be snobbish and to maintain a close relationship with Jehovah.

A person can never really enjoy life when he is not serving the Lord. It is true that such a person would live comfortably and would not have to worry about having to satisfy the basic material necessities as the poor. However, a person who does not have the Spirit of the Lord living in his/her each day with an unfulfilled void. Such a person will not be able to enjoy the inner peace which comes from having the Lord as one's Personal Savior. This void is a result of the fact that man was created to fellowship with Jehovah. This relationship does not end when we die, but we will be spending eternity with Him.

Psalm 49 majors on the state of the wealthy who do not serve the Lord. Verses 16-20 states: *"¹⁶Do not be afraid when some become rich, when the wealth of their houses increases. ¹⁷For when they die they will carry nothing away; their wealth will not go down after them. ¹⁸Though in their lifetime they count themselves happy – for you are praised when you do well for yourself – ¹⁹they will go to the company of their ancestors, who will never again see the light. ²⁰Mortals cannot abide in their pomp; they are like animals that perish."*

We are also reminded of Matthew16:26 and Mark 8:36; the former states: *"²⁶For what will it profit them if they gain the whole world but forfeit their life? Or what will they give in return for their life?"*

Jehovah has created the spirit of man to commune with Him. For this reason *a person who does not have a relationship or is not in right relationship with Him, identifies that there is a void in him which cannot be satisfied by the pleasures of life, the 'comfortable' lifestyle which wealth often creates or any other man-made phenomenon*. Even persons who seek to foster a relationship with Jehovah through religious and other persuasions which are not consistent with Biblical principles would recognize that the void still remains unfulfilled. There is only one way to the Father; that is through His son, Jesus.

A famous maxim states:

"No God, no peace,
Know God, know peace."

It is true that the unrighteous do enjoy some aspects of happiness. A person who drinks alcohol, for example would interact in merriment with his friend during the drinking session. However, the aftereffect of excessive alcohol is often drunkenness, which has resulted in countless persons dying in an accident, poverty, robbery along with personal health and other hazards of the drinker. Similarly, an unsaved person would benefit from providing financial security, acquiring political and other forms of authority. However, such a person would not enjoy the blessings of having the presence of the Lord in their lives, fellowshipping with Him and to enjoying the spiritual and other blessings which we enjoy. There is also the eternal benefit of being with Him in eternity.

Christians managing material wealth

"Can Christians serve the Lord and still be materially wealthy?"

A scripture passage which has been a major obstacle in preventing some persons from optimizing their potential in securing material possessions while serving the Lord since they misinterpret its meaning is Matthew 6:24, where Jesus stated: **24"No one can serve two masters; for a slave will either hate the one and love the other, or be devoted to the one and despise the other. You cannot serve God and wealth (mammon)."**
The passage must be reviewed in the context that Jesus was addressing the disciples and not the multitudes of people. He was discussing 'Kingdom-business' with His disciples. Unless we make Jehovah, the Lord of our lives then we will make the Devil our ruler. Many persons have placed the pursuit of material and other things above serving the Lord. This is idolatry and even though such persons may be religiously inclined, the Lord would not fellowship with them. He is either Lord over all or over none. He would not share His glory with man, the Devil or anything or anyone else. We are reminded of Matthew 6:33 and Luke 12:31 where Jesus instructed His disciples that once they sought the Kingdom of God first all things will be added to them. Jesus told His disciples in verse 19 of Matthew 6 not to store treasures on earth but to store their treasures in heaven since treasure on earth is subject to be stolen or destroyed in some other way. Jesus went on to encourage them that

Jehovah is well able to provide for them above that which He does for the birds and the grass of the field. Christians have been endowed with wisdom, we have the Holy Spirit operating in our lives, the prayer and other forms of support from other congregations, there seems to be no reason why we cannot use the resources at our disposal to accumulate as much wealth as we can manage once we are resolute to be faithful in all of our ways to the Lord.

As we seek the Lord He will bless us in abundance. Once we choose to use His blessings wisely, we will be able to at least 'live comfortably. It may not necessarily be in luxury but at least our basic needs will be satisfied. If we choose to avail ourselves to use His blessings to be wealthy, many more of us can do so.

The wise man Solomon repeatedly stated that wealth is vanity. Of course most of us would prefer to enjoy the 'vanity' of wealth rather than to live in poverty. Psalm 49:16-17 also tell us about the fleeting illusion of wealth, since we will not take the material wealth which we acquire on earth with us when we die. However, Isaiah 60 identified some of the benefits which the righteous will derive when the glory of the Lord comes upon us. Verses 5, 8-10 state: **"⁵Then you shall see and be radiant: because the abundance of the sea shall be brought to you, the wealth of the nations shall come to you…. ⁸Who are these that fly like a cloud, and like doves to their windows? ⁹For the coastlands shall wait for me, the ships of Tarshish first, to bring your children from far away, their silver and gold with them, for the name of the Lord your God, and for the Holy one of Israel, because He has glorified you. ¹⁰Foreigners shall build up your walls, and their kings shall minister to you; for in my wrath I struck you down, but in my favor I have mercy on you."**

This passage relates some of the abundance which Jehovah has decreed for the children of Israel. There are also several individual blessings which are also decreed for the individual believer, even as we serve Him.

Wrong attitude in managing material wealth or resources

"What are some of the wrong attitudes which are used by some persons in managing material resources?"

A classic example of a person who displayed a self-centered attitude in managing material resources, is seen in Jesus' parable of the Rich Fool. Luke 12:13-21 states: **"¹³Someone in the crowd said to Him, "Teacher, tell my brother to divide the family inheritance with me." ¹⁴But He said to him,**

"Friend, who set me to be a judge or arbitrator over you?"
[15]And He said to them, "Take care! Be on your guard against all kinds of greed; for one's life does not consist in the abundance of possessions." [16]Then He told them a parable; "The land of a rich man produced abundantly. [17]And He thought to himself, What should I do, for I have no place to store my crops. [18]Then he said, 'I will do this: I will pull down my barns and build larger ones, and there I will store all my grains and my goods. [19]And I will say to my soul, 'Soul, you have ample goods laid up for many years; relax, eat, drink, be merry.' [20]But God said to him, 'You fool! This very night your life is being demanded of you. And the things you have prepared, whose will they be?' [21]So it is with those who store up treasures for themselves but are not rich towards God."

There are several negatives which Jesus identified in the rich man in this parable, including:

1. **The man displayed an attitude of greed.** Instead of thinking of how he could have used a part of his abundance to offer unto the Lord as tithes and offering and giving to the poor, he was contemplating how he could use it to amass more wealth and comfort for himself.

2. **He did not give thanks to the Lord for His blessings but was attributing the success of his crops to himself,**

3. **His carnal nature of eating, drinking and being merry and to enjoy his material possessions was more important to him than acknowledging God as the source of his blessings and who is able to sustain him,**

We have to recognize that God does not need our money in order to accomplish His will. However, He expects that we manage the resources which He has placed at our disposal in a way which brings glory to Him. The better we are at being stewards of His resources, the more He will allow material and other resources to come our way. There is, however, a limit to what we can do on our own, since our ability to acquire and manage wealth would be restricted by factors such as our health, age and of course, the inevitability of death, unless the Lord returns during our lifetime. The difference comes when we allow the Spirit of the Lord to direct our path as He pours His blessings in our lives.

In Luke 16:11-12 Jesus made the following statement: *"[11]If then you have not been faithful with dishonest wealth, who will entrust to you the true riches? [12]And if you have not been faithful with what belongs to another, who will give you what is your own?"*

Verse 11 implies that there is a connection between the way we manage wealth and our spiritual standing. In many instances, if we cannot pass the money test then we will not be able to graduate into achieving spiritual maturity. The reality of this inference is evident in the lives of many ministers, gospel singers and other Christians who 'backslid' after they acquired much wealth and fame. Many such persons fostered secret dreams and hopes of becoming rich and/or famous. Once they acquired this, they stop serving the Lord. Therefore, when it comes to the point of putting their honesty to the test they failed and were exposed with fraud, tax evasion and other sinful acts. A person who has a serious problem with being honest in managing money, may eventually be exposed for this weakness later in his life, unless he allows the Holy Spirit to deal with it. There are so many examples of ministries breaking up because of the financial impropriety of prominent believers.

Many of the problems which we experience do not necessarily arise from attitudes which are deemed as negative alone. They also arise from thoughts, wishes, dreams and other areas of our lives which are not surrendered to the Lord. Many persons who are poor spend much of their time dreaming of becoming rich and famous. If what a person desire to have or to become is to him a greater life goal or achievement that serving the Lord, he has in fact backslidden.

> The primary mission of money is for it to be acquired honestly and utilized prudently to bless our lives and that of others. For this reasons Luke 6:38 tell us that as we give more will be given to us, pressed down, shaken together and running over will men give to us. For this reason the wealth of the stingy very often is lost in his lifetime or shortly after his death.

Christians blessing others even in material poverty

"Can we as Christians be materially poor and still be a blessing to others?"

Encompassed in the common definition that 'blessing is the empowerment to prosper,' is the fact that blessings is not only need material in nature. This is so because prosperity is not limited to accusation of material resources.

There are several ways a Christian can be a blessing to others which is not financial in nature. They include:

1. **Ministering to them of the saving grace of the Lord.** There is nothing as liberating as the gospel, for once we invite the Lord into our life, we receive the Source of all

blessings.

2. ***Praying and interceding that the Lord intervenes to meet a particular need in another person's life.*** When we use the spiritual authority which the Lord has endowed in us, we are able through the intervention of the Holy Spirit, to see the fulfillment of the needs of others. This include praying for the sick and seeing them recover, providing prophetic direction for others by being in the place where the Holy Spirit can use us.

3. ***Providing council and guidance to persons who are encountering spiritual, financial and other difficulties,***

4. ***Being a good role model in healthy living, members of the family serving the Lord and generally living in a way which challenges others to seek to emulate your lifestyle. Apostle Paul, for example, admonished others to follow him even as he followed Christ.***

5. ***Helping the poor and needy in areas such as the cleaning of their home, yard and by being their friend,***

There seem to be no reason why a Christian should not be able to legitimately acquire a fraction of the wealth of the world, say a few million dollars, and yet remain focused on serving the Lord. How can Christians assist their neighbors with financial and other material need, when the Christians themselves do not have money and other material things for themselves? Peter and John, in Acts Chapter 3, demonstrated a classic example of this principle when they were going to the temple to pray. They met a lame man who was begging alms at the gate called Beautiful. Although they did not have money to give him to God, through the disciples, performed a miracle and the lame man received strength in his feet. This no doubt was more important to him than if they had merely satisfied his temporary financial need.

Can we give a better gift to this sin-sick world than the love of Christ in its totality; healing for the sick, the provision of sound financial advice, rendering assistance to eradicate, or at least significantly reduce poverty and leading them to the path of eternal life? This is also an example where we often mistake what our most pressing needs are and we thus need revelation knowledge from the Holy Spirit to direct us and to assist others. The lame man felt that his most pressing need was money, but Peter knew differently. It was the lack of spiritual and physical vision which caused the man to beg. When he was able to use his limbs, he received the ability to earn a living on his own.

As we preach the Gospel to the poor, we have to follow the example of Jesus who did not only satisfy the spiritual needs of the people but also provided physical food for the hungry. Financial miracles still occur in the lives of Christians and in communities throughout the world. There is also the need for Christians to provide financial assistance to the Body of Christ and to the unsaved.

In many instances when Christians embark on projects such as the construction of a church, they are unable to raise enough money to finance the project through their congregation or other supporting bodies. They often resort to obtaining credit from financial institutions such as a bank or building society. The leaders of some Christian organizations advocate that we should not borrow money or other commodities from other persons or institutions. This principle largely constitutes the activities of some Christians who believe that they should 'live by faith'. The Bible advocates that an adult who can be gainfully employed, but who deliberately chooses not to work when he is well and the employment and other facilities are available for him to do so, should not be given any food. (2 Thessalonians 3:10).

Many Christians believe in the principles of trusting God for miracles in healing and other matters. Yet in emergencies and in business ventures, they may resort to borrowing money from relatives, friends, financial institutions and from the church they attend. Several church bodies have emergency and/or contingency funds to help destitute believers. They provide financial support to believers in times of emergency, help the poor, widows and orphans in the community, and even provide capital for enterprising members. These programs often go a long way to enable believers to emerge from a state of financial lack by engaging in income-generating activities.

While we are in this world, Christians share all of the basic needs as everyone else. We need items such as food, clothing, housing, a high standard of education and for some persons, capital for investment. In many countries Christians follow several traditions of their communities including the financing of elaborate weddings, birthday celebrations, 'naming' or christening ceremony to celebrate the birth of a baby and also the financing of funerals. Financing these activities is often beyond the means of the family. Therefore, unless the Lord provides through sources such as gifts from others, many persons secure credit to meet these expenditures.

In weddings, for example, even for Christians, due to their personal desire and/or the pressure from relatives and friends, elaborate wedding receptions are often held. It is sad to observe that many couples start their marriage with a huge debt that stifles their financial progress for many months, if not longer.

It is true that money plays a very important part in our daily activities. Our role as the light, salt of the earth and other attributes are often essential in areas which do not demand money *per sé*. This is often demonstrated in the operation of the gifts of the Spirit in our lives which produces deliverance which money and other material assets cannot achieve. When a Christian leads a person to the Lord, there is no monetary value that can be attributed to the present and eternal value of this blessed experience.

A person may be healed even after the doctor may pronounce the case as being hopeless, or a drug addict may be set free from his expensive addiction which was ruining his life and that of his family and the wider society. Even so, money is still important in facilitating important aspects of the logistics of sustaining us, and spreading the gospel. However, our spiritual and other functions often go beyond the scope of money. A simple illustration is that many churches which are merely financially strong would not have a significant positive impact on society as one where the believers follow the principles of the Bible such as prayer, fasting and evangelism.

In essence, the answer to the question is yes and no. Lack of financial resources limits a Christian's ability to be a financial blessing. However, one wonders if Peter and James had money (alms) to offer the lame man, whether or not they would not have overlooked his real need, merely to satisfy his want? The lame man's real need was physical sight. However, there are situations where the need is financial and/or other material resources. Prayer and other spiritual interventions may not totally satisfy a particular need. James 2:15-17 states: "**15If a brother or sister is naked and lacks daily food, 16and one of you say to them, "Go in peace; keep warm and eat your fill." And yet you do not supply their bodily needs, what is the good of that? 17So faith by itself, if it has no works, is dead."**

Happiness derived from material wealth

"Isn't it true that being wealthy brings much happiness?"

There are many persons in most communities who are better off than the average person, who can be classified as being wealthy, but whose life are filled with much misery, and they are living in enmity with members of their family, neighbors and other persons. Even though being a Christian does not guarantee that a person would be materially wealth, it does enable a true believer to be content with the material possessions which he has presently, while being challenged to significantly improve his status in life.

Deuteronomy 8:17, 18 God identified the source of lasting wealth which will be of a blessing to the person/s who accumulated it and also to others. It states: *"17Do not say to yourself, "My power and the might of my own hand have gotten me this wealth. 18But remember the Lord your God, for it is He who gives you power to get wealth, so that you may confirm His covenant that He swore to your ancestors, as He is doing today."*

> **There are many wealthy persons whose lives are filled with much misery, and they are living in enmity with members of their family, neighbours and/or other persons. Of course there are persons who are poor and suffer the same fate. Even though being a Christian does not guarantee material wealth, it does enable a true believer to be contented with the material possessions which one has presently, while one will be challenged to significantly improve one status in life in the future.**

Most persons prefer riches to poverty. Some of the benefits of the rich are:

1. They are likely to enjoy a life where they do not have to worry about having access to material needs such as food, clothing and housing,
2. They are able to enjoy a high standard of medical facilities, education, recreation and live in luxury,
3. They are often able to translate their material wealth into obtaining political influence in their society, if they choose to do so. This is seen in the life of the Rockefeller and Kennedy families in the US, for example. This influence has often resulted in the rich taking advantage of the poor and committing crimes and being able to bribe officials and/or hire the best legal team and are freed from indictment or receive very light penalties.
4. They are usually able to use their wealth and influence to invest in economic ventures and generate higher returns than small scale investors. This is so because of the scale of their operation and economic, financial and even political clout.
5. They are usually better able to diversify their investment in their home country and beyond and in several economic ventures in order to prevent a total disaster as if they were investing in one venture which failed,

The life of the rich is often not as glamorous as it appears. Some of the problems which the wealthy encounter are:

1. They have to take extra precaution to safe guard their assets from thieves and deceitful persons who seek to rob them. For this reason many rich persons live behind high fences and other security systems,

2. Many of them also live a life of seclusion as they have grown to mistrust even close relatives and friends who may seek to deceive them,

3. Many of them have come to the realization that even with their wealth, without Christ they are still miserable inside,

4. The children of many wealthy families are snobbish and they find is difficult making friends. Problem such as drug addiction is common among the wealthy.

We have established earlier that there is nothing inherently wrong in being rich, providing we adhere to principles such as recognizing Who is the Source of riches, not making our riches an idol and using our wealth to glorify God.

Spending, a reflection of our personality

"Is it true that the way we spend is often a true reflection of our personality?"

There is a popular maxim which states:

"Show me your check book and I will know what your priorities are."

This maxim can also be related to persons who do not use checks to review how they allocate their budget.

Many persons, even with a well planned budget would still engage in haphazard and impulsive spending and at the end of the month, they are dissatisfied with the way their money was spent. For this reason **we must prioritize our spending and ensure that as far as possible we adhered to a well structured giving, spending, saving and investment program.**

The way we purchase items say quite a lot about our personality, irrespective of if we have much or little money to spend. Many persons purchase items on impulse, without taking consideration of more important factors than the compulsion that the item must be secured 'at any cost'. This state is often as a result of being induced to secure the item as a result of TV advertisement or seeing someone else with it.

There are persons who rush to the store and purchase a piece of exercise equipment, for example, after seeing it advertised as having contributed to the beautiful physique of the beautiful model or outstanding actor, for example. Little do many persons know of the amount of money which the persons who are promoting the item was paid, in many instances merely to affix their support to the promotion of the item which may not have even contributed to the success which the presenters are advertising. After purchasing the item, the gullible consumer may only use it on a few occasions and realize that in order to achieve the level of success which is advertised, a high level of discipline, which the purchaser may not be able to inculcate very easily, is demanded.

There are of course many persons who are inhibited from managing money the way they would have liked to because of budgetary and other constraints. Even then, our personality in dealing with stressful situations is also manifested by the way we spend. There are many persons who simply cannot bring themselves to the discipline of adhering to a budget, irrespective of the financial constraint. This is often a reflection of their inability to discipline their lives in financial management and other areas of their lives.

Maintaining historical financial recording

"How long should financial records such as bills, receipts and used checks be kept?"

The importance of maintaining accurate past financial and other important records cannot be overemphasized. Many persons are in the habit of discarding receipts, bills and other documents as soon as the transaction is completed. This may include receipts for the payments of rent, credit card statements, used checks which the issuer used, which were returned by their bank and other documents which represent the conclusion of particular transactions. In some instances after the document is discarded, we realize that we need it to verify that the transaction occurred. A common example of this practice is when a credit card company is claiming that the value of a particular transaction was much higher than the cardholder can recall. Since the bill was discarded by the cardholder and the seller may be reluctant, or even unable to produce a desirable duplicate receipt, the cardholder may be left in a position where he has to honor the payment. The cardholder may be able to resort to the court to force the seller to produce the record of the transaction. However, the cardholder may prefer to retain the use of the card that he accepts liability in an attempt to resolve the matter.

In many instances we have to produce the bank statement, receipt or other documents to verify the authenticity of a transaction for which a tax deduction is being sought. The legal requirement of some countries is that records should be keep for at least six years in order to verify particular transactions.

Methods use by the Jehovah to meet our material needs

"Is there a fixed way that the Lord relates to His people in the area of meeting our material and other needs?"

It is interesting to observe the methods which God used when dealing with the generation of the children of Israel under Moses and Joshua. Under Moses, God opened the Red Sea for them, manna fell from heaven, Moses struck the rock with his staff and drinking water flowed from it, and other miracles were performed. Under Joshua, it was a different relationship in many respects. The people had to work very hard and fight to expel the hostile nations. He often relate to us in accordance with the spiritual level where we are. We are not expected to remain as spiritual babes but to mature in the things of Christ.

The Lord has provided us with the means to improve our financial position and our general way of life, by giving to us several tools which will enable us to achieve this feat. For this reason there are many things which we do not have to ask and plead to Him to provide for us, since He has already placed them at our disposal. We merely have to thank Him for these and other strategies at our disposal and implement them to achieve the success which He has already given to us. They include:

1. His untenable favor, which He gives to Christians as they walk in right standing before Him. This is illustrated in the life of Daniel, for example. Daniel 1:8, 9 states: **"8But Daniel resolved that he would not defile himself with the royal rations of food and wine, so he asked the palace master to allow him not to defile himself. 9Now God allowed Daniel to receive favor and compassion from the palace master."**

2. Very often opportunities are presented to us that we have no other choice but to recognize that they must have been the Lord presenting the avenue for us to improve our financial situation. This does not infer that every opportunity comes from the Lord, for we must be

discerning in differentiating what is a blessing from the Lord as against a deception from the devil. It should also be stated that the Lord does not always grant His favor freely. In some instances it has to be earned by our faithfulness, persistence and other positive attributes.

3. The word of wisdom, discernment and other spiritual gifts which may manifest in our lives or others from whom we may seek godly council,

4. The weapons of our warfare, many of which we can apply to the management of a business, at our place of employment or whatever method we are using to increase our financial resources,

It is a fact that God often grants us material wealth and other blessings without us having to work specifically for it. This is usually in response to principles such as:

1. Receiving a substantial increase from investments which we have made such as sowing a 'financial seed' giving to the work of the Lord and helping the poor,

2. The blessing of inheritance from our parents, grandparents and other persons,

3. We are saved medical and other expenses, protection from burglars and other catastrophes because of His grace, mercies, favors and other blessings which He extends towards us. This does not infer, however, that as Christians we are insulated from disasters. A frequently used illustration of this occurrence was in the life of Job. In addition, each of us will die, unless the Lord returns before, or we are 'taken up to Heaven' like Enoch, for example. The difference between Christians and the unsaved is that the Lord is with us even through such trials, and we have an eternal assurance that He will never leave us nor forsake us. Hebrew 13:5 states: **"⁵Keep your lives free from the love of money, and be content with what you have; for He has said, "I will never leave you or forsake you."**

This principle needs to be applied since there are several scriptures which attest to the fact that He would not grant us responsibilities above that which He is confident that we have been adequately prepared to manage competently or we have the capacity to grow to. He would also, where necessary, send others to enable us to fulfill our mandate. In view of these factors, we have to abide under the anointing of the

Lord, have a sensitive spirit to know His voice, and be obedient to follow, even as He leads. However, there are many occasions when we have to 'sweat' for it and work hard to ensure that it continues to operate successfully.

4. Addition comes when we seek first the Kingdom of God. This covenant was presented in scripture verses such as Matthew 6:31-33 which states: *"³¹Therefore do not worry, saying, 'What will we eat?' or 'What will we drink'? or 'What will we wear?' ³²For it is the Gentiles who strive for all these things; and indeed your heavenly Father knows that you need all these things. ³³But strive first for the kingdom of God and His righteousness, and all these things will be given to you as well."*

Christians and gambling

"Should Christians engage in Gambling?"

The issue of whether or not Christians should be involved in gambling has split many congregations, families and persons in the wider society. Many governments have legislated gambling and some churches and other organizations support this practice. Therefore, there are established horse racing dens, casinos, national lotteries, bingo and other betting houses and also gambling via the internet. There are several sporting and other activities where betting and other forms of gambling play an essential part. They include horseracing, football and boxing. Several church organizations would host bingo and other activities involving persons 'trying out their luck' in order to win monetary and other prizes. These activities are usually a vital part of their annual fair and other fundraising activities. This may cause dissatisfaction from members who do not agree with these practices.

> God has provided strategies which, if we apply them to our personal lives, business, governments and other institutions will enable us to at least live comfortable on earth if not to be wealthy and prosperous. He will not share His glory with the devil, since He is Jehovah-Jireh, our provider. Therefore, it is no surprise that most Christians even if they choose to be disobedient and indulge in sinful acts such as gambling, never win the jackpot. Yet He continues to meet all of our needs.

It should be noted that there are several references in the Bible of persons 'casting lots' in order to arrive at a crucial decision. This included the choice of a successor for Judas after he committed suicide. In most of these incidents it was stated that the persons who were casting lots prayed before doing so, and the names of the persons from whom the selection had to be made were placed in a container. A member of the group would place his hand in the container and randomly select the name of one candidate. Even though there was no 'scientific' method of selection to determine the candidate, the fact that a prayer was offered before the selection, the process was seen as being directed by God. If, on the other hand, the process is not preceded by prayer and other measures which involved the direction of the Lord, then it is tantamount to gambling. Nevertheless, the practice of praying that one wins the lottery or for a special revelation of the 'lucky' number/s is not supported by scripture.

There are several issues surrounding the act of gambling which render it unscriptural. These include:

1. ***Gambling practices such as bingo and lottery do not usually entail having to use a high level of intelligence or personal ingenuity in order to be able to win***. It is primarily dependent on 'luck and chance', which is not consistent with Biblical principles. Even though **faith** does not depend on our reasoning, intellectual ability and even personal ingenuity, the 'Bible type of faith' does not support gambling. Hebrew 11:1 states: ***"¹Now faith is the assurance of things hoped for, the conviction of things not seen."***

   The remainder of Hebrew 11 outlines examples of what 'Biblical' faith entails. In none of these examples was there any illustration that gambling constituted faith. Some persons have presented an argument that faith is also gambling since it may or may not occur. Our assurance is that once our lives are in good standing with the Lord and what we trust the Lord for is consistent with His will for us, then He will answer our prayers. 1 John 3:21-22 states: ***"²¹Beloved, if our hearts do not condemn us, we have boldness before God; ²²and we receive from Him whatever we ask, because we obey His commandments and do what pleases Him."***

2. ***Most persons who engage in gambling are not doing so with the intention of assisting anyone else*** other than themselves to win the 'jackpot prize.' This obviously is not the Biblical exposition that 'men will give onto our

bosoms.' Philippians 2:3-5 states: *"³Do nothing for selfish ambition or conceit, but in humility regard others as better than yourselves. ⁴Let each of you look not to your own interests, but to the interests of others. ⁵Let the same mind be in you that was in Christ Jesus."*

It is true that many gamblers tithe or at least would give a sizable portion of their winnings to the church, to relatives and friend and/or to charity. Even so, the Bible does not condone gambling.

3. *A very high percentage of persons gamble, become addicted to it,* even though they may not be willing to admit it, or may not have even recognized it. Stopping the practice is often very difficult and they have to undergo deliverance or treatment before they overcome the addiction. Many persons continue to play with the hope that the next game will be the 'big one,' where they will become rich.

4. *Greed fuels gambling,* as the gambler endeavors to acquire more than he would normally be able to earn legally. Colossians 3:5 states: *"⁵Put to death, therefore, whatever in you is earthly; fornication, impurity, passion, evil desire, and greed (which is idolatry). ⁶On account of these the wrath of God is coming on those who are disobedient."*

5. *A large number of gamblers engage in stealing, lying and other sinful acts in order to finance this addiction.* Persons who live with a compulsive gambler can relate to the dramatic mood swings which the gambler experiences as he/she is propelled to take 'just another chance' in an attempt to regain his/her loss or to win 'the big one'. Such persons are usually abusive to those around them as they contemplate on fueling this addiction. Many gamblers end up selling all or most of their valuable assets, their bodies and any other item which they can sell in order to gratify this addiction. Many such persons have to undergo therapy, prayer and deliverance in order to be freed from this demon. Once we are willing to deal with 'lucky numbers' and other issues of chance, the devil and his demons are in the background to lure us further and further into demonic activities unless we denounce these activities.

6. *Gambling lures people into a false state of security* as they fantasize on what they would do, for most gamblers – the ever elusive dream of '*when they win the big one*.' This deception often causes such persons

to spend lavishly and make financial and other decisions which they perceive will reflect their lifestyle 'when they win.' For most gamblers, this is never a reality, at least not to the extent which would make their 'dreams come true.'

7. *Many persons consult fortunetellers, witches and other mediums for their 'lucky number' and other directions on how they should gamble.* Therefore, the money which is paid out is usually 'tainted'. It is true that the same criticism can be leveled at the owners of some businesses and other facilities with which we often do business and conduct other activities. Persons who consult mediums are usually possessed by demons, or at least they are influenced by demons. They may be instructed by these forces to perform various rituals, feed the poor, children and even to donate monetary and other gifts to charitable organizations. Many of these activities are really the devil using counterfeit measures to Biblical principles in an attempt to initially disguise his vicious ploy to make them feel that they are on the right path and gradually lead them into deeper deception which would lead to the damnation of their souls. Therefore, we have to be careful who we accept gifts and favors from, for accepting gifts from Satanists may transfer demonic forces to us.

8. *The average gambler is never satisfied* as he/she endeavors to win higher stakes.

9. *The lives of most gamblers are unhappy even if they win a substantial amount of money or other assets.* This is often so because they find themselves surrounded by relatives and friends whose loyalty and affection may not be genuine and is extended with the aim of receiving a monetary gift or other favors.

10. *Gambling contradicts the very basis of us relying on the principles of God's provision* since it takes our reliance away from God as the gambler seeks to invoke a force other than God to provide the winnings. The same analogy does not apply to us working to earn a living. We are admonished in Proverbs 28:20 that: *"20The faithful will abound with blessings, but one who is in a hurry to be rich will not go unpunished."*

11. After the fall of man in the Garden of Eden, God decreed to men in Genesis 3:19:*"19By the sweat of your face you shall eat bread until you return to the*

ground, for out of it you were taken; you are dust."

Over the years, women have also joined the secular work force, and there is a large number of occupations which can be classified as non-manual labor. The primary principle of work is that it entails the use of our intellect, physical strength, skills, the application of knowledge, experience, training and other faculties to generate a desired output. Usually the element of 'luck and chance' does not enter the main stream of what is classified as work. It is true that very often factors other than market forces may influence the price of a particular item which is sold, however, most of what is classified as work is not dependent on 'luck and chance'. A farmer, for example, may decide to plant a crop outside of the normal planting season and is able to harvest outside of the normal reaping season of the crop and thus generate a high return as a result of the demand for the product due to the shortage in the supply of the item. The breaking away from the tradition may have entailed that he would have had to be more attentive to the crop and possibly use more fertilizer, water or irrigate the land and apply more care and attention to sustain the plants through the adverse weather conditions. However, the outcome was not a result of luck or chance.

> Since the 'flesh' will never be satisfied continually, many persons are hooked on lust, gambling, greed and other sinful activities. Our spirit will find satisfaction only when we are in Christ and as we give Him pre-eminence over every area of our lives.

Spending, a reflection of our **personality**

"Is it possible that we can become too 'heavenly minded and of no earthly good'?"

Many Christians have been accused of being 'too heavenly minded and of no earthly good'. The basis of this accusation is often that far too many of us are living in poverty, even in societies where there is a very high percentage of persons who can be classified as being middle class and wealthy. Many Christians claim that they are forsaking the 'pleasures of this world so as to inherit the blessings of Heaven, where they will be living in mansions and walking on streets made of pure gold'.

It is true that we have a blessed inheritance. However, the important questions which we should address include; does it mean that we cannot enjoy the best of both worlds, here on earth and also in Heaven? Secondly, can financial and other material success be a measure of the closeness of our relationship with the Lord? The answer to many of these issues can be found in Psalm 112:1-10, which states: "*1Praise the Lord! Happy are those who fear the Lord, who greatly delight in His commandments. 2Their descendants will be mighty in the land; the generation of the upright will be blessed. 3Wealth and riches are in their houses, and their righteousness endures forever. 4They rise in the darkness as a light for the upright; they are generous, merciful, and righteous. 5It is well with those who deal generously and lend, who conduct their affairs with justice. 6For the righteous will never be moved; they will be remembered forever. 7They are not afraid of evil tidings; their hearts are firm, secure in the Lord. 8Their hearts are steady, they will not be afraid; in the end they will look in triumph on their foes. 9They have distributed freely, they have given to the poor; their righteousness endures forever; their horn is exhausted in honor. 10The wicked see it and are angry; they gnash their teeth and melt away; the desire of the wicked comes to nothing.*"

There is so much depth in these verses that it would be useful to comment briefly on a few of them. Verses 1, 2 identify some of the blessings which persons who serve the Lord faithfully will receive while they are on earth. Secondly, descendants of the righteous will also inherit blessings as a result of the faithfulness of their ancestors. **A blessing can be defined simply as the empowerment to succeed in whatever area of our life it is directed, be it material and/or spiritual**. The following list presents some items which are commonly classified as blessings.

1. **Wisdom** – this was the blessing which King Solomon asked the Lord for in order to rule the Children of Israel wisely. The Lord granted him this request but also blessed him with much wealth. It is God who gives us wisdom to become wealthy.
2. **Children** are a blessing to their parents and to society. We have the solemn duty to train them to fulfill this Godly responsibility.
3. **Personal physical health, intellectual abilities, success of our businesses, jobs and other undertakings**. Many of us also receive inheritances from our parents, other relatives and even casual acquaintances. Physical blessings include being healthy, the proper functioning of our organs; even where there are sicknesses, God gives us the grace to overcome them cheerfully. Even death for the righteous, is merely a transition 'from the

transient blessings which we enjoy on earth to a higher glory to live eternally with Him.'

4. **There are also spiritual blessings** such as eternal life, the protections of the angels, one or several gifts of the Spirit operating in our lives as well as the fact that we have Jesus interceding to the Father on behalf of all Christians.

5. **It is also a blessing to be living in a country which is affluent**, where there are no major natural and other disasters, where there is religious freedom and citizens enjoy welfare and other benefits. This does not infer that righteous persons cannot live in poor countries; for the Lord blesses us wherever we are.

6. **A happy home** where there is much love and understanding among the couple and their children. A home which is happy, with children who are successful at school and who mature into adults who are successful in their career and fulfill the calling of the Lord for their lives.

7. **Living in a lavishly furnished home in a 'good neighborhood'** is a blessed experience.

Verse 3 confirms that wealth and riches in our homes is a benefit which the righteous will enjoy not merely for their generation, but it will be substantial enough to be passed down to subsequent generations. **Does this infer that there is a seed of material wealth in the lives of every righteous person?** Yes, it is true that there are many believers who are not materially rich in this lifetime. The Bible has numerous examples of righteous persons who were poor. Many of them chose to be poor in order to minister to a specific segment of the society with the gospel. John the Baptist, for example, lived in the wilderness and ate locust and drank wild honey. Other persons are materially poor because there was no other way of earning a living, possibly because of ill health and/or they suffered from some physical challenge. This is illustrated in examples such as Jesus' illustration of Lazarus, the poor man who went to Heaven while the rich man went to hell – Luke 16:19-31.

Some Christians are materially poor because of specific circumstances such as the widow who gave her last coin as an offering to the Lord as a demonstration of her total dependence on Him to meet her every need – 'the parable of the widow's mite' – Mark 12:42-44 and Luke 21:1-4. There were also very wealthy believers such as King Solomon, King David, Job and Abraham. The differences between a believer being materially wealthy or poor are dependent on factors such as his choices, the geographic area or country where he lives, and whether or not he chooses to. It can thus be inferred that not every Christian will be materially wealthy while they are on earth even though the Lord is living in them, and it is He who imparts the ability for a person to become wealthy.

So, does it mean that a Christian who is materially wealthy is more righteous than one who is poor? Can we infer that there is a positive relationship between righteousness and material wealth? Verse 3 confirms that even if a Christian chooses to be materially poor, then his descendants will benefit from the spiritual, material and other blessings of their righteous ancestor, far more than the punishment of the descendants of the unrighteous who do not break the generational curses of their wicked ancestors by living a righteous life.

Verse 4 identifies that the righteous is a beacon not only for holy living but also in the management of material resources where they can extend their generosity to others. If they do not have enough for themselves, then unless they will be consistently giving sacrificially, they will not have enough to give to others. Even if they are giving sacrificially with the right spirit, Jehovah will always replenish their gifts so that they will not only continue to give but also expand their personal resources. The Lord replenishes and grants abundance to the cheerful giver, for when we give to the poor, we are in effect, lending to the Lord.

The separation of the word righteousness at the end of verse 4, seem to reinforce the point that even though there is a spiritual aspect of righteousness, there are also material attributes which should also be evident in the lives of believers. We have a Heavenly Father who has riches untold, why would He withhold His material blessing when we are serving Him faithfully; when He promised that He would not withhold any good thing from those who serve Him? Some Christians choose not to pursue material wealth since they feel more committed to advancing their spiritual growth and they feel that material wealth will be a hindrance to this process.

There are other Christians who simply cannot manage wealth. *Similar to the way the master distributed the money to his servant since he had a foreknowledge of their abilities and attitude towards managing wealth, El-Shaddai knows us. He knows who He can trust with much wealth as against those who can only manage little*. It is easy for us to conclude that since He is all knowing then He knows all of our abilities even before we were born, and allocates wealth in accordance with our abilities to manage it. This does not seem to be an accurate assessment since several scriptures, some of which are highlighted in subsequent sections, attest to the fact that if we are faithful in little things, He will grant us the ability to generate and manage an increase. Secondly, as we give unselfishly, He continues to expand our resources to enable us to be able to give even more.

Verse 5 identifies that Christians who are generous and lend, and who conduct their affairs with justice will receive blessings. What are we to lend, if we ourselves have to borrow? Many preachers use this verse to identify that Christians should not borrow anything, but instead we should be the ones to lend. The fact that it is more blessed to lend than to borrow is often extended by some preachers who contend that we should not even secure a mortgage, purchase items on hire purchase, secure a student, car and/or other loans. Those who are dogmatic would contend that it is a sin to borrow and that **Christians have a right to be debt free**. While this is the ideal situation, for most persons who are able to achieve this coveted state, the process usually is lengthy and demands a consistently disciplined lifestyle. It often require much faith, sacrifice and of course, the blessings of the Lord. It is similar to a person who became obese over a number of years, it often takes months, if not years of consistent exercise, dieting and other healthy lifestyle practices to enable us to regulate and maintain the correct body mass and physique.

There are a number of reasons why persons make an indelible mark in history. They are either extremely wealthy, lived righteous lives and displayed an outstanding talent or conduct some noble or notorious act. Verse 6 relates that the deeds of the righteous will be so significant that they will be remembered forever. It is true that several persons who have made indelible marks in the annals of time are persons from some remote part of the world but who performed extraordinary feats. Even so the lives of many righteous persons have been and are still being crowned by outstanding unselfish giving and miraculous acts which they were used by the Lord to perform.

Verses 7 and 8 identify the fact that the righteous are grounded in their faith, so much so that even when we experience difficulties, we will not be discouraged and turn away from serving the Lord. We need such persons in our homes, church and community and throughout the world, for these are increasingly perilous times which are confronting us. We need men and women who are resolute in their faith who would not only pray for positive changes in our society but who will be willing to give their time, talent, treasury and if necessary, their very lives, to effect positive changes.

Verse 9 states that the righteous have abundance, or at least the hearth of giving so that the poor are also provided for. Such persons do not only receive personal blessings, but it is expanded to their relatives and it is also a testimony of their love of Jehovah. The poor will recognize that the giver of the gift is an instrument who is being used by Jehovah to improve the standard of their lives and is an expression of His love for them. This has challenged many persons to come to the Lord and it also strengthens the lives of believers who receive financial and other gifts from others, since they are reminded of God's promise that He will provide for their every need.

Verse 10 climaxes the exposition of the glory which is exalted in the lives of the righteous. We are aware that the unrighteous are not spiritually discerning. Therefore, even though many persons are converted after seeing miracles and the manifestation of spiritual gifts, most unbelievers are so blinded by Satan that they believe that such acts are false and is another trick used by Christians in their attempt to deceive others that their religion is genuine and/or to lore persons to give them money and/or other favors. Some persons view miracles as another manifestation of natural and/or as a scientifically explainable phenomenon. Many persons are also suspicious that persons who extend kindness to them are doing so with the aim of getting something in return, to impress on-lookers, or for some other selfish reason. However, when they see a Christian who is very wealthy, and they are convinced that that person did not amass the wealth from unjust practices, it made them jealous. Since the Lord preserves the resources of His people, the wealth of the righteous becomes a snare to the eyes of the unrighteous who are struggling to make ends meet and who have to engage in devious acts in order to accumulate and maintain wealth.

> **Goodness and mercies is a part of our inheritance**

"Can Christianity derive material and other benefits on account of being God's children?"

Many Christians would not feel convicted if they visit a medical doctor or use medication in an attempt to overcome or prevent an illness. Once we recognize the Lord as the source of the wisdom of the doctor and the practice by the physician is not contrary to the Word, for example, visiting the doctor is scriptural. However, there may be special situations such as when the finding of the physicians is that the condition of the patient is terminal, where we may be forced to rely on the miracle working power of the Holy Spirit. The application of faith is not only in situations when 'all else fails.'

Even in the example of a person who has to undergo a surgery, for example, the patient and others can still be walking in faith in believing that the Lord will guide the hands of the surgeon and that the medical condition would be corrected. The level of faith of persons differs. Therefore, the level of one person's faith may be to believe that the Lord would guide the hands of a surgeon, while another person has enough faith to believe that the Lord would heal them. They may both be operating in obedience based on their relationship with the Lord. Nevertheless, care must be taken that what we refer to as faith does not contradict the word of God. It is a sin to contend that we believe that God is so merciful that no one would go to hell, so we live like the devil and trust that the mercies of God allow us to inherit eternal life with Him. We are also reminded of the Gift of Faith, which is one of the spiritual gifts (1 Corinthians 12:9).

Many Christians have enough faith and they rely on God to prevent accidents and sickness; and healing when they are ill. Some persons even feel that it is a sin to visit a doctor and to take medication, resulting in the death of family members. There are several examples where such parents received criminal charges when a child or other love one died or became seriously ill when a parent or guardian denied them access to the necessary medication and treatment. Secondly, even as we work, we have to recognize that He is the One who guides and protects us as we go to and from work and on the job. He also grants us special favor with those in authority over us. James 5:15 states: **"15The prayer of faith will save the sick, and the Lord will raise them up; and anyone who committed sins will be forgiven."**

God's desire is that we should be in good health, even as our soul prospers. Salvation does not stop with spiritual liberation. It also includes financial, health and the total well being of every aspect of our lives. There are, however, several important principles which we have to adhere to and practice on a consistent basis. They include being in continuous communication with Him, and following His leadership. As Christians we are admonished in 1 Thessalonians 4:11 to work with our hands and not to depend on anyone. We also have a responsibility to humanity and ourselves to encourage the expansion of the Gospel, to pursue financially rewarding careers and to excel in all our financial and other endeavors.

Many prominent preachers have expounded on what they sometimes call the '**theology of prosperity**.' One preacher propagated that: "**If pimps and drug lords can drive fancy cars, live in the best houses, wear the most expensive clothing and eat the best foods, then Christians should enjoy even more.**" His rationale is that our Heavenly Father has riches untold, and as heirs and joint-heirs with Jesus, we should enjoy a part of this fortune on earth. We have a Heavenly Father who is far more loving and caring than any earthly father. Hence, according to this theology, poor Christians:

1. May not be receiving the correct teaching on this important issue,
2. Lack enough faith to claim what is rightfully theirs. Hebrew 11:1 states: "**¹Now faith is the assurance of things hoped for, the conviction of things not seen.**"
   Faith is taking God at His word and proving the truth of word by upholding it. Our relationship with the Lord is dependent on faith. We are also reminded that we cannot please God unless we exercise our faith.
3. May not be living according with Biblical principles of financial prosperity, unless they deliberately prefer to live financially humble lives,

The premise of our relationship is having faith in Him. Every blessing which we receive from Him is as a result of our relationship with Him. The Lord also blesses us on account of His love and mercy.

Christians and the accumulation and management of wealth

"**Is earthly wealth and Christianity mutually exclusive, that is, once a person is a true believer they should not maintain or seek to acquire material wealth?**"

Passages such as Exodus 9:29, Psalm 24:1-2, and 1 Corinthians 10:26 refer to the fact that the earth and everything in it is the Lord's. Psalm 24:1, 2 states that: "**¹The earth is the Lord's and all that is in it, the world, and those who live in it; ²for He has founded it on the seas, and established it on the rivers.**"

This being so, are we as Christians to allow the unsaved to rule over the wealth of our Heavenly Father? It seems unfair for a child of a rich man to live in abject poverty when his father is rich. As a matter of fact, Jesus addressed this issue in Matthew 7:7-11 and Luke 11:9-13. The latter passage states: **⁹"So I say to** *you, Ask, and it will be given to you; search, and you will find; knock, and the door will be opened for you. [10]For everyone who asks receives, and everyone who searches finds, and for everyone who knocks, the door will be opened. [11]Is there anyone among you who, if your child asks for a fish will give a snake instead of a fish? [12]Or if the child asks for an egg, will give a scorpion? [13]If you then, who are evil. Know how to give good gifts to your children, how much more will the heavenly Father give the Holy Spirit to those who ask Him!"*

> *Some persons are materially wealthy yet they are humble, while others are poor and haughty. Christians, who are wealthy, by their very nature, should be humble and use their wealth to bless their relatives, help the poor, contribute to the spreading of the gospel and finance other noble acts.*

The more conservative, and possibly the more popular view, is that we should not be engrossed in acquiring wealth. In Luke 18:18-30 Jesus discussed several principles on the management of material wealth as He responded to a rich ruler who was questioning Him on what he should do to inherit eternal life. Jesus reminded him of the commandments which he should follow. When the rich man told Jesus that he had been following the commandments from His youth, verses 22-25 states: *"[22]When Jesus heard this, He said to him, "There is still one thing lacking. Sell all you own and distribute the money to the poor, and you will have treasures in heaven; then come follow me." [23]But when he heard this, he became sad; for he was very rich. [24]Jesus looked at him and said. "How hard it is for those who have wealth to enter the kingdom God! [25]Indeed it is easier for a camel to go through the eye of a needle than for someone who is rich to enter the kingdom of God."*

Verse 24 confirms that even though it is difficult for a rich man to serve the Lord, that **it is possible for a rich man to enter heaven, once he is willing to prioritize the Lord over his wealth and other aspects of his life.** The difference is dependent on the level of importance which we attribute to material things and whether or not we are prepared to follow the Lord in all of our ways. Some persons engage in dishonest practices to acquire, maintain and expand their material resources and may in fact idolize their wealth. It would appear that Jesus identified that the rich ruler was in fact idolizing his wealth. When Jesus instructed him to sell his possessions and to follow Him, he rejected Jesus' offer.

There are numerous examples of persons who served

Jehovah who were very wealthy in accordance with the material standards of their day. They included Abraham, Job, King David and King Solomon. Even though Jesus may not have been extremely wealthy, there is ample evidence that His cloak, for example, was very expensive. In addition, carpentry was an occupation which commanded high wage and much respect among the community. One also wonders what happened with all of the gifts which Jesus received when He was a baby. In addition, several wealthy persons supported Jesus' ministry.

> Jehovah is the creator of the universe and everything which is in it, is His. We are His heirs and joint heirs. Once we are in good standing with Him, is it too much for us to expect to receive a few million dollars of His wealth, even in this present life? Since He knows that most of us will not be able to manage such wealth and still serve Him, He would not allow all of us to have it. Another reason which every Christian will not be materially wealthy is that in order for most of us to fulfil His will for our lives, we do not need to be wealthy.

In the early Church, as described in the book of Acts, those who had material possessions such as houses and land, either shared them where possible, or sold them and shared the proceeds with others. There is no evidence to suggest that Christianity is synonymous with living in material poverty. If that were so, how then will we fulfill our obligations to adequately cater for the financial needs of our families, assist the needy and support the spreading of the Gospel? The upkeep of ministries and the spreading of the Gospel also have high financial demands. Can we as believers expect the unrighteous to finance the spreading of the Gospel? Secondly, does it bring glory to God when we have to beg the unsaved to fund the Lord's work?

> 1Timothy 6:6-10 states: "6Of course, there is great gain in Godliness combined with contentment, 7for we brought nothing into the world, so that we can take nothing out of it; 8but if we have food and clothing, we have to be content with these. 9But those who want to be rich fall into temptation and are trapped by many senseless and harmful desires that plunge people into ruin and destruction. 10For the love of money is a root of all kinds of evil, and in their eagerness to be rich some have wandered away from the faith and pierced themselves with many pains."

Once we are able to understand that **money is a tool and not a means in itself**, we are on our way to manage money as the Lord expects us to. On a macro level, money (capital) is used to finance the provision of services such as medical, education and other social services, infrastructure facilities such as roads, portable water and other amenities by the government. These facilities are financed from taxes, the sale of treasury bills, debentures, bonds and other securities. Bilateral, multilateral aid, grants, loans and other contributions may also be supplied by international agencies, other governments, Non Government Organizations (NGOs) and from other agencies. Money (capital) is also important to finance the production of goods and services which we need.

On the micro level, money is also needed by the family to purchase items such as food and clothing and for the payment of services such as utility bills and the cost of transportation. Money is also needed to perform spiritual functions such the payment of tithes and the giving of offering, helping the poor and for supporting missionaries and other methods of spreading the Gospel.

> There is no evidence to suggest that Christianity is synonymous with living in material poverty. If that were so, how then will we fulfil our obligations to adequately cater for the financial needs of our families, assist the needy and support the spreading of the Gospel?

Strategies to manage inflation

"Inflation is a reality in many countries. Are there strategies which we can use to derive financial benefits even during an inflationary period?"

Many countries undergo a period of inflation in most decades. It is therefore important that we plan for such an eventuality since Jehovah is Lord over every situation which confronts us. Some of the strategies which have been successfully employed by many persons who have emerged substantially better off after inflation are:

1. Decrease spending and/or increasing their income, hence, increasing their cash flow. This makes more funds available for saving and investment, which would generate higher than normal returns.
2. Avoiding, or at least dramatically reducing borrowings, particularly for consumer items since interest rates will be higher than normal. A savings account which pays 3% interest per annum during normal times, may pay

12% per annum during an inflation. The additional returns generated by savers and investors would be quite substantial when the economy returns to normal.

3. Avoid impulsive buying, particularly of large purchases. Many persons succumb to the delusion that the prices for commodities would not decrease, at least over the short-run. Therefore, they shop extensively, because of the fear that prices will increase dramatically over the short-run.

High inflation usually has a serious negative effect on an economy over the long-run. However, at least we can manage the situation over the short and medium-term and derive substantial returns. Jehovah is Lord over every situation and He prospers His people irrespective of the economic or other situations.

The distribution of the 'talents'

"I am from a developing country; therefore I am at a more serious disadvantage financially than persons from developed countries. Would the Lord expect that I would be as productive in the returns from managing my financial resources as that of other Christians from developed countries?"

There are several factors which we have to consider when addressing the above issues.

1. The blessings of the Lord are not restricted by economic, political, geographical, social and other conditions,

2. The Lord has promised to bless His people irrespective of where they live. However, I have not seen any Scripture passage which states that the Lord has promised that all Christian will enjoy an equal standard of living or that we will all be very wealthy while we are on earth. We are reminded, for example, of the widow who had her last 'mite' and gave it as an offering to the Lord.

3. The Lord has placed us in various locations so that we can minister to others wherever we are. We are all expected to maximize our returns and allow the Lord to bless and multiply it.

Many books written on financial management, even from a Christian perspective, neglect the peculiar financial position of the extremely poor, the homeless, refugees and other categories of poor persons. Many such persons do not have a source of income but their livelihood is dependent on handout and alms from other persons and organizations. The Lord has placed the responsibility of meeting the need of such persons on the 'Body of Christ –

Principles Governing Acquisition of Prosperity

INTRODUCION

T here are several principles which have been presented by persons in an attempt to capture the primary parameters of Biblical prosperity. Two of these presentations are discussed in this section.

The Seven Laws of Prosperity

"What are the so-called 'Seven Laws of Prosperity'?"

There are several principles in the Bible which the Lord has established for us to use as a guide to enable us to achieve the blessings which He have placed at our disposal. A combination of these principles has been popularized as the Seven Laws of Prosperity. It should be noted that these practices are not restricted to material prosperity but are also essential tools to foster our spiritual growth. Many of these issues are detailed in other sections, nevertheless, a brief discussion will be conducted on a sample of them. Christians are expected to practice them every day of our lives.

1. **Obedience.** This principle requires that we have to be in close communion with the Lord since He does not establish a covenant with persons who do not abide in Him. A covenant relationship, and therefore, direct benefits as a consequence, commences with

salvation. There are several Biblical principles which even if they are practiced by persons who are not Christians would derive some benefits from observing them. A common example is that persons who assist the poor and invest wisely, will derive some form of compensation for their efforts, for God is no man's debtor. The difference is that the unrighteous would not derive the full extent, and in many instances not at all, from some blessings which are specified in passages such as Matthew 5:3-11 – the Beatitudes. Blessings such as continuous protection and eternal life are reserved to the righteous. Even if the unrighteous were to gain the whole world and loose his soul, he would have wasted his life.

Once we remain as a branch from the Vine, then we will be able to draw the sustenance and empowerment which is in Him to enable us to succeed. The act of obedience will only be implemented if we know what is expected of us and we walk in that path. For this reason we must spend quality time studying the word, and implementing these principles, in communion with Him in prayer and praise, and spreading His word.

2. **Meditation**. If we are not grounded in the ways of the Lord we can easily be swayed by 'every doctrine.' The closer our relationship is with the Father, the closer will our walk with the Lord be and the more we will know and understand the will and direction of the Lord. Meditation from a Christian perspective does not entail 'emptying' our mind of all thoughts and tapping into our 'inner self' as yoga and other Eastern teaching propagates. It rather entails principles such as:

I. **Tuning our spirits to the Spirit of the Lord.** We will be able to achieve this by eradicating barriers such as sin, which hinders the relationship.

II. **Studying the Word of God.** Quality time must be spent reading and applying the Word to our lives on a consistent basis where we allow Him to minister the secrets of His Word to us where we will learn of His will and His ways and be able to apply them to our lives.

III. **Prayer and supplication**. As we spend quality time worshipping and glorifying Him, He imparts glorious truths into our lives which will enable us to break any form of bondage such as poverty, and generation curses which hinder us from receiving His glory for our lives even while we are on earth.

IV. **Doing His work** - as we put into practice the glorious truths of His word, it increases our communication with Him. He does not expect us to only be hearers of the Word but also to be doers by keeping His commandments. This is the most practical demonstration of our relationship with Him.

3. **Work** - the issue of work was the first instruction which God gave to man in the form of beautification of the Garden of Eden. Even though God related to Adam after the fall of man that he will eat by the sweat of his brow, the Lord still extends blessings on His children who are conscientious workers. Work is a spiritual obligation for persons who are able to do so and where appropriate employment is available. The Bible is full of examples of persons who received a special visitation from the Lord after they had been actively involved in doing something which was consistent with His will for their lives. I cannot recall any example where the Lord blessed someone who was consistently lazy.

   There are for example, several references to the fact that the Lord resented persons who did not adequately provide for their families even though they had the means at their disposal to do so. Persons who do not adequately provide for their families when they have the capacity to do so are also categorized as an outcast of the faith. Proverbs 10:4 states: "*4A slack hand causes poverty, but the hand of the diligent makes rich.*"

   The parable of the talents also demonstrated that the blessings went to those who produced more. This does not mean that He would not bless persons who are sick, disabled or for other reasons unable to work. However, once we can, we should produce at our maximum, of course, balancing it with our spiritual, family life and other obligations.

4. **Giving -** the issue of giving relates to giving to the Lord in the form of our tithes, talents and treasury and also in assisting others who are in need. As we give to the poor, we in fact lend to the Lord. Since He is no man's debtor, He will repay us in the form of material, spiritual and other types of blessings.

5. **Agreement** is also an import ingredient in realizing the blessings of the Lord. Agreement is important from several perspective:

I. Our lives must be in agreement or conformity with the Word of God. This would require that we know the word of God and apply the principles of the Word to our lives on a consistent basis.

II. We will usually be able to achieve more as a group if we are in one accord with our spouse, praying partner and other persons who would support us and agree with us in praying, working together and other areas of unison. Under the condition of agreement the revelation and other gifts of the Spirit will operate which offer direction to our personal lives, business and other aspects of our lives. This would have a positive effect to increase our financial and other areas of our lives. Reference of the importance of agreement is confirmed in scripture verses such as Matthew 18:18-20, where Jesus stated: *"18Truly I tell you, whatever you bind on earth will be bound in heaven, and whatever you loose on earth will be loosed in heaven. 19Again, truly I tell you, if two of you agree on earth about anything you ask, it would be done for you by my Father in heaven. 20For where two or three are gathered in my name, I am there among them."*

Many of us live defeated lives because we do not know of, or tap into, or appreciate the magnitude of the power of the Lord which is manifested when we operate in an atmosphere of unity. The negative effect of unity was illustrated where God highlighted the authority which man had when they united to build the tower of Babel. Hence, He confused their language and in disunity they destroyed the tower and migrated to different parts of the earth in their various language groups. Conversely, when the early church was in unity on the day of Pentecost, the Holy Spirit descended and filled the believers in the Upper Room and miracles and wonders were performed thereafter in an unprecedented way.

Satan often sow discord which results in the severing of the relationship between us and God, where we do not have the deep meaningful relationship with Him. There is also disunity between members of families, the church and other bodies which prevents us from approaching the throne of God so that He can grant us the desires of our hearts.

Agreement also entails making positive confessions of our faith and also in the fact that the Lord has already done what He said that He will do. All we have to do to actualize the fulfillment of these manifestations in the natural realm is to fulfill the conditions including having faith 'like a mustard seed' believing His word and applying the Biblical principles to the situation.

6. *Patience and Persistence* – we are reminded of Isaiah 40:31 which states: *"³¹.....but those who wait for the Lord shall renew their strength, they shall mount up with wings like eagle, they shall run and not be weary, they shall walk and not faint."*

We need the refreshing presence of the Lord throughout the day to keep us on the right track and to enable us to achieve our goals. We must be able to differentiate between *patience verses laziness* and *persistence verses presumptuousness* (from a negative perspective). A summary of some aspects of these principles are highlighted as follows:

1. *Patience* relates to waiting in calm confidence and expectation, knowing that it is only a matter of time before the fulfillment of the objectives which the person, others and/or the Lord has set in motion for the realization of the objective.

2. *Laziness,* on the other hand, refers to the attitude of one who deliberately fails to make a conscious effort to realize a given objective, even though he has the ability to at least attempt to achieve it.

3. *Persistence* connotes making a fervent effort to achieve a given objective and overcoming any obstacles which may seek to prevent the attainment of the ultimate goal.

4. *Presumptuousness* (from a negative perspective) is an indication that one is consciously conducting an act which is inconsistent with the will of the Lord, for example.

In mastering these essential qualities, we will know the precise time when the Spirit of the Lord wants us to take advantage of situations which confront us. We will not rush ahead of God and attempt to 'help God out' when in actual fact He desire that we wait on His precise time and occasion to 'strike the iron when it is hot.'

> The true character of the Christian is shown even during periods of adversities. Job, for example, did not commit suicide, which is so common among wealthy unbelievers who experience catastrophic occurrence in their lives. Because Job knew who His God was, and that there was no adversary too great for Him to overcome.

1. **Fasting** - fasting is an essential discipline which promotes spiritual growth and development of our Christian life. This is a practice which has been established in the Old Testament and there are numerous references to fasting in the New Testament also. Two notable examples of fasting in the Bible are:
   I. Queen Esther asked Mordecai to gather the Jewish community to hold a fast for three days after which she would approach King Ahasuerus to spare the lives of the Jews who were about to be killed because of Haman's wicked plot,
   II. Jesus fasted for forty days and forty nights after which He overcame the temptation of the devil,

   Fasting is a very powerful tool which is an important way of showing the Lord that nothing is more important to us than serving Him. There are however, several guidelines which we are instructed to follow so that the fasting would not be dishonorable to the Lord. These include issues such as not:
   a. Publicizing it, possibly beyond one's spouse, relatives and/or close associates,
   b. Boasting about one's 'superior spiritual ability,'
   c. Wearing a sad countenance, as the Scribes and Pharisees did when they fasted,

There are several types of fasting. They include a partial fast where a person may abstain from solid food, while consuming water and fruit juices; to a total fast of abstention from food, water, sexual and other activities which distract, us from being in total submission to the Lord. A classic example of the importance of fasting was illustrated when the disciples were unable to cast the demon out of the man who was possessed. After Jesus cast the demon out He, told His disciples that there are instances when fasting is required to break the bondage of satanic activities over our lives and that of other persons (Mark 9:29). There are times when we have to be desperate and intercede with prayer and fasting so that the Lord would interview on our behalf. The breaking of the bondage of financial lack often requires this degree of desperation.

The Four Principles of Prosperity

"I have also heard of the Four Principles of Prosperity, what are they?"

Here again there is no scripture verse which specifically refers to any specific four laws or principles of prosperity. However, these are Biblical principles which persons have applied to their lives and/or observed in the lives of others which have granted them much material success. A brief discussion on these principles is as follows:

1. **Giving** – this involves giving to the Lord in the form of tithes and offering, using one's financial and other resources to help the poor, spreading the gospel and engaging in other activities which are pleasing to the Lord.

2. **Sowing** – this issue is often viewed from the context of working to earn a living, budgeting wisely, saving and investing to increase our net worth. Persons who invest their time, talent and treasury wisely will reap the benefits not only in terms of material rewards but also will derive spiritual benefits from the Lord.

3. **Reaping** – we should have the correct spirit when the Lord is using others to bless our lives and/or when He is doing this directly by opening doors to enable us to achieve success in various endeavors. We should reap what we sow or we will be branded a thief. If we keep sowing but never reap, then we would have to find out what is hindering the cycle of the 'water bring blessings back to us'. Some of the common source of such hindrance includes giving in the wrong spirit, sowing on barren ground and having the wrong spirit in receiving, such as greed and selfishness.

4. **Receiving** – some persons display a false sense of modesty in not accepting gifts which persons give to them out of a genuine sense of appreciation and not as a form of bribery or to use the gift as a way of manipulating the receiver in any way. If we fail to discern a genuine gift and reject the offer, we will be forfeiting the process which the Lord is using to provide

a blessing. We will also stifle the receipt of the blessings of the giver.

There are several scripture passages which present principles which are important guidelines to enable us to achieve financial and other forms of blessings. A popular passage is 2 Corinthians 9:6-12 which states: ***"6The point is this; the one who sows sparingly will also reap sparingly, and the one who sows bountifully will also reap bountifully. 7Each of you must give as you have made up your mind, not reluctantly or under compulsion, for God loves a cheerful giver. 8And God is able to provide you with every blessing in abundance, so that by always having enough of everything, you may share abundantly in every good work. 9As it is written, "He scatters abroad, He gives to the poor; his righteousness endures forever." 10He who supplies seed to the sower and bread for food will supply and multiply your seed for sowing and increase the harvest of your righteousness. 11You will be enriched in every way for your great generosity, which will produce thanksgiving to God through us; 12for the rendering of this ministry not only supplies the needs of the saints but also overflows with many thanksgivings to God "***

The remainder of this chapter continues to present principles which are important for our financial, spiritual and other aspects of our well being.

Time Management

The way we manage our time has a profound impact on several important aspect of our lives, including our relationship with the Lord, relationship with our associates, success in preparation and realization of success at our career. It is therefore important that emphasis is focused on this important facet as it relates to the acquisition and management of material resources.

Attributing a monetary value to time management

"Is the maxim 'time is money' really true?"

Since important aspects of time management are presented in several sections of this book, only brief mention is made of this important issue in this section. There is a famous maxim which states that '***time is money***'. The rationale for this is that the length of time it takes and the price of the resources used to produce a particular item or to provide a service, is often one of the most important factors in determining its price. (The demand and supply of the commodity also affects its price). The monetary value of time is seen, for example, where advertisement during prime time on the radio or television is usually more expensive than during off-peak periods. Similarly, the way we spend our time often has positive or negative financial implications on our lives. Most persons who waste their time during the 'summer' of their lives (during our youth) in unrighteous living, will suffer during the 'winter' of their lives (during old age). A popular example of this eventuality was presented in Jesus' parable of the Prodigal Son. Proverbs 6:10, 11 also warns us that: **"¹⁰A little sleep, a little slumber, a little folding of the hands to rest, ¹¹and poverty will come upon you like a robber, and want, like an armed warrior."**

As it is in the physical, even so importance is attributed to time management in the spiritual arena, even though a different slant may be adopted in many instances. The way we manage our time on earth determines the level of spirituality rewards which we will receive while on earth and also in the life hereafter, even though such 'treasures' in the afterlife, cannot be measured in earthly financial terms. We cannot, for example, affix a financial value to eternal life, the crown of glory or being with the Lord forever and ever. We are expected to make good use of every moment. Our time should be prudently apportioned to ensure that maximum use is made of this most valuable asset which is at our disposal. For this reason much reference is made in the Bible, to the need for us to ensure that we are not slothful, lazy or manifest other traits of persons who are not practicing efficient and effective time management principles. It should be noted, however, that we cannot quantity time and money in every situation. For example, how can we quantity the cost to Jehovah for creating the world in six days, or what does it cost Him to transfer our lives from 'the gutter to the His righteousness?

Effective time management can be measured from the perspective of what one has achieved over a given time-frame, given factors such as one's age, maturity, academic accreditation, financial resources and spiritual maturity. The amount of time which is usefully spent by a person in pursuit of his/her career, for example, would have a significant impact on his/her success in acquiring the necessary qualifications and skills, which are very important in determining the level of success which will be achieved in one's career. Many persons who attempt to take shortcuts by not investing adequate time and resources necessary to acquire success in a highly recognized profession often end up:

1. Having to accept mediocre jobs,
2. Remaining unemployed,
3. Engaging in dishonest practices to acquire finance or awarded a promotion, for example,
4. As beggars when they are old,

A general principle of life is that we reap what we sow; if we sow our time wisely, we will reap positive benefits and vice versa. Of course thieves such as sickness, natural and man-made disasters such as war and other misfortunes sometimes hamper persons from acquiring the full benefits from investments which they have made. On the other hand, we often benefit from investments made by others and of course Christians benefit from the blessings of the Lord and other spiritual and other favors which are beyond scope of the benefits of our investment or personal achievements.

Time management is also important in how we apportion our time during the day, for the results will be manifested in what we have achieved at the end of the day and the benefits received in the future from investments which were made. Many persons have a well organized system of planning and recording, at least the major activities which they have to embark on for the day, very early in the morning or sometime before they commence the main stream of their activities and work assiduously to achieve at least the more important aspects of the plan.

No one can accurately determine the exact way that events of the day will unfold. The closest one may be to achieving this feat is if one is possibly confined to a prison or operates in other environments where a rigid system of activities are maintained or enforced. Even in such circumstances, there are often variations from the normal routine. At the same time it would be unrealistic if one attempts to rigidly follow a diary of events which are planned for the day, when as situations of the day unfold, there is a need to make major adjustments to the time table. The Lord expects us to plan in our pursuit to do His will. However, there must be some flexibility in our plan to cater for the inclusion of unplanned important events which may have to take precedence over the planned program. The Lord may also input some of His dynamism in our plans which we have to be receptive to and follow His direction.

It would be interesting to analyze how we spend an average day in an attempt to determine how effective we are in managing our time. The average person sleeps at least eight hours per day even though many situations such as demands of work or studies cause many persons to live for extended periods on a dramatically reduced period of sleep. At the other end of the spectrum we have babies and smaller children, the elderly and persons who are ill who sleep for longer hours. There are also lazy persons who sleep their lives away, very often contributing to, or further worsening their state of extremely obese and other forms of unhealthy life styles. It is obviously important that we have enough sleep each day to give the organs and other parts of our body a rest and to allow the rejuvenation of new cells, for example. However, if one becomes addicted to sleeping for long hours or suffers from sleeping disorders such as insomnia; then sleep becomes detrimental to our health and well being.

Other ways in which we can misuse time include:

1. Spending much time reading comic and other books which may not contribute very much to our academic development and improve our reading skill or creativity, for example. It is important that a person engages in some form of leisure as a way of reducing stress, exercise, socializing and other positive effects which various leisure activities produces. We must, however, be able to differentiate between leisure, which is useful relaxation, verses slothfulness, which is complacency, and thus unproductive.

2. Watching at soap operas and other television programs for extended periods which are not in keeping with our personal development and which do not inspire us to live very productive lives. In many instances we admire the success stories of others, without seriously endeavoring to improve our own lives. It is true that many persons have been inspired by some aspects of the lives of some of these characters and effected positive changes in their lives also. However, this does not pertain to the majority of persons who faithfully look at these soap operas day after day. Soap operas have a negative effect on many persons who are addicted to them. Many such persons live in a fantasy world where characters in the soap operas have a negative influence on their lives. They often spend much of their money on products which are advertised during the intermission periods and many of them are obese after spending hours each day watching television instead of exercising and engaging in other productive activities.

3. Gossiping, instead of trying to use our time to upgrade our lives and that of others,

4. Worrying, instead of seeking positive solutions from the Lord, and other sources,

5. Constantly changing one's career path, resulting in much time, energy and money being wasted on moving from one career path to another. Younger people are particularly susceptible to such actions. In order to overcome this weakness they need the assistance of prudent parental guidance, qualified counselors and they should learn to know and rely on the direction of the Holy Spirit in every area of their lives.

Having analyzed the above factors, it can be observed that many persons who have achieved prominence in their career, business and in other secular and religious activities have implemented effective time management principles in their lives. Very few persons have achieved outstanding feats without hard work and a period of intensive training, and other forms of preparation. Of course there must be room for the blessings of the Lord to be prominent in our lives since we will not achieve lasting success in our own strength or wisdom. Prominent Bible characters such as the Apostle Paul did not achieve instantaneous transformation from Saul the prosecutor of Christians to the very successful Apostle Paul. Galatians Chapters One and Two identify that his process of preparation for the ministry occurred over a period of more than fourteen years. Even while he had achieved international prominence, he was still receiving new revelations from the Lord. Even Jesus underwent a period of preparation before He launched His ministry when He was thirty years old. Prominent ministers of the Gospel today usually attend seminary and/or other programs of training. It is true that the best teacher is the Holy Spirit and the more time we spend in His presence, the more effective we would be in the area/s where He has called us to walk in. There are persons who have been called to consistent intercession who would spend hours in prayer and praise to the Lord.

The value attached to the time of various individuals differs based on their profession, how they are able to 'sell' themselves, and other factors. One may be familiar with the heavy weight boxing where boxers such as Mike Tyson earned over US$10 million for knocking out an opponent in a matter of minutes after the commencement of the first round. Prominent personalities are also paid handsomely for public appearances and other activities which are determined by the amount of time they have to expend preparing and making such presentations. Even though the average person may not be paid a huge amount for one's working day and skills, it is at least important to seek avenues where one is paid at least at a level which is commensurate with the amount of time and effort which was needed to successfully conduct the task.

Principles of effective time management

"What are some of the things that we can do to maximize our effective use of time?"

We can use our time effectively to accomplish several essential tasks on a consistent basis. From a macro spiritual perspective we can conclude that we can spend out time doing things which are good or evil. Among the good things are promoting peace among humanity, promoting economic growth and development, preventing the spread of AIDS, Cancer and other diseases. There are several things which we can do to maximize the way in which we use our time. A brief list of some of them is as follows:

1. *Know the perfect will of God for one's life and staying on that course*. As with Abraham, Joseph, David and many other great men of God, He reveals the end of the journey but never give the specific details of the in-between. It is features such as this which makes living by faith essential.

2. *Live each day of our lives as if it is our last one*. This is a Biblical principle which Jesus reiterated that we should work diligently since we do not know the time or the hour when the Son of Man (Jesus) will return. This is not only a spiritual principle, but it also has material implications. In achieving the maximum material possessions one ensures that it is used for our family and also for the furtherance of the proclamation of the Gospel.

3. *Delegate responsibilities to others* such as other members of the family and colleagues at work, so that you can accomplish tasks for which you are more competent to perform and which would generate higher returns to your ministry, spiritual growth, employment, personal fulfillment and in other areas. The Midianite Priest, for example, encouraged Moses to institute this principle since Moses was tiring himself out judging all of the disputes between the Children of Israel when they were in the Wilderness. The example

stated shows the benefits of reducing your workload, particularly in non-essential areas and tasks and the importance of equipping others to carry out the work should you be gone for any reason and also to train them in principles of practical management. It also reduces a person's stress level.

4. **Engage in leisure**; our day should be so well structured that we have enough time not only to sleep but also to indulge in some of the activities which we deem as relaxation. For some persons this include reading their Bible and other books, praying, exercising, playing games which you enjoy and other activities which would enable you to recuperate from a hectic lifestyle and plan effectively for the future.

5. **Count the cost**, and embark only on activities which they can realistically accomplish in the most cost effective and efficient way, taking cognizance of spiritual and other implications. Some persons are in the habit of trying to do everything and at the end of the day accomplish very little. It is often better to undertake little tasks, accomplish them and progress to bigger ones.

CONCLUSION

It is true that many persons who are not Christians have used prudent investment strategies and have amassed a huge amount of wealth honestly. Many of them enjoy a life of luxury, pleasure of this world; economic, social, political, intellectual and other forms of power to the admiration and even envy of other persons. If many persons are given the choice between earthly riches and poverty, most would choose riches. The sad reality is that many rich persons find it difficult to acquire, maintain and even expand their wealth in a manner that is pleasing to the Lord. Several scriptures passages, including admonishments of Jesus, have emphasized on the difficulty which most persons encounter in their attempt to manage their wealth and serve the Lord. There are also Christians who have used Biblical principles and have become wealthy. One of the fundamental differences between the two groups is that the former has not allowed the Lord to direct their ways, while the latter has. Both groups would derive enjoyment from their riches and they may both assist the needy and engage in other noteworthy causes. Nevertheless, their relationship with the Lord and subsequently humanity makes the difference in their lives on earth and after death.

The Bible admonishes us to be good stewards of the financial and other resources which the Lord has placed at our disposal. It is therefore necessary that Christians are good stewards of the resources which the Lord has placed at our disposal. Non-Christians are challenged that their wealth would not provide them with a right relationship with their Creator. It does not matter how wealthy a person is, if he does not enjoy a right relationship with his Jehovah, he will always experience an unfulfilled void which would only be satisfied when his spirit is united with the Spirit of the Lord. Even if a person was to 'have it all' materially and still does not know the Lord, he will be separated from Him in this life and spend eternity in Hell, which was made for Satan and his rebellious angels who were thrown out of Heaven.

There are Christians who are materially poor, due to problems in the economy where they live, wars and other factors. Many such persons still maintained a loving relationship with the Lord and persons with whom they come into close contact since they recognize that He is Lord of every situation and that their source is not their job, the economy of other earthly channels. The Lord is our source and once we put our trust in Him and obey His word, He will deliver us from any circumstance which is contrary to His will for our lives. His blessings to His people transcend economic, social and other earthly constraints. The Lord does not compromise on His promises such as to bless those who give to the poor, since they lend to Him. Even if He has to use a raven to feed His people, He will never leave us nor forsake us; His promise is for abundance.

NOTES

****

Chapter 3: DEBT MANAGEMENT

INTRODUCTION

T he movement from being under the burden of debt, to a place where we experience complete financial liberation demands that the best choices are made as we seek to move from the darkness of being debt-ridden to living in freedom when our financial and other resources work for us. For the large majority of us, there is usually no quick fix principle in managing our financial and other resources. Most persons have to undergo a period of unlearning many of the negative principles which has been instilled in our minds by well intended but misguided persons, years of indiscipline and other oppressions by the devil to implementing the principle of the Bible with regards to financial management to our lives.

The discipline of conforming to the Word of God can be just as painful if we do not have enough faith and are willing to accept His word in its totality. The process of being broken, melted, and made into vessels of honor is very often just as painful as shedding weight and getting in peak physical shape. The same process is often applicable as we seek to achieve and maintain control over financial and other resources. For the very reason that we have to daily mortify our flesh, even so we have to daily eradicate unhealthy financial and other practices and implement Biblical principles in order to manage our resources as well. Very often when a person undergoes a stringent dietary and exercise program there is usually an initial accelerated weight loss as the unsettled fat is quickly burnt. However, it usually takes the implementation of well structured, and consistent, concentrated exercise; dietary and other healthy lifestyle practices to burn the fat in areas which are more difficult to reach. Similarly, the mastery over our financial resources demands the application of an extended financial management program which is consistent to the Word of God.

Fundamentals of Debt Management

Most of the financial problems which we experience are primarily manifestation of years of neglect of fundamental Biblical principles, many of which were discussed in Chapter 1. Some of the problems and manifestations are:

Negative Principles	Consequences
Failure to tithe and give of our offerings;	The protection provision, other blessings of the Lord are inhibited, if not completely withdrawn.
Not a giver, or gives very miserly;	If we sow nothing, we will receive nothing in return. If we sow little we will receive little return also. It is true that the Lord does not follow every natural law at all times, as demonstrated when the Red Sea opened to allow the Children of Israel to cross over on dry land, and when Jesus walked on water for example. However, there are several natural laws such as sowing and reaping which are also applicable in the spiritual realm. It is important to note, however, that we may suffer the consequences of the actions of our parents and other persons if we follow their lifestyle.
A thief	Be a loser, financially and/or in other aspects of one's life;
Not saving where there is abundance;	Not having any or at least enough money to meet urgent financial requirements;
Not investing or not doing so prudently;	Always be in need
Not lending or doing so grudgingly, when one has the means to so;	Always be a borrower
Not giving with a cheerful heart	Not receiving in abundance

Table 3.1:   Consequences of not Adhering to Biblical Principles in Relation to Financial Management

Many persons who have adopted and consistently apply prudent financial management principles such as budgeting wisely, engaging in a healthy savings and investment program from when they were very young have been able to be debt free in their forties when they may have been able to repay for their home, car, education and other major expenditures. Such persons may have also streamlined their pension program, so that even if they decide to retire early, they can still enjoy a comfortable retirement. Even so, the 'locust and cankerworm' will destroy the best human financial and other plan, unless we adhere to Biblical principles such as giving of our tithe and offering and assisting the poor. There is no doubt that only financial, economic, spiritual and other programs which are consistent to Biblical principles will guarantee lasting success in this life and in eternity. Even the 'Bill Gates and Warren Buffett" of this world have not become wealthy overnight. It is true that many persons have won a large lottery and received an inheritance and became rich instantly. However, for the majority of persons the process of financial liberation is achieved over a number of years of adhering to a financially disciplined life.

The Elimination of Waste Adds up Over Time

Some aspects of waste include:
1. *Over eating, wastage of food and other items,*
2. *Overspending and purchasing items which are not necessary or neglecting better bargains which are available,*
3. *Failure to save in an account which generates the highest possible return and not investing prudently,*
4. *Not managing your bank account* and having to pay banking and other charges and losing your creditability by having your checks returned. There is usually a cost associated with paying checks which cause the account to be overdrawn and even for the bank to return your check due to insufficient funds on the account. A chare may also be allocated by the agency which was issued the check and they may refer the check to a debt collector or the police, where the issuer may be prosecuted.
5. *Incorrectly filing income tax returns* and not claiming returns which are due to you. The result may be a heavy penalty for tax evasion and loss of income.
6. *Wasting time* which could have been used productively to earn and additional source of income, work for the Lord, helping the poor, for example. The Lord provides financial and other blessings when we invest in His work.

Biblical guidance on the management of debt

"What are some of the issues related to debt which are recorded in the Bible?"

The Bible highlights several important issues on debt management. They include:

1. *If debt is secured among His people, they should be short term*; Deuteronomy 15:1 highlights that every seven years a remission should be granted where debtors be forgiven any outstanding debt to their creditors. However, the Jews were allowed to demand the entire amount from foreigners.
2. *Lending to fellow believers should be interest free –* Exodus 22:25,

3. *A blessing from the Lord is manifested in His people lending to many nations instead of borrowing* – Deuteronomy 15:6,

4. *Borrowing is financial enslavement* – Proverbs 22:7. This passage is viewed in areas such as unless the borrower is willing to adhere to the requirements of the lender, the credit facility is withheld. In addition, failure to honor the repayment schedule and satisfy other requirements may result in the foreclosure and the security is confiscated if the borrower is unable to repay the entire outstanding balance, plus in many instances the legal and other fees as a result of a court judgment. There are also many clauses in the loan agreement which the borrowers often sign in their eagerness and/or without reading and/or fully understanding, which grants the lender unfair advantage over them. This may include the right to increase the interest rate very high without notifying them and the right to foreclose on the loan at short notice.

5. *God's best method of provision may not include a person getting into debt which he cannot repay or for which the Lord will not perform a miracle to enable the debt to be repaid.* We have seen that 'the blessing of the Lord makes us rich and adds no sorrow.' Even though debt per sé is not classified as a sinful act unless it is a manifestation of greed or other sinful roots, it is not His best method of provision when we walk in His ways and trust Him. Examples of this principle are seen in the lives of righteous Bible characters such as King Solomon, Job and Abraham. If we are to be liberated in our financial management, it would entail being able to manage our debt, and even better, to be debt free.

6. *We should not stand as guarantor (surety) for strangers.* Unfortunately, in today's world the 'stranger' may be our own children and other close relatives and 'friends'. Many parents would, unwisely, give a credit card to an irresponsible youth only to find that he went on a massive spending spree and incurred a huge debt. When the youth who incurred the debt is unable to pay, payment will be demanded from the guarantor.

7. *We should not incur so much debt that we are unable to give of our tithes and give our offering, in order to*

service our debt and other life-style practices. If we cannot give to the Lord but we have to pay our creditors, it could be an indication that we are idolaters in putting the satisfaction of material desire before being obedient to the command of the Lord. *This is tantamount to robbing God in order to pay man*.

It is sad to see that many churches encourage their members to incur debt to finance the building fund of the church or other projects, when they should be assisting members to be debt free.

I have not found any scripture passage which declares that it is a sin to borrow. However, there are several passages which warn us against borrowing, particularly more than we can repay comfortably. Because of his indebtedness, the borrower becomes subject to the 'beck and call' of the lender. Very often there is a clause in the loan agreement where the lender can increase the interest rate and impose other clauses on the loan repayment and the borrower has to comply with them or the entire outstanding balance is demanded and the security confiscated if he does not comply. Similarly, even if the borrower is undergoing a period of hardship, the lender may refuse to be sympathetic and agree on a moratorium on the loan repayment until the borrower is in a position to continue to repay it. The result is that the house or other assets pledged as security is sold at an auction, very often for far lower than their market value; the bank pays off the loan and the borrower receives any remaining amount. In view of reasons such as these, Christians should be very careful who they borrow from and the amount they borrow.

Philippians 4:19, for example states: *"¹⁹And my God will fully satisfy every need of yours according to His riches in glory in Christ Jesus."*

If God is able to supply, according to His riches, isn't it a defeat to His word when we jump ahead of His provision and incur huge debt on our own? Among the names which the God declares Himself as is Jehovah-Jireh and El Shaddai, that is *'The Lord Will Provide'* and *'The All Mighty God'*, respectively. This first name declares that God will not hesitate to provide and the second reinforces the truth that nothing or no one has the power to hinder God from doing what He promises. God is our source, not our education, job, parent, business, investment or any created being or thing. He is also Jehovah-Shalom, *'The God of Peace'* who grants His peace when we heed the guidance of the Holy Spirit and Godly council from others and make financial and other decisions which are consistent with His will for our lives.

Debt related issues are the primary financial problems which affect a majority of persons directly or indirectly. One of the indirect effects of debt on nations is that the government of both developed and developing countries tax their income earners, consumers and other groups in order to defray debt incurred by the government. The national debt of the US, for example, is computed electronically by the second and displayed on monitors around Time Square and other locations. A newborn child is saddled with a debt repayment for debt which the child knows nothing about. The justification by some governments for this practice is that the infrastructure programs such as significantly improved medical facilities, roads, and education programs which have in some way contributed to the safe delivery of the child and during its growth, is testimony that the child has already began to benefit from the proceeds of debt incurred by the government and other agencies which were secured even before the child was born.

> There are two methods which can be used to get out of debt. That is to increase our inflow of income and/or to reduce our expenditure to the level which would enable us to have enough money to honor the repayment of the debt.

Debt and greed

Isn't debt a symptom of greed, therefore, Christians should avoid it?

Debt is usually the symptom of a deeper problem experienced by a person, family, corporate entity, nation and other entities. There are several reasons why persons get into debt. They include one or a combination of factors such as:

1. They are not earning enough to satisfy the basic nutritional and other items needed by their family,

2. Many persons are living beyond their means in that their expenditure consistently exceeds their income because of materialism and their desire to have items which may be beyond the capability of their immediate income.

3. There is an acute shortage of job opportunities in the society and they cannot find a higher paying job to enable them to provide enough funds to support their family.

Once a person gets into debt, unless they receive a large injection of money possibly from an inheritance, it usually would take a much longer time to get out of the debt, even with the implementation of a strict adherence to a disciplined budget. The difficult question which often goes unanswered until it is too late is, how does a person recognize that he is experiencing a debt problem? We often make promises that we will make this last purchase on the credit card or hire purchases, for example, and yet it goes on perpetually. Some of the first symptoms which a person caught in the debt trap may manifest are:

1. One is unable to meet monthly repayments and have enough money remaining to purchase food and other necessities for the month.
2. The inability of the holder of credit cards, for example, to fully repay it at the end of the month without having to neglect other important expenditure.

Some unscriptural reasons why some persons secure debt are greed, fear, impatience, self indulgence and lack of discipline.

*Debt - **easy to get into but often difficult to get out of***

"Is getting out and staying out of debt as easy as many television evangelists and other preachers contend?"

Many persons seek to emerge out of debt by mortgaging their home or refinancing their mortgage to secure the money they need to repay their debt. Once the persons involved are prepared to adopt a disciplined spending program, they may be able to emerge out of the debt. Sadly, many persons end up incurring more debt and may even lose their home since they are unable to maintain the monthly repayment. This is an example where the debt was a symptom of a deep rooted problem for which the person may not have been willing to seek or adhere to godly council and to adopt a disciplined budgetary program. For this reason, women in particular are very skeptical about mortgaging their home to repay a debt or even to use it as surety for an investment, unless there is concrete evidence that they may not end up losing it.

Many persons and corporate bodies use the avenue of declaring **bankruptcy** in order to avoid repaying a debt which they incurred. There are genuine instances where this is the only way out because of circumstances which were beyond the control of the debtor. For Christians, this should be the last resort, since we are obligated to honor our pledge since this is a good testimony and a direct command from the Lord. A person who declares bankruptcy would have that record on his credit record for five to ten years, depending on the country in which he lives. This becomes public knowledge and it contradicts any testimony of God's provision, personal prudence and financial discipline. For this reasons many Christians endeavor to avoid debt, even if it entails having to sell some of their assets and live at a lower level or take another job, for example. The issue of taking a second or third job in order to satisfy an inflated lifestyle is very dangerous. This is because the extra money may not compensate for the negative effects of the stress which is created as a result of being involved in so many activities outside of the home.

Many persons incur short term debt in order to invest over the long term. If one is a skilful investor and is able to secure a lucrative investment, this could be a profitable strategy. Commercial banks, for example, derive much profit by mismatching deposits and investments. If this strategy is not managed, it would be very unprofitable, for interest on short term credit is usually higher than on long term credit. For this reason when commercial banks experience liquidity difficulties they have to purchase short term financial instruments such as certificate of deposits (CDs) and incur inter-bank loans which carry high rate of interest. This reduces their profitability.

A person or business should secures an **overdraft**, for example, to finance working capital activities such as purchasing stocks and paying wages and utilities during the production process or in managing the office, until adequate revenue is generated from the sale of their goods and/or service, in order to repay the debt. If the capital from the overdraft is used to purchase fixed assets such as to factory, for example, the company is likely to suffer from cash flow difficulties. It is usually better to secure a **loan** for this purpose since a low monthly payment would be better to manage.

A question which a Christian who has a huge debt frequently asks is if one should make the repayment of the debt a priority over his tithes, saving and investments? It is true that the debt burden is quite heavy; particularly when it is past due and creditors are calling you on the phone, visiting your home and may even be in contact with your employers. Three popular methods which a person may use to manage this undesirable state are:

1. **Increase the income of the family** – this includes methods such as one or both spouses taking a second job, securing a higher paying job and/or engaging in some business activity which generates additional income. A wife who was previously working from home may secure a part time or permanent job. These options must be reviewed carefully since they may have a negative impact on other areas of our lives. Parents who, for example, spend lengthy hours working away from home would have far less time to spend with their children and each other. Unless they are able to hire the services of a baby sitter when it is cost effective to do so, or a competent relative who possibly volunteers to do so, the family will encounter financial, discipline and other problems.

2. **Decrease their expenditure** – this process will not be achieve instantaneously, since they may have become accustomed to a certain standard of living and even reducing it gradually may demand several major adjustments to accommodate the 'tightening of their belts'. Unless this is a commitment to the success of this process, there usually is much conflict in the home as they conserve on their spending. It is common for couples who are not seriously committed to their marriage to experience serious marital difficulties and even divorce during this period.

3. **Renegotiate the terms of repayment** - this could include strategies such as:

4. **Requesting a grace period or moratorium on the payment of the principal and even the interest on the loan over a reasonable period**. This is particularly applicable during the construction of a business premises or other activities where it would not be generating enough income to service the principle and even the interest on the loan repayment. In other instances a request for a lower loan payment during the off-peak, or low income period of the business and increase the amount paid during the high season, for example.

5. **Extending the repayment period, thus reducing the monthly repayment**. The wisdom of the strategy employed must be weighed against the additional

cost which is usually incurred and the supplier should be at least cautious in granting credit in the future unless it is ascertained that the crisis is no longer likely to reoccur.

A payment can be made on a pre-dated check. A person who is in a cash strapped position but would still like to maintain a good relationship with a supplier may request that even though the check is issued it will not be cashed until an agreed future date. If this is a large amount from a reputed person or agency, the recipient of the check may negotiate with a financial institution to have the check discounted and they will receive the funds even though the customer's account will not be debited until the date of the clearance of the check. *A standard check also has an inherent credit element associated with it. Once a check is issued, it provides credit to the issuer until it is cashed.* Other important debt management techniques include:

1. *It is always better to contact the agency before the repayment is due and negotiate a feasible rescheduling of the repayment.* This may include negotiating a lower monthly repayment and/or a period of moratorium where you service the interest only, for example. In the interim efforts should be made to have the additional finance to meet future payments.

2. *Some persons adopt the prudent strategy of consolidating their debt with one institution which offers a lower monthly repayment than the individual creditors from several institutions.* This principle also reduces the time and energy spent in making payment to several institutions during different days in the month. Debt consolidation can often be negotiated where several debts are repaid by one financial institution and a more comfortable repayment schedule granted to the debtor. This strategy is particularly favorable where one or several credit card debts are repaid with a loan with a lower interest rate and over a longer period. Care must be taken in an attempt to implement this strategy since during the process a debt with a low interest rate may be repaid in full with another debt which has high interest attached to it. Some persons consciously incur this loss with the comfort of having to make one payment on the consolidated debt.

3. *As far as possible, persons on a tight budget should avoid purchasing items over a given amount, say one hundred dollars, on impulse.* It is better to pray about the wisdom of the purchase and discuss it with your spouse or other persons before purchasing it. Very often the moment of reflection allows us to exam other options of payment, or whether or not a cheaper substitute cannot be secured. This principle is highlighted in Proverbs 21:5 which states: *"⁵The plans of the diligent lead surely to abundance, but everyone who is hasty comes only to want (poverty)."*

4. *Increase the time for paying creditors (persons who you owe) and decrease the time to receive payment from debtors (persons who owe you).* These two principles are commonly used by business entities to manage their cash flow. The benefit may not be as significant for an individual where the transitions are usually small but is significant for persons and businesses who deal with large financial transaction. If we are able to delay payment for a month or two with the consent of the creditor, particularly if it does not include incurring additional charges, it would have a positive impact on our cash flow. Similarly, receiving payment cash on delivery (COD) or over a short time would increase our cash flow.

5. *Where possible solicit assistance from a relative, friend or even a fellow Christian or the church council. It may also be possible to secure a short term loan from a relative or friend.* These are several methods which can be used to alleviate the predicament temporarily. The better long term solution would be to be more discipline in managing the budget. We are reminded of the old Chinese proverb which expounds on the wisdom of *teaching a person to fish, rather than merely giving him a fish.* In teaching him to fish he will be able to provide for himself and if he so desires, to use this as an economic venture to earn a living rather than to merely satisfy an immediate need by giving him the fish and he is perpetually dependant on handouts in order to survive. Particularly for business entities two additional features are usually added. They are:

6. *By increasing the time for the settlement of accounts payable*, that is, *delay forwarding payments to suppliers.*

7. ***Reducing the time for accounts receivables***, where they request cash or prompt payments when purchases are made by customers instead of granting credit, or at least do so over a lengthy period. This practice is questionable from a scriptural perspective, since we should 'do unto others as we would like them to do unto us'. However, if the supplier and purchaser are prepared to accept those conditions, they can be effective in reducing severe cash flow difficulties.

> ***Debt to most persons is like the Venus flytrap to insects; easy to get in, very often impossible to get out.*** (A Venus flytrap is a flower which traps and kills insects which enter its enfolding petals. The flower would shut tightly and suffocate the insect which was attracted by the sweet smell of the flower and its quest to collect nectar. The flower would then absorb the water and other nutrients from the decaying body of the insect).

We have established that it is the perfect will of God that His children are free from financial debt since we are not to remain as slaves, but live in the liberty in which Christ has set us free. This freedom is not only spiritual, but includes liberation from all forms of oppression, including financial bondage such as the hideous burden of debt which has contributed to the destruction of many persons, families and nations. We have an obligation to give of our tithes to the Lord and give offerings and to serve the Lord faithfully in every aspect of our lives. In return, He will provide protection, health, material and other blessings to us and our family and to the wider community. An important strategy which has been successfully employed by millions of persons who are embroiled in the debt trap is to ***sow their way out of Debt***.

2 Corinthians 9:6-8 states: ***"⁶The point is this; the one who sows sparingly will also reap sparingly, and the one who sows bountifully will also reap bountifully. ⁷Each of you must give as you have made up your mind, not reluctantly or under compulsion, for God loves a cheerful giver. ⁸And God is able to provide you with every blessing in abundance, so that by always having enough of everything, you may share abundantly in every good work."***

This is merely one of the hundreds of promises which the Lord has established with His children. If we would only be obedient to these commands, we will experience the overwhelmingly abundance of blessings in our lives. Since the

Lord is not like man that He would lie, then we have to take Him at His word and experience the abundance of His blessings which are in the Bible and which so many persons have testified of their reality.

> Once we stay committed and focused on fulfilling God's will for our lives and we are walking in accordance with His ways; then we have nothing to worry about. We can cast all of our burdens on Him and He will look after the provision to enable us to succeed.

The ability of most persons to live on their income is not as feasible as they would like. As a result, a number of persons and financial institutions have existed on the basis that they have been providing credit to persons and institutions that have immediate financial demands which they cannot currently meet, but which they have the potential to honor at a future date. The credit culture is dominant in the US and several other countries where credit agencies offer attractive packages to members of the public who would end up in many instances in a worse financial position than before they accepted the credit facilities. The credit card industry has contributed to the serious financial difficulties of many families in these societies.

> Very often we make unwise purchases because we have the option to purchase the item on credit. When most persons have to make large cash payments for an item, they are more likely to review other more lucrative ways of spending the money. There is usually less pressure when we use credit faculties such as hire purchase and credit card.

'Good' versus bad debts

"Is there such a thing as a 'good' and/or bad debt?"

The Bible does not totally condemn the use of debt, instead, guidelines are presented on the management of debt, as discussed in Chapter 1. The fact that the Lord declared a year of Jubilee for the Israelites and that they should not take interest for debt to other Israelites but that they can do so for non-Israelites, are some of the illustrations that debt should be managed in a Biblical framework.

It is a fact that many persons incur debt where the repayment is so strenuous that they are forced to neglect to give of their tithes and offering to the Lord in order to pay their debt and to meet other expenditures. The word of the Lord which came to the prophet Haggai in Haggai 1:6,9,10 identifies some of the frustration which persons experience (in this instant because they did not build a house for the Lord) when they spend money on their personal well being and pleasure and neglect to obey the Lord: *"⁶You have sown much, and harvest little; you eat, but never have enough; you drink, but never have your fill; you clothe yourselves, but no one is warm; and you that earn wages earn wages to put them into a bag with holes....⁹You have looked for much, and, lo, it came to little; and when you brought it home, I blew it away. Why? says the Lord of host. Because my house lies in ruins while all of you hurry off to your own houses. ¹⁰Therfore the heavens above you have withheld the dew, and the earth has withheld its produce."*

We are also reminded in Malachi Chapter 3 of some of our financial obligations to the Lord and the blessings we will enjoy from obeying them versus the consequences of disobeying them. We should therefore seriously assess the likely implications on our relationship with the Lord and others before we incur debt and make other important financial and other decisions. Serious consideration before incurring debt include how does the monthly loan payment affect the amount available for tithes and offering, the cash flow of the family and funds available for leisure.

The following are three important issues which should be considered when reviewing some of the fundamental principles of managing material resources:

1. The Lord deals with us on an individual basis, as can be noted in the parable where the master gave his servants talents which were consistent with his assessment of their ability to manage money. It is my view that it was not coincidental that he gave one five talents and another only one.

2. Even though persons will receive special blessings for giving to the poor, being faithful in tithing and offering, for example, a person who does not manage his financial resources, is not automatically condemned to hell, unless such a person also commits the unpardonable sin, of blaspheming against the Holy Spirit.

3. Similar to the life of Job, we do not have full control over every aspect of our financial resources and life in general.

There are volumes of books written on strategies which we should implement in an attempt to get out and stay out of the debt trap. A common theme among genuine Christian writers on the issue of debt management is that apart from a miracle such a relative leaving a large inheritance, a debt write-off from the financial institution, winning the jackpot from the lottery (gambling is not sanctioned by the Bible), there is no financial strategy which can be used to transform a person instantaneously from being heavily indebted to being debt-free. Since events occur in the spiritual realm before they are manifested naturally, inherent in the plan of salvation is the freedom from the debt burden. Hence, even though we may experience the physical symptoms of the debt (such as the deprivation of even necessities), we should cast our cares, including the debt burden, on Him, for He has already borne all of our burdens and set us free.

It is important that a person who receives a miracle and a debt was written off, for example, should not look down on another person who the Lord directs to work smart and avoid debt but instead to purchase cash. The Lord may be teaching different lessons to the two persons. It is similar to the fact that Moses prayed and the Lord performed many miracles; when Joshua took over the leadership of the children of Israel he had to fight several wars and to lead the people into cultivating the land, for example.

Knowing Your Need, Want and Desire:

1. **Need** - an essential item which is tantamount to a life and death scenario such as food and fresh air. We also have material and other needs such as to have adequate housing, amount of clothes, standard of education, friendship, companionship, source of income, spiritual growth and development.
2. **Want** - the desire to have an item which is of secondary importance,
3. **Desire** - something which a person longs or hopes for,

In our strategy to move from a state of being heavily dependent on debt to one of being debt free, we may still have to incur some debt even though we may have a more structured approach to managing it. Some of the debts which many persons view as necessary at least in the short and medium term are:

1. **The purchase of furniture and other necessities at the initial stage of their marriage.** This is usually because the couple may not have been able to accumulate enough savings to pay for their wedding and other

expenses and still have enough to purchase all the requirements for their home with cash.

2. **A mortgage to secure their home**. This is usually weighed against paying a rent to a home owner, when one can be making an investment into one's own home. The financial situation of the couple may be so grave that the couple may have to secure a loan from one institution in order to make the down payment and to cover legal and other expenses associated with the mortgage and a loan from another financial institution for the remaining amount. Thankfully, many financial institutions are now providing 100% financing for first time and other home owners, particularly for low income applicants whose mortgage is within a given ceiling.

3. **The purchase of a private jet, yacht (of course there are Christians who purchase these items), car, motor cycle and/other mode of transportation** is a major expense for many families. The repayment of the loan may have to be extended from three to five years to enable them to be able to service the loan and still live comfortably.

4. **The payment of fees and other expenses associated with our education and/or the children's**. Many parents began to save for the college fund of their children even before they are born. Sadly, even in such instance due to inflation, the growing cost of fees and other expenses, they are not able to save enough to cover all of the costs. Therefore, they have to resort to borrowing to meet such shortfalls.

5. **The payment of medical expenses, funeral expenses of a loved one and other emergencies which may arise.** Unless we earn enough and are able to save enough to cover the cost of emergencies, for most of us when emergencies arise where we have to incur huge expenses, we have to borrow to meet those financial commitments.

Generally, debt which is incurred merely for consumption and does not generate additional income but is merely to fulfill greed, in an attempt to 'live up' to the life style of others and other sinful practices, can be classified as undesirable debt.

Steps toward debt freedom

"What are some of the important steps which can be pursued in order to be debt free?"

Having recognized that we should be debt free, there are several principles which we can follow in order to be debt free and stay out of debt permanently. They include:

1. **Stage 1:** Recognize that you have a debt problem and be committed to get out of debt with the help of the Lord, prudent management of the debt and adhering to godly council. This is a common practice among organizations such as the Alcoholic Anonymous, where when a new member attends the first meeting, as part of the introductory speech they state, "I am an alcoholic." Reorganization of one's state of addiction is an important first step in the progression of the healing process.

   There are three examples of burdens/yokes which I can recall the Bible instructing us to have. They are:

   I. Spouses being yoked (joint) together,

   II. We should bear each other's burdens (empathize with the sufferings of others, provide financial and other forms of assistance to those in need). In this example we are yoked to them in that we can be empathic with their challenge, stand with them in prayer and seek to assist them in whatever way we can.

   III. We should be yoked to Christ – follow the Lord, we should be guided by Him and learn what it is to rest in Him, for example.

   We were never instructed to go through this life being under the yoke or burden of debt. We are instead encouraged for us to rely on the wisdom, guidance, strength and other attributes which the Lord has endowed in us to work ardently at eradicating our debt. He also gives us favor, blessings and other forms of assistance which is beyond our capabilities.

2. **Stage 2:** List the extent of the debt. This can be done in a format as highlighted below:

Debt Schedule of the Robertson Family ($)					
List of Debtors	**Purpose**	**Amount Borrowed**	**Amount Due**	**Monthly Payment**	**Interest Rate %**
Family Mortgage Inc.	Mortgage	250,000	225,326	1,556	9.25
Rest Motors Inc.	Motor car	65,000	56,285	456	17
Ace College	Ann's Fee	48,000	23,542	350	5.5
A to Z Variety Store	Vanity set, bed, fridge & stove	25,500	18,126	526	15

Credit card	Miscellaneous	15,000	14,600	325	23
Uncle Jake	Wedding expenses	4,500	3,875	125	5
Total		**$408,000**	**$341,754**	**$3,338**	

Table 3.2 A Schedule of the Debt of the Robinson Family

This table shows the debt of the Roberson family. Several other columns could have been added to this table such as one highlighting the maturity date of each loan. At the same time, even though a debt schedule does not have to be as complex as this one, it is important that it is structured to highlight the essentials of each debt so that a systematic strategy can be adopted in order to eradicate this burden. It becomes a challenge to speed up the process as one sees the balances decline.

As the family recognizes the magnitude of the debt burden they can seek to increase their income and/or decrease their spending and contribute more towards the loan payment.

3. **Stage 3:** Depending on the financial resources of the family, their discipline and commitment to work in unison and other factors of an individual family, this process may take a few months for some families or a number of years for others.

4. **Stage 4:** Work ardently to eliminate each debt. This principle includes seeking and securing the type of job which would enable you to earn enough money to be able to repay the debt, adopting a disciplined lifestyle of budgeting and living within your means. In the process, it would take much discipline and faith in the Lord to avoid getting into new debt. As each debt is repaid and it is omitted from the list, it would be a source of joy for the family as they recognize that the end of their struggle is drawing near. This will challenge them to eliminate the others.

The issue of being debt free is particularly difficult for poorer families to embrace, even though many wealthier families also adopt a lifestyle which is beyond their means because of greed, indulgence and other lifestyle patterns. However, the solution to being debt free is reinforced by the fact that in every aspect of our lives, the Lord expects us to work conscientiously and also to trust Him to see us through every difficult situation. We cannot please Him without having faith in Him and working with Him and those persons and institutions which He has placed at our disposal to assist us in this process.

| Caught in a debt trap |

"What are some of the symptoms of a person or family caught in the debt trap?"

Financial analysts have formulated several methods of determining whether or not a person or corporate entity is experiencing a debt management crisis and the extent and severity of this situation. These include:

1. *The Liquidity ratio which expresses the current asset as a percentage of the current liability.* This is a simple measure of the ability of the debtor to honor payments which are due within a number of days, weeks and/or months, depending on the financial requirements of the family or business and the urgency of their demand to meet current expenditure. In terms of an individual or family it can be related to the ability of their income to meet monthly repayments which are due and still live comfortable. The severity of this problem is dependent on factors such as the ability of the family to reduce their expenditure and/or secure adequate short-term funding in order to survive until the next payday. If they cannot meet their current debt obligation and are unable to repay their debt/s, the result may be that the creditor repossesses to the item/s or foreclose on the security, such as their home.

2. *There are so many families who are merely one pay day away from bankruptcy and who are unable to maintain their normal standard of living for at least one year from their savings.*

3. *The inability of a person to repay the entire balance on their credit card at the end of the month.* Many persons prefer to use their credit card to meet short-term expenditure such as to purchase groceries. They do not mind the service and other charges at the end of the month because of the convenience and safety of the credit card. This method is particularly useful to persons who are not disciplined enough to adhere to purchasing items from a list and they do not want to use a calculator at the shopping centre to assist them to stay within their budget and more specifically, the amount of cash which they took with them to the store.

4. *When the repayment of the loan has to take precedence over the payment of tithes, offering, utility bills, financing health requirements and other essential*

expenditure on a consistent basis. Many Christians experience an occasional situation when an emergency arises where it may be necessary to defer payment of their tithes in order to meet the urgent expense. This practice should be avoided as much as possible and instead we should exercise our faith in the promise of the Lord to satisfy all of our needs while paying careful attention not to habitually live well beyond our needs. We must carefully analyze our circumstances and see whether they are the result of a mistake, an emergency or an unnecessary lifestyle habit such as extravagant spending beyond our budget. If it is the latter, it is our responsibility to uproot the mindset which encourages it.

It should be noted that many of the symptoms identified in a person or family caught in the debt trap can be extended to a society, country and region. An example of this feature is shown in the Heavily Indebted Poor Countries (HIPIC), for example, where much emphasis is increasingly been focused by the international community to write off or reschedule their debt and to provide other concessions to enable them to emerge from their impoverishment. Many of them have received heavy investment from international donor agencies and other governments in developing infrastructural programs such as health, education, the construction and maintenance of 'all-weather' roads, the establishment of communication network and the establishment and expansion of the operations of export oriented industries. The assistance received is often not enough since many of these nations are so underdeveloped that these concessions are not enough to enable them to emerge from poverty since many of these endeavors are hampered by the corrupt political system and poor human rights practices by many governments of poorer countries.

"Covered *under the blood' from financial woes*

"As Christians, aren't we protected by the Lord from financial and other crises?"

Matthew 5: 45(b) states: ***"45 (b)....for He makes His sun rise on the evil and on the good, and sends rain on the righteous and on the unrighteous."***

It is a misconception for us to believe that as Christians we are entitled to a 'bed of roses' while we are on earth. There are so many scripture verses which inform us that as Christians we will be prosecuted and that some of us will be put to death on account of the gospel. Luke 21:16-36 identified some of the perilous experiences which will befall the world, including Christians. Some Christians will be imprisoned and even be put to death for the sake of the gospel. We also have the famous story of the life of Job who fell from riches to rags but whose wealth was reinstated in a greater measure. We also have the example of the family of the prophet who died and left them in debt to the extent where his sons would have been sold into slavery to repay his debt. Elijah intervened and the Lord performed the miracle of filling the oil jars which, in accordance with the prophet's instructions, the late prophet's wife borrowed. They were filled miraculously as she poured oil from her oil jar. These examples are highlighted to identify that Christians also suffer from financial and other crises. Christian parents and children also die from road accidents and other tragedies and their families are often left with grief, financial and other difficulties.

Christians have several support mechanisms which non-Christians do not have. Three differences between Christians and non-Christians in the area of managing crises are:
1. The steps of believers are ordered by the Lord, that is, 'nothing happens by chance.'
2. We have the support of loved ones, other believers, there are so many comforting and reassuring passages in the Bible, and the Holy Spirit strengthens us and provides us with direction. Secondly, we have a hope of eternal life after we leave this earth.

Each person experiences financial and other challenges in one form or another at various stages of their lives. This dilemma is not only applicable to persons who are living below the poverty line in developing countries but also for persons in affluent societies. Very often a person who is born in an impoverished family is better able to cope with financial and other difficulties since they have been accustomed to surviving on very little. Conversely, many persons in affluent societies are prone to experience mental depression and may even commit suicide when confronted with financial difficulties since they cannot imagine living well below the affluence which they have been accustomed to and the prestige which their status commands.

The devastating effect of financial difficulties is so profound on the lives of individuals, families and nations that it has, and continues to be one of the primary reasons for much of the difficulties which affect our society. As was alluded to in

Chapter 1, money is important because of factors such as:

1. It enables us to conduct the financial transactions which enable us to get the items which are essential for our sustenance such as adequate quantity and quality of food, housing, education, clothing and opportunities to increase our standard of living to a satisfactory level.

2. It determines to a great extent the educational status we will be able to attain, the level of health care we will receive, the neighborhood in which we live, the type of house we live in and the furnishing, the type of transportation facility, if any, which we can afford.

Our social status is to a great extent influenced by our financial position. Very often political and other prominent positions in society are influenced by the financial standing of both the incumbent candidate and his/her supporters. This is often so because the person who is able to get things done would inject personal funds (equity) or at least be influential enough to secure the financial support from another source.

Several financial problems which affect families have been highlighted in various sections of this book. It is useful to have a section which focuses exclusively on some of the more common problems and some methods which have been successfully used to resolve them. This is important since Christians experience many of the difficulties related to financial and other aspects of our lives. They include:

1. Living in an impoverished society where there are very limited opportunities to earn a reasonable standard of living. Many such families live in poverty and their state is worsening as they incur debt in order to survive. It is common even in impoverished countries for persons to lose their cattle, land and other assets as a result of being unable to repay debt.

2. The inability of the income of the breadwinner/s of the family to satisfy the basic needs of the family such as the provision of adequate quantity and quality of food, clothing, housing, educational, health and other essential areas. The church and other Christian organizations have often been instrumental in assisting persons to emerge from poverty. It may begin by instructing the society of their spiritual responsibilities to serve the Lord, seek His face, pray and to turn from our wicked ways. These principles extend to working with the government in providing

grants through non-governmental organizations (NGOs), credit schemes, health, education and other community development programs.

3. Spouses who are grossly dissatisfied with the standard of living of the family and are working for long hours, neglecting each other and the children or have resorted to extramarital affairs or other sinful methods to secure money, repay huge debt, 'relaxation' and/or other forms of gratification.

4. A wife may request, or even demand that her husband provides her with a separate 'spousal allowance' even if he is meeting other financial needs of the family. If there is efficient budgeting in the family and everyone is reasonably satisfied, one would not normally expect such episodes. However, when the husband is a miser, stingy, and not earning enough to meet the financial needs of the family, for example, this situation is common. There are also some wives who are not willing to live within the limitation of the budget, even as the family endeavors to increase their financial position. Where effective budgeting is practiced, each member of the family should have their financial and other needs met in accordance with the 'size of the pie.'

5. Children who are dissatisfied with the standard of living of their family may become rebellious and may even resort to a life of crime to satisfy their financial wants. Parents have the responsibility to teach their children prudent money management and other principles as illustrated in the Bible and also by referring to secular practices which are consistent with the teachings of the Bible, and more importantly, live these examples. Even as we prayerfully play our part, we have to give our children over to the Lord for Him to instill His word and direction in their lives.

6. One or both partners of a marriage who are lavish spenders and would not adhere to the discipline of a well-planned budget and living within their means. This is usually a receipt for one or both of them to incur huge debts in order to finance their life style.

7. A spouse who is domineering and would seek to impose his/her beliefs dictates in financial and other matters on the other. A husband who is the sole breadwinner of the family may be particularly prone to this practice. Similarly, a discontented wife may

continually make financial and other demands on her husband which he may be unable or unwilling to fulfill. The source of this action may not necessarily have anything to do with, per sé but a misguided mindset which needs to be changed.

8. A person, and more seriously, a family living without concrete financial and other goals which would challenge them to structure their activities to enable them to achieve their goals and continually trust the Lord for His abundant blessings beyond their abilities. We have to plan and seek to execute Godly principles in every area of our lives including our **health** by eating correctly, exercising and indulging in other healthy lifestyle practices; **financial management** including formulating and executing short, medium and long term goals; our **personal growth and development** in areas such as our career, family life; and **spiritual growth and development.**

9. Members of a family who prostitute their bodies, beg and/or do menial jobs such as working in a 'sweat shop' under inhumane conditions and with low wages in order to survive. Christians have to live above merely existing and instead come into the abundance which the Lord has brought us into. We have to be obedient to His Word and trust Him to fulfill His glorious promises in our lives, that of our family and the nations.

10. Members of a family who have to live in perpetual debt in order to survive. This may be as a result of one or several members of the family having to finance an addiction such as illegal drugs, alcohol, cigarettes, and greed, which propel them to make credit purchases which are far beyond their ability to provide. For far too many Christians, life is primarily a state of constant borrowing, repaying loans and living under the burden of perpetual debt. The Lord has delivered us from sin and the consequence of sin including material, spiritual and other forms of bondage.

11. Some families suffer from financial difficulties due to severe sickness and other forms of incapacitation of one or several members of the family.

12. The following are some of the factors which cause persons to incur debt:
    a. Weddings expenses,

b. To purchase a home,
c. To establishing or expanding a business,
d. For the burial of a member of the family,
e. To finance a member or several members of the family traveling to a foreign country,

Debt erodes the financial freedom of families as they seek to meet the monthly repayments.

Some Christian families go through life so poverty-stricken that there is hardly a time when they can truly enjoy spending money to enjoy the simple things in life; instead they are perpetually bowed-down, scavenging to exist from moment-to-moment, day-to-day. Yet we are serving a God who has created the world and all that is in it. Whatever the need, we serve a God who is well able to meet all of our financial and other needs which are consistent with His will. We also have Christian financial counselors and other professionals who are specially trained to guide us in this and other important areas of our lives. God has given us His Word; we have direct access to Him via the channel of prayer, praise and worship. We also have intercessors, the body ministry of the church, the five-fold ministry, our spiritual weapons and other assets to see us through financial and other difficulties. We must put our trust in the Lord and take Him at his word.

Once we are His children and keep His commands in areas such as delighting ourselves in Him, asking, seeking and knocking, giving from a generous heart, giving thanks to Him, trusting in Him, putting Him to the test, being poor in spirit and so many other areas which He has decreed to enable us to receive the things which we need. Since we are not our own, but were bought with a price, the precious blood of Jesus, we are no longer our own, we have to cast our cares on Him and see Him 'come through for us'. He has promised to bless us beyond our ability and even more than we can think or imagine. We will usually achieve victory over debt as we trust in Jehovah to meet our every need.

Many Christians are disillusioned with their life since even though we have everything at our 'fingertip' yet we have not learnt how to 'tap into it.' This fact is illustrated in the life of the 'Prodigal Son Number Two' who worked as a servant not as an owner. He had everything at his disposal and could have killed any calf he wanted, whenever he wanted and host as many parties as he wanted, of course within limits, yet he was jealous when his father hosted a party for his adventurous brother. In many Christian circles, servant-hood and ownership are seen as opposites, even though Christ united these functions. Christ demonstrated this by becoming a servant and carrying out the will of His Father even though He was the owner of the world. We will see Him in His majesty as He celebrates with His bride, the church, on His second coming.

The primary reason for the financial, spiritual and other deprivations suffered by Christians is due to the way we see ourselves and live accordingly. For many of us the issue of being the chosen generation, royal priesthood, a peculiar people and all of the other titles and positions which Christ has given us, is empty boasting. The dominance of our fleshly nature still wars against our spiritual nature since we are not prepared to 'go the extra mile' and extend our faith and take the Lord at His word and see Him perform the miraculous. We cannot please God without faith, yet we are not prepared to allow our faith to grow like the mustard seed, but for far too many of us our faith in God does not go very far beyond salvation and believing in eternal life. There are so many examples in the Bible where we can identify that **God does not respond to a need but rather to faith. We have to knock and seek in order to find.** We often limit God to what we can achieve on our own and never seek to extend our faith to allow the Lord to perform the supernatural in our lives. We do not get in the place where we allow the Lord to perform the miraculous to bless us and those around us. This is what brings most glory to God not merely what we can do in our own strength but when we invite Him to take us beyond our capabilities into the supernatural. This is what brings most glory to the Lord, bless the lives of those around us and also challenges the unsaved to come to the Lord. This is not merely a state of achieving enormous material wealth but also in areas of healing and other operation of the other gifts of the Spirit.

1. **God is our Source**. He may change the supplier, which may include our job, business, a widow or even a raven (Elijah). However, all good gifts come from Him.
2. If Elijah can command the sun to stand, and the Lord enabled his request to be fulfilled, why can't we trust the Lord to enable us to be debt free and to enjoy other blessing?
3. **Prosperity is not about money, it is about obedience.** Delight yourself in the Lord and He will give you the desires of your heart.

Managing Debt from Financial Institutions

The use of debt instruments such as a mortgage, hire purchase, leasing, credit card and consumer loans are very popular in most countries and communities in the developed and developing countries. Even in rural communities such as in Bangladesh, micro-finance credit though institutions such as the Grameen Bank are very popular. Similarly, credit through money lenders and other traditional mechanisms are also popular even in rural communities in developing countries. In view of these factors, many Christians do not view debt as inherently bad or good but would focus on factors such as the purpose of the facility, the reason why the debt option is explored, the interest rate and repayment period of the facility and the ability of the applicant to comfortably manage the debt.

"Easy' credit and Christians

"Should Christians use credit cards and accept 'easy' credit offers?"

Even among many persons who oppose the general usage of credit cards, they may be obtained for purposes such as the following:

1. When a person has to travel to another country or even to another location locally, it is often safer to have a credit card rather than to carry cash which could be easily stolen. Even if the credit card is stolen, it could be reported to the Credit Card Company and further transaction stopped until the card is recovered or a replacement issued.

2. Some agencies grant discount if a credit card is used. Once the cardholder is disciplined enough and is able to replace the amounts purchased before the end of the month, there is usually only a minimal service charge which may be payable.

Credit cards are commonly used in developed countries such as the US, Canada and among several EU countries and among the upper and middle classes of the population of many developing countries. Increasingly, persons are being offered several credit cards via the internet and by banks and credit card companies which use telemarketing, mail offers and other strategies to lure potential customers to patronize this service. Credit card companies offer clients easy access to credit. There are also many circumstances such as when one is traveling to another state or country when it is usually more convenient to use a credit card than to carry around cash which can be easily stolen or lost.

If a credit card is misplaced, the card holder can report it to the credit card company which will nullify the activity on the card and prevent an unauthorized person from debiting the account. Persons who are indiscipline and those who are confronted with serious financial situations which they cannot find immediate solutions for, often utilize these facilities to the maximum in anticipation that they will be able to fully repay the debt in the short-run. The reality is that a large percentage of persons become so addicted to using credit cards that they go on frequent shopping sprees with the honest intention of repaying in due course. Very often such persons end up accepting several credit cards and other forms of credit facilities in an attempt to repay outstanding debts. In other words, they 'dig a hole to fill a hole.' It is customary to find such persons accumulating credit on one card to repay outstanding debt on another when the payment is past due.

In credit driven societies such as the US, it is usually easy to acquire a credit card without having to undergo extensive background checks or in some countries, young adults who are not even working and cannot adequately service such a facility are offered credit cards. Such persons often obtain a bad credit rating even before they had the opportunity to start earning a decent wage. The question is often asked who is to be blamed for such an unfortunate situation. The answer is usually both the credit card companies whose primary concern is usually to issue as much credit as possible and the gullible customer for accepting these offers at face value without seeking wise council and carefully weighing the consequences of their actions.

It is true that a credit card may come in very handy in situations such as purchasing items on the internet, even though the risk of using it to purchase on some sites may be risky since it may be illegally debited for other unsolicited purchases or the sites may not be secure and other persons may have access to the number. It is very convenient and safe to use a credit card when one is traveling since it offers safety where if it is stolen, it is usually easy to stop any payment on the card by merely reporting it to the credit card company. However, a debit card offers the same facilities without the additional high interest charge on transaction undertaken since the cost of the transaction is merely debited from the account of the user.

Particularly for the undisciplined spender, the best ways of managing debt include practices such as:

1. Not having a credit card, or only use it in emergencies and not to purchase items where the entire balance of the card can be fully repaid by the end of the month. It is a statistical fact that the there is a likelihood for the average credit card holders to spend more than 20% than they normally would have spent if they were making cash payments.

2. Not to purchase any item on credit unless it can be promptly repaid for by the end of the current month.

Proverbs 11:15 states: *"¹⁵Guarantee loans for a stranger brings trouble, but there is safety in refusing to do so."*

Even though not every stranger will be dishonest, there is a higher probability that a person with whom one is familiar, will usually endeavor to honor a commitment which is guaranteed by a relative or at least someone who knows them. Failure to do so may result in members of one family, friend and other persons pressurizing the defaulter to honor his/her commitment. This may not be possible with a stranger and one may end up losing the collateral or one's good name may be tarnished.

Unless a person can manage his finance in ways such as budgeting wisely, and as far as possible live within that budget, avoid unnecessary spending and implement a disciplined savings program; it is wise that credit card and other forms of credit, particularly for consumer items be avoided. *The important consideration should be a commitment by each member of the family to live within the discipline of the budget*. There should also be a commitment from the parents to endeavor to manage the resources which they have, even as they save and invest wisely to acquire the things which they need.

There was a recent advertisement for a washing machine where consumers were offered the follow options:

1. A cash payment of $1,999.00
2. Term payment as follows:
   a. Down payment of $1.00, or an amount that one can afford to pay,

b. 30 monthly payments of $100.00. (The monthly payment would be smaller with a higher deposit, since a smaller interest will be payable).

Many persons would be attracted to the second offer since it does not put immediate pressure on them to find the cash payment. However, in taking this option they have to consider issues such as the following:

1. They would enjoy the privilege of using the washer even though they were not willing or able to expend all of the money to fully pay for it immediately,

2. They should negotiate to have the warranty on the washer extended to at least the period of the repayment. They should demand that any problem which may be encountered is repaired quickly by even threatening to withhold further payments until the problem is rectified.

   The total cost of the washing machine at the end of the two and a half years is $3,001.00. The cost of the washer would be $1,001.00 or 14.3% more that the cash price. Important tips to observe when purchasing items on hire purchase, similar to any other credit scheme is that, the higher the down payment, the lower the monthly payment and interest will be.

3. If the purchaser is unable to meet the full payment of the washing machine and the company is forced to repossess it, it would affect one's credit rating. This may jeopardize one's chances of securing further credit from this and other companies in the near future (under ten years). This feature is referred to as the **Opportunity Cost** of conducting the activities, *vise a vie* others. The concept of Opportunity Cost can be illustrated simply by comparing the financial advantage in investing one dollar in **Business A** where the profit is twenty five cents, as against **Business B** where the profit is fifty cents. The opportunity cost of investing in **Business A** is twenty five cents (0.50 to 0.25) by forgoing **Business B**.

4. Once the prospective purchaser is able to invest the $1,001.00 and generate a net profit of more than 14.3% for two and a half years, it may be a worthwhile investment to secure the item on credit. A word of caution must be interjected, since the net profit is not merely the selling price minus the buying price. Accurate account must be made of inputs such as labor, time and other input by the investor. **Even though the cash purchase may be the better option (at least**

for the wealthy), other considerations often render the hire purchase as practically the only other option other than waiting a number of months to purchase the item, the price of which may have in fact escalated significantly.

Since credit facilities by their very nature require that we incur interest, service charge and other costs, we have to weigh the advantages and disadvantages before engaging in any credit transaction. Many persons have encountered situations where it is more profitable to purchase an item on credit and utilize one's cash to engage in an investment, for example, which generates a higher return than the amount we would pay for the credit facility. There are even situations where an item such as the purchase of the home, car, the payment for the education of a child is beyond our immediate financial capability and a credit has to be sought. It is a fact, however, that the lives of far too many persons are ruined or at least are less than satisfactory because persons make poor credit and other decisions. It is important that we count the cost before we engage in any financial and other decisions.

Two fundamental limitations of borrowing are that:

1. We are making presumptions that we will live long enough and retain the ability to repay the loan.
2. It limits the demonstration of the power of the Lord to provide for us in other ways.

Do's *and don'ts when seeking a mortgage*

"What are some of the costs and other factors which we should consider when securing a mortgage?"

If a person or family were to secure a **mortgage for a property**, some of the initial costs which would be incurred are as follows:

1. Valuation of the property,
2. Solicitor fees, this is usually for representing the interest of the mortgagee in favor of the mortgage company,

3. The registration of the mortgage in favor of the mortgage company, for example, for a mortgage of $250,000.00, the title deeds of the property will be registered to have a charge of $250,000.00 in favor of the mortgage company. If the mortgagee defaults on the loan repayment, the mortgage company can take the matter to court and be granted the authority to sell the property and to recover the $250,000.00 plus any legal and other charges incurred,
4. Facility fee charged by the mortgage company,
5. Insurance of the building,
6. The purchase of new furniture, utensils, blinds and other necessities, and the cost and logistics of transporting them to the new home. The process of moving house is usually very stressful for most families and it usually takes a number of months before they become settled into the new environment. For this reason the process has to be managed and persons have to be tolerant, accommodating and supportive of each other. This may include the children changing school, becoming familiar with the location of shops and supermarkets, new neighbors and making friends with new church members.

Once the applicant qualifies for the mortgage, the other major consideration is usually the obligation to honor the monthly payments, failing which, unless they are able to negotiate for a moratorium on their repayment and/or other favorable concessions until they are in a better financial position to resume their repayment, they could lose the property. Many persons also take a second mortgage or refinance an existing mortgage on their home in order to conduct activities such as repairs or renovation to their home and to finance the education of their children.

Many persons debate the issue of which institution is best suited for them to secure a mortgage to purchase or build a house. The options which are available include a credit union, building society, insurance company or commercial bank. There are also some agencies which provide housing loans for staff of the institution with highly concessional terms. In many instances the credit union and the building societies would offer attractive interest rates even though the ceiling of the amount they lend usually is lower than that of commercial banks. The interest rates on mortgages from a commercial bank may be higher than other financial institutions and they may require a higher percentage contribution than other financial institutions.

Customers may also have to pay commitment and other fees, and their interest rates may be floating at a given percentage above the bank's prime interest rate. Unless a cap is agreed to, this would prove to be very expensive once the interest rates increases significantly.

The acquisition of one or several homes is the biggest financial investment for a large number of couples. This may only be second to the investment in business ventures which some couples or a member of a family may engage in. For this reason it is imperative that the couple be very careful in choosing which house to purchase since factors such as the architectural design, number of rooms, size of the land and building, and neighborhood where it is located are important in determining the selling price and value of the property.

Many persons debate whether to accept a **fixed rate or an adjustable rate mortgage**. For most persons it is more advantageous to secure an adjustable rate mortgage since they will benefit from having to pay less interest when the interest rate is low. However, they will also have to pay a higher rate when the interest rate is high. For this reason, even with an adjustable rate of interest mortgage, it is prudent to negotiate an interest rate cap, where charges will not exceed a given amount, say 3% above prime.

It is usually better to repay the mortgages or other credit facilities by consistently making the monthly payment along with additional payments to the principal. Once the principle is reduced, then the interest charge will also be reduced. There are, however, some credit facilities where there is a penalty for early repayment. This is usually done since the institution would lose by not being able to collect the projected interest had the repayment been completed as scheduled.

In an effort to avoid paying a high mortgage, while securing the asset of a permanent home, many families purchase a mobile home, a condominium or flat as interim accommodation. One advantage of purchasing a condominium or flat is that the maintenance of the facility will be undertaken by the person or company who/which manages the building complex. This may be particularly attractive for persons who do not want the worry of contracting the services of individual maintenance persons or agencies. When they are more financially secured they may choose to rent the former facility or sell it and use the proceeds for a down payment on a mortgage for a house. Persons who are wealthier may purchase one or several condominiums or other housing facilities in a holiday resort in their country or another country as a vacation home and/or as an investment. It may be rented by an agency which manages it during the period when the owner is not using it.

The computation of a 30 year mortgage for a property which was purchased for $300,000, with an interest rate of 8% per annum is computed as follows:

Mortgage	$792,466
Legal and other fees	28,500
Total cost	**$820,966**
Principal	$300,000
Interest payment	$520,966
Monthly payment	**$2,201.00**

Table 3.3 Computation of Total Mortgage Payment

Notes: Legal and other fees are calculated at 9.5% of the principal of the mortgage. This may be higher or lower in accordance with the law of the country and the policy of the financial institution.

The cost incurred in servicing the mortgage is quite a substantial investment and homeowner could have purchased at least another house and one could have been rented to generate an additional source of income. It is noted that the entire repayment to the financial institution does not constitute profit to the financial institution, since management would have incurred a cost by providing the capital, along with administration and other costs.

Other important considerations which should be made before securing a mortgage include:

1. It is better to avoid a mortgage if you can afford to do so. Since most of us can't we should endeavor to accelerate the repayment to complete the payment well before the period stipulated in order to reduce the amount of interest which would be paid,

2. It may be better to rent a house in a low income housing scheme or live with relatives, while saving to at least make a substantial deposit towards the mortgage,

3. The amount of interest paid on a mortgage is usually very high. Even though the value of the property may have appreciated substantially over the period, it may not be as much as the amount paid. Unless the property is sold and the proceeds realized, the purchase cannot be seen as an investment which generates returns other than the security of a home, and savings from rent being paid to a land lord.

Even though the financial institution usually makes a large profit by providing the mortgage, most families would find it very difficult to accumulate enough money from their savings to secure a home in middle and upper income complex.

Some of the important factors which should be considered before purchasing or building a house using a mortgage are:

1. ***What is the primary purpose for securing the property?*** Many families purchase a property, live in it for a short time during which they develop it and later sell it at a substantial profit. This could be quite unsettling since moving from one house to another is very traumatic, particularly for spouses who have a number of children and a large number of furniture and other items. It also takes a long time for a family to become comfortable in their new environment as they familiarize themselves with the location of the school, church and other building and as they socialize with persons of the new community. A property can be purchased for the purpose of investing without the family having to live in it.

2. ***The cost involved in closing the transaction*** - this usually includes legal fees, commitment fees from the bank or mortgage company,

3. ***The proximity of the building to important facilities such as the school for the children, medical facilities, place of employment, supermarket and the church,***

4. ***Obtain a mortgage which the family can afford comfortably even on one spouse's salary.*** It is important that a well-suited balance is found between one's 'dream-home' and being able to comfortably maintain the mortgage over the long-run. Many persons are misled into accepting the terms of repayment once the financial institution approves the mortgage. It is common for some credit or mortgage officers to misrepresent the true financial position of the applicant in an attempt to attain his target on the amount of new mortgages approved and disbursed each year. Hence, the new property owner is saddled with the task of making huge sacrifices merely to maintain the mortgage payment.

5. ***The ability of the family to meet expenses such as property insurance, rates and taxes on the property, maintenance and other costs,.***

6. ***Seek to contribute the highest deposit which the family can comfortably afford towards owning the property.*** This contribution is important, since the lower the

principal of the mortgage is, the lower the monthly repayment would be. Unfortunately, many persons have to secure a loan for the deposit, which they have to service in addition to the mortgage payment.

7. Mortgagee/s can usually accelerating the repayment from bonus and other cash inflows.

8. **Many families take the option of renting a part of the property in order to supplement the mortgage payment,**

9. The type of mortgage which is negotiated. There are several types of mortgages such as the **Adjustable Rate Mortgage** (ARM) and **Fixed Rate Mortgage** (FRM). With the ARM the client is given a rate which may be lowered over a given period, after which it fluctuates. A protective clause may be included in the agreement, whereby the rate is not allowed to rise beyond a given ceiling. Care must be taken that the repayment is not so low that it does not adequately service the interest and principal on the loan.

10. The tax deduction on the repayment would be subtracted at the earlier years of the mortgage since it is primarily the payment on the interest which occurs during this period.

The computation of the payment of a 30 years mortgage at various principle amounts and interest rates is presented in the following table:

%	$100,000	$150,000	$200,000	$250,000	$300,000	$350,000
6	600	899	1,199	1,499	1,799	2,098
6.5	632	948	1,264	1,580	1,896	2,212
7	655	998	1,331	1,663	1,996	2,329
7.5	699	1,049	1,398	1,748	2,098	2,447
8	734	1,101	1,468	1,834	2,201	2,568
8.5	769	1,153	1,538	1,922	2,307	2,691
9	805	1,207	1,609	2,012	2,414	2,816
9.5	841	1,261	1,682	2,102	2,523	2,943
10	878	1,316	1,755	2,194	2,633	3,072

Table 3.4 Monthly payment on a 30 year mortgage at various interest rates

The above monthly payments do not include fees such as mortgage protection insurance, property insurance, property rates and taxes, maintenance and other costs which are usually associated with the management and maintenance of the property. Very often the mortgage company would quote the price of the property insurance and other fees in the total monthly payment instead of quoting them as separate entities.

Impulsive purchases and *purchasing on credit* are two serious hindrances to the growth of the savings and investment capacity of a large percentage of persons. The result of these two actions is usually that even when they are able to increase their net income, the excess is not saved or invested but used to satisfy their uncontrolled craving to spend it all on things which heightens their inflated need to 'live like the Jones'

Do's **and don'ts of purchasing a motor vehicle**

"What are some of the guidelines which we should follow when contemplating to purchase a motor vehicle and/or incur other large debts?"

Many couples in affluent societies have more than two motor cars in their lifetime. The amount of money spent on the purchase, maintenance and repairs of motor vehicles, cause motor vehicles to be rated as the second largest expenditure for many families. The model of vehicle which a person purchases is usually determined by factors such as his preference for a particular make of vehicle and the availability and price of cheap spares. There is also the practice of some wealthy persons who purchase vintage and other expensive motor vehicles because of their love for particular models of classic vehicles, the resale value of the vehicles and/or owning them merely as collector items.

For many persons it is prudent to purchase a good secondhand rather than a new motor vehicle which would be expensive and could significantly deplete their personal savings, and/or have a monthly repayment that is too high for their budget to accommodate. It is also important to know the conditions under which it is better to trade in or sell a vehicle. For persons with a serious budgetary constraint, this decision should not be arrived at as fashion dictates but in accordance with the peace from the Lord which a person receives when the decision is consistent with the will of the Lord. A vehicle which is more than ten years old usually have a very high maintenance cost which makes it uneconomical to operate it.

There are several prominent preachers and other Biblical scholars who have a number of publications and also preach extensively on the necessity for **Christians to be debt free and stay out of debt.** They have expounded on several scripture verses which emphasizes that the perfect will of Yahweh is that His children should rely on His provision and not be 'enslaved' by the burden of debt. It is true that the inability of many persons to manage their financial activities, leads to huge debt which they cannot service without causing a severe strain on meeting other essential expenditure of the family. This state has led to the disintegration of many families and individuals resorting to illegal activities in order to payoff their debt. Many Christians even compromise their faith by engaging in stealing and other unscriptural practices in order to meet their loan payments. However, when we are able to manage personal and corporate debt it contributes significantly to the acquisition and expansion of our assets. This does not infer that we should not rely of the provision of the Lord to enable us to acquire and manage our assets.

If a person feels that it is essential to engage in a debt transaction, it is always better to have the direction of the Lord before indulging in it. In embarking on, or expanding a business entity for example, the option is usually either to utilize a debt instrument or expand the ownership of the business in the form of issuing shares. Since the present owner may not be desirous of extending the ownership of the entity to other persons, as in the offer of additional shares, for example, to whom they would have to share their profit, then the option is usually to engage in debt.

The Lord's best is for us to be debt free and be able to have abundance to give for the furtherance of His work. However, provision is given for those of us who have not been able to attain this state to incur debt which does not jeopardize our relationship with the Lord, our family and to live comfortably. Many Christians still incur several types of debt in order to survive in this world where easy credit is the order of the day. As a matter of fact, very often if a person does not have a credit history it is difficult for them to secure a large credit facility when they need it the most. (There is no doubt that current financial, economic, political and other events in our world today is a prelude to the end times before the second coming of the Lord where unless a person has the 'mark of the beast' he would not be able to engage in economic activity).

There are several factors which a person should consider before applying for a loan. They include:

1. *Finding out from the Lord if the desire to purchase the item or the investment to be made is fuelled by greed, lust, or other unscriptural practices,*

2. *Ensure that the purpose for which the credit facility is being sought is consistent with the will of the Lord for your life,*

3. *At least the primary parties who are involved in the transaction should pray about the matter, discuss it thoroughly with persons who are knowledgeable on the credit related matters and the activity/item to be financed,*

4. *There should be a clear and workable strategy to service the facility which would not place them and/or their family or other persons concerned, in unnecessary difficulties,*

5. *Before assets such as a property is offered as security for a loan, the husband, wife, older children and/or other persons who will be affected by this transaction should be in agreement with this decision.* They should be aware of the possibility of losing it in the event that the borrower is unable to adequately service the debt. A contingency plan should be in place to ensure that even if the principal source of the loan repayment fails that there is some other source from which the repayment will be secured. Failing to honor the loan repayment may result in the bank selling the home.

6. *Calling up and enquiring on prices and visiting stores or other suppliers to ensure that one is in a position to make the best possible selection of the item.*

7. *Soliciting expert advice on making the best selection of the item.* It is important when purchasing major items such as a car, house, electrical appliances, heating and air conditioning units, for example, to secure the unbiased advise of experts in that specific field. It is unwise to undergo an investment to secure a major asset only to find out a short time after the purchase that it has major defects, particularly if the contract protects the seller from liabilities after the purchase is made. To avoid such catastrophes, it is prudent to invest a fraction of the cost of the item to pay for the advice of an expert in the field, unless one can secure the unbiased advice from a relative, friend or someone else for free.

8. *Ensuring that one has the necessary financial resources to make a cash purchase, or is able to negotiate it without having to undergo undue pressure to secure the down-payment and maintain the repayment schedule,*

9. *Contracts should be carefully examined by one's attorney, or at least by someone who is knowledgeable enough to provide competent advice on the protection of the consumer, before signing the contract.* Important issues to look for include the provision of an acceptable warranty, or at least some recourse that the consumer can take in the event of dissatisfaction with the product or the service of the institution.

10. *For items such as electrical and other appliances and motor vehicles, it is usually necessary to ensure that acceptable levels of after sales services and essential spares are available to ensure that there is not a lengthy down-time when a problem cannot be rectified due to the unavailability of spares.* For this reason many consumers prefer to purchase 'brand name' products even though the price may be a little more than others. Many persons, who can afford to, may purchase spares for parts which are likely to be defective in the near future.

> *The management of debt is one of the primary factors which would increase the cash flow of a person, family, corporation and other entities.*

Credit appraisal by financial institutions

"What are some of the issues which are considered by credit institutions to determine the eligibility of applicants who have applied for a credit facility?"

Three important criteria which creditors use to determine the credit worthiness of an applicant are:

1. *Character* – in order to verify whether past credit has been honored satisfactorily, credit institutions usually access the credit scores of the applicant which highlights factors such as the promptness of honoring past payment, whether the person filed for bankruptcy,

and whether or not there are any judgments which were successfully filed by a former or existing credit agency. This process is usually facilitated by the institution sending a written credit enquiry to sister credit institutions, checking the credit rating on the applicant from reputable credit rating institutions and by personally contacting associates in other credit institutions. Character references are usually contacted.

2. **Capacity** – for salaried employees, the applicant usually has to produce a copy of a recent pay slip or statement of employment, at least one income statement and, statement of indebtedness to other institutions.

3. **Collateral** – most commercial creditors would maintain ownership of the asset being purchased, leased or hire purchased or other credit arrangements and take a lien (Bill of Sale, Mortgage, Debenture or even an informal agreement is undertaken) over other collateral with an acceptable value to cover the amount being lent or item purchased. A lien is executed over the collateral so that in the event that the debtor is unable, or refuses to honor his repayment obligation, then the creditor can if he so chooses (usually with the authority of the court or as per a legal contract) confiscate the security or repossess the item bought under the credit arrangement. Nevertheless, there are dishonest debtors who would falsify information, move to another location without providing a forwarding address, and engage in other activities which cause many financial institutions to lose much money due to bad debt each year.

It is recognized that it is the perfect will of God for Christians not only be debt free, but for us to have enough that we can be a blessing to those around us and to engage in the financing of the gospel nationally and internationally, where possible. Even though most Christians will not have as much financial resources to be able to contribute millions of dollars towards the spreading of the Gospel, we still have an essential part to play by giving of our tithes and offering, prayer, and other activities which will collectively contribute significantly towards world evangelism. Jehovah is able to take even the little that we have and multiply it to be a blessing to a multitude. 2 Corinthians 8:10-12 states: *"¹⁰And in this matter I am giving my advice; it is appropriate for you who began last year not only to do something but even to desire to do something –* *¹¹now finish doing it, so that our eagerness may be matched by completing it according to your means. ¹²For if the eagerness is there, the gift is acceptable according to what one has – not according to what one does not have.*

CONCLUSION

It is the desire of the Lord that every Christian live debt-free. We are made totally liberated from every form of bondage including the debt trap when we accept the Lord into our lives. The difficulty of moving from where we are to where we should be is often paved with much hardship since we may not be fully aware of the correct strategy which the Lord has outlined in His Word for us to follow in order to achieve this target. There is no scripture which states that if we are not debt free we will not go to heaven. However, our effectiveness as givers is primarily dependant on our willingness to give to the Lord and to others. The concept of willingness is highlighted since it very often does not depend on how much we give but the state of our heart. This statement is substantiated when we compare the fact that the widow who gave of her 'mite' received commendation while Ananias and Sapphira, for example, were killed even though they sold their home and gave what must have been a substantial amount of money to the work of the Lord but they lied to the Holy Spirit on how much the house was sold for.

Many financial and other blessings which the Bibles states that we will receive are prevented from being manifested in our lives since we are burdened with debt and other problems which we do not give to the Lord and trust Him to take us out of those difficulties. The onus is on every Christian to implement the principles of the Word to bring us out and keep us out of debt. Every Christian will not be materially rich on earth, nor will we all be debt free, even though we have the potential to achieve these feats.

Many Christian fail to obey the teachings of the Bible in the vital area of financial, and more specifically debt management, hence, they mismanage the resources which the Lord placed at our disposal. Many of us have become involved in sinful activities in an attempt to amass wealth and these sinful acts are exposed to the ridicule of the world Many persons also become stingy as their material affluence increases and they do not give to the work of the Lord and to help those in need. The result is that they do not benefit from the overwhelming blessings of the Lord and may end up in a worse financial position than where the Lord delivered them from.

Many persons, particularly in developed countries, cannot envisage themselves living without debt. This often includes several credit cards, a mortgage, car and student loans, to finance their annual vacation, furniture, groceries and other items. Persons are even rewarded when they have successfully repaid a number of debts over the years, by being able to negotiate a mortgage and other credit facilities on more favorable terms than others who has not had any, or only small amounts of credit, even if they were paying cash for everything which they owned. Thankfully, as more persons mature in years and are better able to manage their finances, they are able to repay all of their credit facilities and live debt free. This is in contrast to those persons who continue to accumulate huge debt even in their advance years and their children and/other relatives have to continually assist them to repay loans or they would lose their home and other assets due to foreclosure by credit agencies.

It is not God's will that we should be perpetually saddled with the burden of debt. This state seriously hampers us from allocating more of our financial and other resources to save, invest, assist others who are in financial and other material need and also to contribute more to financing the spreading of the gospel and fulfill spiritual and other obligations. We must heed Biblical council in areas such as to avoid making rash financial decisions, not to guarantee loans of strangers and to seek to be debt free as soon as possible. Where it is absolutely necessary to incur financial debt, to seek to repay all of it and to desist from incurring more long term debt in particular, since we cannot predict the future, and unless we can establish adequate insurance cover, we may saddle our children and others with debt which they may not be able to repay. Parents should not seek to saddle their children with debt, which should have been avoided in the first place. Even if it property, attempts should be made to ensure that if it is left as an inheritance that it is debt free.

NOTES

****

Chapter 4
SAVING AND INVESTING PRUDENTLY

INTRODUCTION

More than 40% of the population of the world live in abject poverty. The disparity in the distribution of wealth (the Gini Coefficient) even among the richer countries is so skewed that in many countries less than 10% of the population live in luxury, another 40% or so, are classified as middle class, while the remaining 50% live in poverty. The severity of the poverty suffered by the citizen of various countries varies depending on factors such as the per capita income of the country, the availability of free or at least cheap medical care, social security and other benefits as well as the severity of adverse climatic and other conditions. A large percentage of the population of Christians suffer severe poverty even though we are grafted into the Abrahamic covenant and we are called to be a blessing to all nations. The Bible has so many principles which we can apply to our personal lives, activities in our communities, nationally and internationally which would significantly improve our standard of living on this earth.

For a large percentage of Christians and even non-Christians, their primary financial problem is how to escape the cycle of poverty. It is true that many of the communities and countries where we live in are poor and as a result there are not many lucrative economic opportunities available to assist us to emerge from poverty. We are reminded that we serve a God who is not a respecter of persons, economic situations nor other earthly limitations. His blessings transcend the state where His hands of provision could reach us wherever we are. Even if it means taking us to another location, we will be blessed once we serve the Lord in faithfully.

There are several tools which have been placed at our disposal to assist us to manage the material and other resources which the Lord provides for us. Several of them are discussed in this chapter.

> *"They that sow in tears shall reap in joy."* **The act of saving, including giving sacrificially, working smarter, longer hours, studying the extra hour, and living on humble means in order to achieve long-term objectives. When we do our part, the Lord will come in to fill the gap and grant us the increase which we seek.**

Maximizing Returns from Our Saving

INTRODUCTION

As attractive as the interest rate of many financial institutions are, many persons still retain some cash at home in the event of an emergency and depending on the society and temperament of the person, for purchasing of groceries and other consumer items. However, with the increasing use of debit, credit and other 'plastic cards' many persons seek to maximize their returns from savings and investments. As the savings and investment climate of societies increases, even so does the opportunity for persons and institutions to generate higher returns from savings. The amount saved, the financial instrument used and the discipline and ability of the saver to maintain the instrument to maturity are some of the primary factors which determine the success or failure of the saver to realize their short, medium and long-term goals.

Managing compound interest

"How do I make compound interest work for me rather than against me?"

Compound interest is the system of charging or deriving interest not only on the principle but also on the interest which accrues on the principal. We benefit tremendously when the principle of compound interest is working in our favor. The interest of several saving instruments can be 'rolled over' where after the maturity date, the interest which is accumulated for the previous year is added to the principal, and the interest for the next period is calculated on the new principal (which is the sum of the old principle and the interest from the last period). Conversely, when we borrow from several institutions we have to pay compound interest on the amount borrowed. In this computation the interest computed over the period of the loan at the stipulated interest rate is added on to the principal and the interest rate is computed on the original principal and interest over the life of the loan.

The famous **Rule of 72** provides us with an indication of the amount we would have to save over a specified time for our savings to double. This can be illustrated as follows:

$$72 \div 3 = 24$$

In other words if you were to save $72.00 for 24 years at interest rate of 3% per annum in 24 years it would accumulate interest of an additional $72.00, less tax and/or other charges. This rule can be used as a guide to assist us in determining how to achieve our savings target. It is true that if the $72.00 is invested prudently in a higher yielding financial instrument or other investment you are likely to earn far more over a shorter period. However, many persons attempt to earn a higher rate of return and end up losing all or most of their investments.

The rule of 72 can be illustrates as follows: If the interest rate on an account is 3%, and you deposit $10,000.00 on the account, it would take **72 ÷ 3 = 24** years for it to accumulate $10,000 interest. This amount excludes any taxes or other charges which may be leveled on the account. This is a good guide for persons who are desirous of attaining particular long-term targets such as saving for retirement. Of course it is more advantageous to save on a higher yielding account such as government debenture and treasury bills.

By using the **Rule of 72**, it would assist us to determine how much we can earn in a savings or investment account to generate the level of funds we desire at retirement or some other time in the future. This is not an accurate presentation, since interest rates usually change over time, resulting in the return being more or less than projected. In addition, this principle does not take into consideration the effect of inflation on the projected amount and it does not include the levy of any tax or other deduction on the accumulated amount. Nevertheless, it is a reasonable guide to assist in our future financial plan.

If a person is desirous of investing $1,000.00 in a savings account which pays 4% interest per annum, he would receive the following returns:

Year	Amount Injected ($)	Principal at Year End ($)
1	$1,000	$1,040
2	$2,000	$2,080
3	$4,000	$4,160

Table 4.1 Returns on Savings

This rule assists us in several ways including the fact that it tells us that:

It is recognized that this is only for $1,000.00, where as if the person is consistent, he would be saving other amounts each year, which would also generate interest. This principle highlights the importance of budgeting wisely and saving and investing prudently. This may seem as a laborious way of accumulating money. Sadly, many persons have sought after 'get rich quick' schemes and have ended up with little or no return over the same period as against a person who saved a little consistently over an extended number of years. In this regards we are reminded of Proverbs 21:5 which states: "**5The plans if the diligent lead surely to abundance, but everyone who is hasty comes only to want.**"

The Rule of 72
The number 72 divided by the interest rate on a particular saving account would tell us of the number of years it would take a principal amount to double.

A Time, Money Yield table can be used to calculate this amount also:

INVESTING A LUMP SUM OF $10,000.00

	Years							
	5	10	15	20	25	30	35	40
2	$11,041	$12,190	$13,459	$14,859	$16,406	$18,114	$19,999	$22,080
4	12,167	14,802	18,009	21,911	26,658	32,434	39,460	48,010
6	13,382	17,908	23,966	32,071	42,919	57,435	76,861	102,857
8	14,693	21,589	31,722	46,610	68,485	100,627	147,853	217,245
10	16,105	25,937	41,772	67,275	108,347	174,494	281,024	452,593
12	17,623	31,058	54,736	96,463	170,001	299,599	527,996	930,510
14	19,254	37,072	71,379	137,435	264,619	509,502	981,002	1,888,835
16	21,003	44,114	92,655	197,608	408,742	858,499	1,803,141	3,787,212
18	22,878	52,338	119,737	273,930	626,686	1,433,706	3,279,973	7,503,783
20	24,883	61,917	154,070	383,376	953,962	2,373,763	5,906,682	14,697,716
22	27,028	73,046	197,423	533,576	1,442,101	3,897,579	10,534,018	28,470,378
24	29,316	85,944	251,956	738,641	2,165,420	6,348,199	18,610,540	54,559,126
25	30,518	93,132	284,217	867,362	2,646,978	8,077,936	24,651,903	75,231,638

Source: Ron Blue, 1991, p. 37.

Table 4.2.1 Compounding, Time and Money Yield

$1,000 deposited each year:

%	Years							
	5	10	15	20	25	30	35	40
2	$5,204	$10,950	$17,293	$24,297	$32,030	$40,568	$49,994	$60,402
4	5,416	12,006	20,024	29,778	41,646	56,085	73,652	95,026
6	5,637	13,181	23,276	36,786	54,865	79,058	111,435	154,762
8	5,867	14,487	27,152	45,762	73,106	113,283	172,317	259,057
10	6,105	15,937	31,772	57,275	98,347	164,494	271,024	442,593
12	6,353	17,549	37,280	72,052	133,334	241,333	431,663	767,091
14	6,610	19,337	43,842	91,025	181,871	356,787	693,573	1,342,025
16	6,877	21,321	51,660	115,380	249,214	530,312	1,120,713	2,360,757
18	7,154	23,521	60,965	146,628	342,603	790,948	1,816,652	4,163,213
20	7,442	25,959	72,035	186,688	471,981	1,181,882	2,948,341	7,343,858
22	7,740	28,657	85,192	237,989	650,955	1,767,081	4,783,645	12,936,535
24	8,048	31,643	100,815	303,601	898,092	2,640,916	7,750,225	22,728,803
25	8,207	33,253	109,687	342,945	1,054,791	3,227,174	9,856,761	30,088,655

Source: Ron Blue, 1991, p. 37.

Table 4.2.2 Compounding End of Year Values

When we understand Tables 4.1 and 4.2 it could be a challenge to assist us in charting our financial future. Depending on the financial instruments which exist in our country or which we have access to, our ability to save and other factors, we can determine the amount of money we will be able to earn over a given time period. If a person is able to save $10,000.00 on a Fixed Deposit, which pays interest of 4% per annum and it matures in 5 years the amount he will receive in $12,167.00, less any taxes (from Table 4.1). Conversely, if you deposit $1,000.00 per year on a Fixed Deposit which pays interest of 4% per annum, at the end of 10 years you will receive $12,006.00; this is an accumulated interest of $2,006.00 (Table 4.2).

When some commercial banks compute the interest rate on their loans they do so using 'add-on' rather than simple interest. We may be familiar with the following formula:

$$(P + I) \times I$$

Similarly, it is no secret that it is far more economical to purchase a house at the cash price rather than to secure a mortgage. A simple calculation would identify this disadvantage. In securing a mortgage of $250,000.00 for 30 years at a mortgage rate of 6.3% per annum, for example, would result in the total mortgage payment of $557,076.00 at the end of the 30 years. Over the thirty years the actual cost of the house is $307,076.00 or 123% more than the purchase price. This does not take into account the legal fee, commitment fee, insurance premium (even though this is important even if the house were paid for cash), maintenance and other costs which were incurred as a result of the mortgage. In effect this is a poor investment when we consider that two houses at $250,000.00 could have been bought at the cash price instead of securing a mortgage. This is not only a gloomy picture, since it is likely that the value of the house would have appreciated to more than the $557,076.00 at the end of 30 years, which would result in a profit. In addition, a large percentage of persons and families cannot afford to purchase a house for cash and even if they choose to rent in the interim, they may lose more when they try to save along with paying a rent.

Some couples choose to live with their in-laws or rent a modest home and implement a discipline saving culture so that they can make a large down payment and reduce the interest cost involved in the mortgage and/or they can purchase a larger house and rent a part of it, for example, in order to supplement their mortgage payment. These options have to be reviewed carefully since living with relatives, renting one's property to others and similar cost cutting measures each has its disadvantages.

The investor who is able to purchase the house cash would have the advantage of owning two houses valued in excess of $554,146 after thirty years. Hence, it is far more advantageous to stretch one's finances and purchase two houses and possibly rent one, providing the rent is high enough to pay for at least one of the houses and a part of the other. In this way the owner of the houses would be virtually living 'rent free.' We are reminded of the maxim that "**the rich are getting richer and the poor, poorer**" in this imperfect world system. The severe disadvantage of the mortgage rate can be lessened by accelerating the mortgage payment by paying more than the prescribed monthly payment and requesting that the additional amount be paid to reduce the principal.

The principles of simple interest are highlighted in the famous formula:

$$SI = (P \times R \times T) \div 100$$

Where: **SI** = simple interest,   **P** = principle,
        R = rate of interest,   **T** = time

This formula can be illustrated by using a loan of $50,000.00 granted for ten years at a rate of interest of 12% per annum as follows:

Interest = ($50,000.00 × 12% × 10) ÷ 100 = $600.00

The debtor will have to repay a total of $50,600.00 over the ten years or $421.67 per month.

If the compound rate of interest were charged, the repayment would be $717.35 per month. This is quite a significant difference since the payment is not calculated on a declining balance. The total amount paid using compound interest would be $86,082.00. This is a difference of $35,482.00. This is a huge difference. In order to reduce this huge wastage, we must attempt to repay the loan in as short a time as possible, thus reducing the interest charge. In order to reduce their loss in the event of an early payoff by customers, some financial institution would include a clause in the loan agreement which states that the debtor would have to pay a penalty fee if one decided to repay the loan before the maturity date.

There are various categories of investments which are characterized by the level of risks which the investor incurs. There is an inverse relation between a 'rational' risk and the level of return which is usually derived. They are:

1. *Investment in 'risk free' financial instruments* such as treasury bills and government debentures or that of a statutory body which are usually guaranteed by the government or a statutory body. The investor in these instruments is guaranteed a given level of return which is usually negotiated when the security is purchased.

2. *Primary financial instruments such as bank deposits* where returns may be higher than that of the risk free instruments, but the return is usually guaranteed, even though the interest rate usually fluctuates.

3. *Secondary financial instruments* such as shares, mortgage certificate and certificates of deposit (CDs) which are traded on the stock exchange or secondary markets. The returns are subject to volatile changes due to the influence of market forces and other mechanisms. The returns from these financial instruments are usually higher than the two other financial instruments, even though an investor may lose all, or a greater part of his portfolio in an acute financial crisis.

Compounding should work for, and not Against you

One of the important features of **compounding** is that interest is earned on the principal amount plus the accumulated interest. This principle works for us when we are saving in an interest bearing account. However, it works against us when we borrow, particularly when the purpose is not to directly or indirectly generate enough income to cover the cost of borrowing.

> *Credit unions versus commercial banks*

"Are there advantages in banking with a credit union rather than a commercial bank?"

The passage from a debt ridden crisis to living under God's desired state of being debt free usually require the adaptation and continual living of a disciplined lifestyle. The credit union is one organization which has been and continues to be successfully used by millions of persons worldwide to assist them through this process. Credit unions are organizations which are managed by members such as teachers, nurses and other associations, the Private Sector Commission, Public Workers church organizations and other similar bodies. Membership in many of these organizations is restricted to persons who are affiliated with the parent body of the organization. The membership may be allowed to continue even after a person leaves the organization, even though there may be special conditions attached to their continual affiliation to the organization. There are several features which are common in a large number of credit unions. They include:

1. Members may be given the option of purchasing shares and/or participating in one or several saving accounts. The interest earned from the savings account is usually higher than that of the savings accounts of commercial banks and other financial institutions. The dividends from the shares are also usually very attractive since management may be investing on the stock market and other high interest earning financial instruments.

2. There is usually a stipulated period over which the member must be saving with the institution before they can access credit. This is usually between 3 to 6 months to enable the management of the financial

institution to gain some indication of the savings capacity of the member.

3. The organization often grants credit at a specified percentage in proportion to the amount of savings which the member has. In many instances it is between three to ten times the amounts saved. If, for example, the credit union lends at a ratio of in excess of 1:5, where member who has a savings of $1,000.00, and is desirous of borrowing $5,000.00, the credit union would hold the $1,000.00 as partial security and lend the member the $5,000.00. If the member wants an amount above this ratio, a tangible security such as a Bill of Sale over furniture, and other assets, or a mortgage may be required.

4. A credit union often approve an amount of unsecured credit to a member which is far above the amount that person would have been able to access, even with adequate security, from a commercial bank due to their low income.

5. The interest rate on loans from a credit union may be calculated using simple interest on the reducing balance, while commercial bank, may charge a compounded interest rate computed on the principal. Commercial banks may also charge a commitment fee and other charges for processing the credit facility. Members may also benefit from a tax rebate from a percentage of the interest paid on a loan.

6. It is a waste of money for a member or a credit union to purchase an item on hire purchase and incur the high interest and other charges, when they could secure a loan from the credit union at a very low rate of interest and make cash payment for the item.

7. Members in many instances have to pay a small amount of insurance premium proportionate to the amount of their debit with the debt with the credit union. It may be as minimal as $45.00 per thousand dollars. The benefit of this insurance coverage may include features such as:

   a. If the member becomes ill or becomes unemployed, for example, the insurance company may continue to make the monthly payment on the loan over a given number of months until the insured person is able to resume servicing the credit facility, or the company will repay the entire amount if he is unable to complete repaying the facility due to death or a serious incapacitation.

b. If the member dies and there is an outstanding balance, the insurance company will repay the loan.

c. The insurance company will provide a given amount of money towards the burial expense of the member. The beneficiary of the deceased member may also be paid in some instances a given percentage more than the savings of the deceased member.

Funds saved in the credit union over a financial year are tax deductible in many countries. This is a method which some governments use to assist the poorer segment of the population to increase their savings and investment and subsequently increase their standard of living. In this way a person who saves with a credit union may be able to claim an amount to a given ceiling in the preceding year of saving. This tax saving can be deposited into the account with the credit union when the refund is received from the tax office or used as he chooses. Alternatively, the member may be allowed a reduced tax deduction with the commitment that the member would deposit this amount along with their regular savings with the credit union. The more established credit unions may have ATM machines located at several branches, checking accounts and other facilities which are similar to that of commercial banks.

Some persons are deterred from becoming a member of a credit union which is managed by their employer, church or other organization with which they are closely associated. The reason for this is that they may feel that persons who may be closely associated with them would have knowledge of their personal affairs which can be used in a negative way by unscrupulous persons. Notwithstanding this, the services of a credit union is highly recommended, members would feel comfortable interacting with the officers since they often work at the same institution.

By spending less than we earn and implementing wise saving and investment programs (of course, while still observing spiritual principles such as tithing and giving one's offering) over a number of years is a primary recipe to achieve financial success.

Making the right financial decisions

"I was confronted with the following situation, should I purchase a lawn cutter for $475.00 or allow someone to cut the grass at $15.00 per month? If I decide to purchase it, would it be prudent to purchase it by hire purchase where I would have to pay $30.00 per month for two years, since I cannot afford to pay the cash price now?"

Since there is more than a financial consideration that has to be taken into account in addressing these issues, the following analysis is presented:

1. Purchasing the grass cutter by hire purchase would cost $720.00 over the two years and in the end you own the machine. This is quite expensive, and it would be prudent to secure a loan with a lower interest rate, possibly from a credit union and purchase the grass cutter at the cash price and honor the monthly loan payment with the credit union.

2. Consideration would have to be taken of the fact that you would have incurred additional cost for the petrol and any maintenance of the cutter.

3. Account also has to be taken of the time which you or another member of the family would have to expend to cut the grass and clean and store it in a safe place to avoid it from being stolen or damaged.

4. There is also a danger associated with using the cutter and protective items such as a goggle or at least a pair of sunglasses, boots and gloves may also be necessary to prevent pebbles and other materials from causing the user harm.

5. There are some health benefits from the exercise while mowing or cutter the lawn, weeding and engaging in other related activities. However, all of us are not so inclined to derive pleasure from engaging in such activities. Hence, some persons are of the opinion that it would be more profitable to engage in an income generating activity which would be more profitable that the savings generated from cutting the lawn personally. Others would prefer to engage in a leisure activity rather that benefit from the saving from mowing the lawn personally. Some persons may prefer

the option of paying a member of the family, rather than a stranger to cut the grass.

6. Paying to cut the grass would cost $360.00 over the two years and in the end you still do not own the grass cutter.

The best strategy is to continue to pay to cut the grass, while you are intensifying your savings towards the purchase of the grass cutter at the cash price.

Arriving at the correct portfolio mix of liquid and long-term

"Is it better to hold liquid assets or to hold long term high earning assets?"

A balanced portfolio would have a combination of both sets of assets spread over various financial instruments and other assets and even other markets and countryies where possible. The percentage of each in the portfolio is dependent on factors such as the availability of funds, the types of investment opportunities which are available, investment temperature of holding/s of the assets and even age of the investment/s. The majority of us, even in developed countries, are too preoccupied on surviving from month to month, and at the extreme, from day to day, to even be very concerned about the mix of our portfolio. A person who has a portfolio of any substance, should focus on maximizing the return from the assets which they have at their disposal.

The age of the investor very often influences their temperament in investing. Younger persons are usually more inclined to hold liquid assets and take advantage of risky investment. This reality is evident in many brokerage firms where younger investors are often the ones to build up a large portfolio since they are more inclined to take more risks than older brokers. Very often as a person ages and they have additional responsibilities such as a large family, they are usually less inclined to take a larger degree of risk than they would have done when they were younger. The rationale for this is that rather than a single person suffering the financial and other loss and embarrassment as a result of a bad investment, a larger number of persons would be adversely affected when there is a large family.

In many communities persons who have money which they are desirous of investing have access to a small number of investment opportunities where they can generate a substantial financial return. The choice may be to save at a bank or other financial institution where the interest rate is marginal. There are however, investment opportunities such as purchasing or leasing farm land or investing in other areas which can generate substantial returns once it is managed. Persons who have cash may also be able to purchase raw gold and other minerals and other items and engage in trading.

Among the advantages of holding liquid assets such as cash and other assets such as checks, credit card and certificate of deposits which can be easily converted into cash, are that:

1. These can be used to take advantage of investment opportunities which are readily available. This include purchasing items at an auction and being able to receive a discount from cash, check or credit card payment. This flexibility does not exist when we hold fixed and other long term assets, even though these assets may be used as collateral to guarantee loans and other credit facilities.

2. Another advantage of holding liquid assets is that money can be lent for short periods at high rate because of the desperate need of the borrower. Christians have to be very watchful to be able to accurately differentiate between a genuine investment opportunity as against exploiting persons who are in grave situations and who need a helping hand.

Among the advantage of holding assets is that the returns are usually minimal if any at all. Conversely, investing in long-term assets usually generate a high level of return or yield, even though they are less flexibility to be converted to liquid assets.

Sources of Raising Capital

This section discusses some of the more prominent methods which are used by entrepreneurs to raise capital when the need to finance personal and/or business ventures. Attention is not focused on illegitimate methods of raising capital, since many unscrupulous persons use methods such as channeling the proceeds of illegal activities such as drug smuggling and money laundering into legitimate business operations.

Sources of raising capital

"What are some of the sources of securing financing

from informal institutions?"

Similar to other members of society, Christians are often unable to satisfy the requirements to secure a loan from commercial financial institutions. Therefore, many of us, (particularly in rural areas) would engage in securing credit from traditional or informal financial institutions such as moneylenders and pawnshops. Among the disadvantages of securing credit from these institutions is that the loans have high interest rates. Interest rates on credit from moneylenders may be high as 50% or more. Collateral such as jewelry, cattle or a lien over property or a motor vehicle, for example, is demanded. These items may be seized if repayments are not made as scheduled. The question which is often paramount in such circumstances is if the investment would generate enough profits to adequately cover the high cost of the credit facility. Activities such as petty trading often generate huge profits in the short run once it is managed, thereby enabling the borrower to repay the high cost. Very often persons do not have another choice than to resort to borrowing from moneylenders since the moneylender may be the only source of credit that they can secure.

There are examples, particularly in developing countries, where groups within a congregation practice saving techniques commonly called **Osusu** (in The Gambia), **Susu** (in Trinidad and Tobago), **Box** (in Guyana) and **Meeting Money** (in Barbados), for example. The basic principle governing this system is that a group of persons decide on a fixed amount of money that each member can realistically contribute to the pool of funds of the group for each period, which they compute in days, weeks or months. The whole pool is given to a pre-selected member on each of the maturity dates and rotated, until each member of the group receives his or her share. Some groups have the system where a small amount (usually less than 1% of the principle) is retained in a pool which is kept by the treasurer to increase the capital of the group. The amount retained, along with membership fees and money generated from fund raising activities organized by the group is also used as loans to members and/or donated to worthy causes.

A principle which often comes in handy in finding specific areas which the Lord is leading us is to:

Obey the general principles of the Bible and the Lord will lead us to the specifics of what He wants us to do.

Irrespective of how well we plan, very often emergencies arise at a time when we are not in a position to meet such financial demands. Therefore, one may be compelled to seek financial assistance in order to defray these urgent expenses. These may include situations such as:

1. The Christian entrepreneur may need capital to embark on a business venture or to expand an existing business venture which necessitates that capital be acquired.

2. A Christian student who is unable to secure a scholarship or whose parents are not in a position to provide adequate financial assistance, often has to borrow money for tuition, books, living and other expenses at college or university.

3. The Christian entering marriage often has to resort to securing a mortgage and other forms of credit to purchase or build a house.

The overwhelming rationale seems to be that it is not sinful for Christians to borrow sensibly, particularly for major items such as a house and car which may be beyond the ability of the average couple to purchase at the cash price. However, care must be taken that unnecessary and excessive credit, particularity for nonessential consumer items, is avoided as much as possible. We should also work ardently, with the help of the Lord, at reaching a state of being debt free. For most of us this process is achieved over a number of years of trusting in the Lord and applying prudent Biblical principles.

Among the things that Jehovah was angry about, as highlighted in Nehemiah Chapter 5, was the practice of paying interest among His people. Jesus also said in Acts 20:35[b] that giving is better than receiving. This admonition is ever present in our lives, for most people are usually ashamed when they have to ask favours from neighbours, colleagues at work and even to negotiate a loan, particularly to purchase consumer items. We often feel at least at that particular moment of negotiating the loan that the appraiser has some degree of power over us, in that he/she can accept or reject the loan application. This issue was reiterated in Proverbs 22:7[b] which states: *"7(b)...and the borrower is the slave of the lender."*

There are some unscrupulous, unsaved loan officers who are dishonest and may only approve an application when the applicant agrees to pay a bribe in the form of cash and/or kind. Christians are well aware that we should not accept or pay bribes or indulge in any dishonest transactions.

> Taking the business idea successfully from conception to a long-term reality

"I have what I consider, and what has been substantiated by two creditable financial advisors, to be an excellent business idea. How do I take the idea from just being that, to a fruitful business venture?"

It is commendable that you have decided to take at least the first two steps in actualizing the fulfillment of the business venture. The Lord has birthed what can be proven to be a brilliant business in the hearts of many Christians who for one reason or another, have allowed it to die. This is similar to the 'parable of the Talents' which Jesus told. Some persons never do anything about their dreams and they die with these unfulfilled dreams which could have been instrumental in changing the course of their lives, that of other persons and bringing much glory to the kingdom of the Lord. Many persons who receive a business idea may be intimidated at the magnitude of the responsibility of taking it from conceptualization to a reality. Some of the challenges which they would be confronted with include:

1. Would the service to be provided and/or product produced be economically enough to be able to generate the high levels of returns to justify the project?
2. Where would they acquire the capital needed to finance the project?
3. How would the other factors of production such as land and office space be secured?
4. Particularly for large projects, where would the specialized labor be secured?
5. What is the best strategy of marketing the produce?

We should not be intimidated by the challenges which would confront us as we pursue our 'God given dreams'. The Lord does not challenge us with a vision unless He has already placed the mechanisms in place to guarantee its success. We should not expect a 'bed of roses' since He has to prepare us to confront what is usually a hostile business environment. However, He often creates situations and brings us into contact with persons who would direct us along the path of success. We are reminded that all things work together for good for them that love the Lord.

> Sources of raising capital

"What are some of the best options available to secure capital to start or expand a business venture?"

There are several methods which investors use to raise capital. The primary methods are:

1. ***Debt instruments*** - this is the financing of the operations of a business with capital which is not owned by the business. Common debt instruments include the various types of loan facilities such as term, pinnacle or personal loans. **Commercial Loans** are usually to finance capital investments and a repayment schedule is computed based on the ability of the debtor and/or the commercial activity being undertaken to generate the cash flow necessary to adequately service the debt. A commercial bank may charge interest rate of prime, for their best customers and on facilities which are secured by cash or other highly liquid assets which can be realized if the customer is unable to service the credit facility.

   An **overdraft**, on the other hand, is usually allocated for working capital requirements. This is where the bank agrees to grant permission for a current account to be overdrawn to the extent of an authorized limit. Interest on the overdraft facility is usually calculated on the debit balance at the end of each day and deducted from the account at the end of the month. Thus, the customers would only pay interest on the amount which is used. Other debt instruments include **guarantees** and **letters of credit.**

2. ***Equity*** represents the assets owned by the shareholders of the business. This would include cash injection, land, building, machinery, entrepreneurial skills, goodwill and other assets which belong to the owner/s of the business. Some of the advantages of equity financing are:

   a. Since the owners injected the capital, there is usually no pressure for the management of the company to meet monthly loan repayments, as would obtain in debt funding.

   b. The extent of their share in the company. There are, however, incidents where a law suit may be brought against the shareholders of a company.
   There are several disadvantages of owning shares and other assets in a company. They include:

I. In the event of the failure of the company, compulsion to repay the capital over a short time-frame or not at all, as is common with debt financing. The result is that management has more scope to turn over the capital over a longer timeframe without the added pressure to repay it.

II. The business has the opportunity to reinvest the retained earnings and profit made which is not paid to the shareholders of the business to further generate profit.

III. The cost of capital is usually cheaper with equity financing since the interest rates of most commercial institutions are very high.

IV. The shareholders of limited liability companies, for example, are only normally liable to the extent of their shareholding in the company. Therefore, if the company is being sued for negligence, for example, the shareholders can usually lose a maximum of the extent of the value of their shareholding in the company and are usually the last to be repaid from the sale of any remaining assets.

V. The payment of dividends, and the amount which is paid, even when the company realizes a huge profit is at the discretion of the Board of that company.

VI. The value of the shares is often determined by factors which are beyond the control of the company. This includes inflation, the exchange rate of the country and even the world market prices of the commodity.

A disadvantage of debt financing is that the cost of debt is usually more expensive than equity financing. In addition, if the borrower is unable to honor the repayment schedule as per the credit agreement, the credit institution may place a levy on the asset which is pledged as surety for the facility.

3. **_Leasing_** to some extent is an extension of the hire purchase arrangement where the owner allows the lessee to use the asset for a fee. At the end of the period of the lease, the lessee may negotiate to extend the contract, purchase the asset at a discount price or acquire another. This arrangement is attractive to many investors who may be able to negotiate the servicing of assets such as a piece of machinery, motor vehicles and

the maintenance of buildings at the expense of the leaser.

It is important that one carefully reads the lease contract before signing it. It may seem an attractive option to secure a lease for a motor car, for example, without having to make a large cash injection before securing the vehicle. Once the applicant qualifies for the lease, all that he may be required to do is to sign the necessary documentation, pay the first monthly installment, and drive away with the vehicle. The attractiveness of this option often obscures the lessee from reading the 'fine print' of the lease contract. One document which is usually presented is an authorization from the employer of the lessee to continue paying the monthly installment until the entire sum is repaid or when the institution presents written consent to discontinue the payment. This clause is important particularly if the lessee is desirous of breaking the contract. Even if the purchaser changes job, the mere fact that one is indebted, carries an obligation to repay.

Leasing companies usually have a battery of solicitors who would pursue clients who refuse to pay or who attempt to get out of the contract. Of course there are circumstances which most leasing companies would consider as being genuine enough for them to agree to a cancellation of a contract. These may include if the lessee becomes unemployed and is unable to secure another job after a number of months or the death of the spouse of the lessee, for example.

If the lessee is desirous of trading in the vehicle or discontinuing the agreement, one may encounter penalties. These may be penalties such as the lessee having to pay the company the equivalent of a number of monthly installments, for breaking the contract. In some instances there may be some concessions such as, if the vehicle is defective or the customer is trading the vehicle in for another.

Many persons who have achieved financial freedom would attest to having consistently saved and prudently invested in excess of 10% of their income over a number of years.

Leasing financing

"What are some of the advantages and disadvantages of leasing?"

Some persons prefer the 'luxury' to trade in or sell the old car every three years or so and effect a cash purchase, lease, or take a new one on hire purchase. There are several advantages associated with this practice.

1. They are afforded the opportunity of always having a trouble free car, since most new cars will not normally experience major mechanical and other defects unless it was involved in a major accident and/or it was subjected to gross neglect or is otherwise seriously defective.
2. It may add to their flamboyant life style of always being in the fashion, since this practice enables them to lease vehicles which are fashionable at that time.
3. They avoid spending much money on repairs and maintenance due to major wear and tear.

Unless one is very wealthy, this option is often not the best since a car which is serviced as scheduled, with no major accidents and properly maintained, may be able to run for more than five years before major problems such as the need to overhaul the engine and/or re-spray it, occurs. Savings from an owner driven vehicle can be channeled into other areas of the family budget. At the end of the lease, the holder usually has the option to purchase the vehicle, trade it in for another or terminate the contract.

In many instances, a senior executive enjoys the privilege of being given a company vehicle to drive, thus one does not have to worry about paying for maintenance or even purchasing petrol from one's salary. This privilege may be extended where a senior executive may be chauffeur-driven, enjoy all expenses paid holiday for himself and family members and provided with a house or housing allowance and other benefits. Such benefits should challenge us to work hard at one's career and achieve the best that we possibly can. Christians should endeavor to be the head of private, governmental, corporate and other agencies and enjoy the privileges which such offices afford.

It is remarkable how haphazard our control mechanism usually is when there is no clearly defined target which the couple is pursing. Manifestations of unmanaged budget include:

1. Items which may not really be important would be purchased and investments which are not lucrative may be undertaken, simply because a couple did not have a specific objective to attain.

2. There is much duplication in the items which the couple purchases, very often in an attempt to outdo each other in what they purchase.
3. They usually save separately and they are very cagey and apprehensive about disclosing their savings and spending.
4. One partner may try to persuade the other to take care of the major expenditures which will enable them to save more.
5. Major items are purchased in the name of the spouse who contributed most of the cash or who will be paying the higher purchase account, for example. There may also be bickering about who owns which items and thus should have exclusive or more use of it.
6. The couple lives together for an extended number of years and does not have much evidence that they have attained many material possessions. Their life together is tantamount to that of the foolish servant who hid his talent instead of investing prudently since they neglected to maximize the significant increase which their combined resources would have afforded.

International financing

"What are some of the international financial and business opportunities which are available to us?"

With the increased prominence given to globalization, several international financial centers have been adopting similar principles governing their operations. Many governments have also implemented economic and other policies in an attempt to attract more local and foreign investors. This phenomenon is becoming popular in both developed and developing countries.

Several catastrophes have recently affected international financial centers. The notorious **Third World Debt Crisis** and **the Asian Economic Crisis** are examples of how phony investors and bad business decisions are plaguing national and international financial centers. The Third World Debt Crisis was caused when governments and private investors (many of whom were guaranteed by their respective governments) sought to invest in the industrialization trust of their economies. Some large debtor nations including Brazil, Argentina, Kenya and Tanzania still owe billions of dollars to banks in the US, UK and other European countries. A greater part of their capital was mismanaged and many projects failed. The result is that the governments of these countries are saddled with the Herculean task of servicing debt in the wake of serious global, national, economic and social problems which affect their economies. Fortunately, several of these loans have been written off by creditors and softer terms such as a moratorium and debt/equity swaps have been applied to many of them.

Traditionally, the movement of money in international financial centers has been characterized by **transnational companies** that operate in developing countries using transfer payment and laundering money from these countries to their parent companies in the developed world. Although this trend has decreased because of stricter governmental control in several countries, many of these companies have developed other devious methods to repatriate their profits with the host country deriving a disproportionately smaller benefit from the operations of foreign companies.

It is a common practice for well-established **drug traffickers** to launder the proceeds from their corrupt dealings through the official financial system in an attempt to cloud their activities. Offshore banks are often used in an attempt to hide the illegal transactions of dishonest managers of companies, government officials and other individuals. Thankfully, Interpol and other policing agencies are apprehending many racketeers. Several governments have also established legislation to impose harsh penalties and confiscate assets of persons convicted of such illegal activities.

Some persons and institutions invest in securities (that is, shares, treasury bills and debentures, for example) in several international financial centers. This is often viewed as a prudent method of **diversification of their investment risk** of possible default or failure which investors would be exposed to when investing in a single financial center or in one line of product. However, financial theory advocates that this principle becomes less efficient as the portfolio is diversified beyond a certain point, called beta (β). After this point the returns as a percentage of the investment declines and eventually becomes negative (diminishing marginal returns).

The internet has opened a new world of communication, research materials, commercial activities, photography and other features to our disposal 'at the touch of a key.' There are so many activities which we can conduct from our computer terminal that it has dramatically reduced the distance between the supplier and the consumer. In many countries we can now access our bank account online, engage in the purchase and sale of items online where payments can be made by deducting the credit card of the purchaser or via other methods. Trading of stocks, the securing of credit facilities and other banking transactions are increasing being conducted online. Even though these transactions are becoming increasingly popular, many persons are still maintaining their relationship with financial and other institutions since they prefer the personal contact of a person whom they can see rather than communicating with a person merely with an internet address. For this reason many institutions are using digital cameras where customers with this facility can see the persons with who they are communicating and *visé versa*.

The internet has resulted in the loss of thousands of jobs in several traditional areas of customer service. However, new jobs are created to support many of the services provided by the internet businesses. Trading in stocks, for example, reduces the need for the customer to interact with a physical broker. However, there is still the need for financial advisors to conduct market analysis and make recommendations on the best options available to customers.

Some common mistakes made by investors:

1. *Using private and/or borrowing funds to invest in business ventures which they are not familiar with, or for which they have been ill-advised.*
2. *Not seeking and/or adhering to Godly counsel.* It is true that many investors realize a huge profit after acting on a 'gut feeling.' Christians have an obligation to verify the source of their inspiration. If it is from the Lord, then it is a sure winner.
3. *Employing and retaining staff and business associates who are dishonest and who seek to promote their self interest rather than the success of the business.*
4. *Not relying on Godly counsel from our spouse, pastor, business advisor and/or other competent persons.*
5. *Dishonest practices such as tax evasion, failing to disclose the true content and/or other important information on the product produced or service provided or lying about them.*
6. *Misappropriation of funds and not maintaining accurate accounting information.* Recent examples of this practice have led to the prosecution of several senior executives and other persons of companies in the US and other countries.
7. *Inappropriate use of funds* such as borrowing short-term to invest on a project which would generate income over the long-term. This usually results in a severe financial squeeze on the liquidity of the business to meet repayments in the short and medium term.

We are close to commerce being controlled by the 'one world government'

"The financial sector is often viewed as being under the control of Satan. An example of this is the introduction of

many activities in the financial sector which points to the fulfillment of activities surrounding the 'mark of the beast' and other end time prophecies as revealed in the Book of Revelation and other books of the Bible. In view of this, should Christians engage in banking?"

This section reviews several aspects of banking activities which are very important to the lives of individuals, families and the Body of Christ. Banking activities are commonly practiced widely by Christians and non-Christians throughout the world. There are several different types of banks including commercial, central, investment, offshore and development banks.

There are two broad types of commercial banks; retail and wholesale commercial banks. Wholesale commercial banks deal only with very large financial transactions (usually in millions of dollars) and they engage in maturity matching of loans with deposits. That is, a loan for six months is usually given against a fixed deposit of the same principal amount for six months. Retail commercial banks, on the other hand, accept small deposit and withdrawals can usually be conducted without prior notification to the bank. Some common transactions conducted in retail commercial banks include:

1. The operation of savings accounts on which interest is paid semiannually or annually.
2. In several banks, interest is not paid at all (or at a minimal level) on a direct debit or checking accounts.
3. Customers are usually able to negotiate personal and/or business (corporate) credit facilities from them.

Some Christians have an aversion to using some facilities of retail commercial banks and other financial institutions. Several Christians view such financial innovations as electronic banking, for example, with a high level of suspicion. Electronic banking has advanced to the point where the need to hold a large sum of notes and coins is rapidly fading in the more developed countries. Nevertheless, the uneducated poor, in particular, often feel that the banking environment is too sophisticated and formal for them. Therefore, they often feel alienated from the world of the established financial system.

> *It is in our interest to use a combination of savings and returns from prudent investment programs when planning for retirement. Savings are an accumulation of wealth to meet needs which may arise, whereas prudent investment programs should generate higher returns than from savings.*

The arrival of advanced financial instruments such as

checks, debit and credit cards, Automated Teller Machines (ATMs), and telephone and electronic transfer systems has rapidly revolutionized the world of finance. It is common to walk into a supermarket and purchase a trolley of groceries and present a plastic debit or credit card to the cashier. Transfer of the cost of the purchase can be made from the bank or a credit card company to the supermarket. Individuals and companies also transfer millions of dollars and other currencies daily between international money and capital markets.

Several analysts have found that many of these financial innovations are subject to possible frauds and errors which often result in the loss of large amounts of money and embarrassment to the financial institutions and customers. There are also many reports of teenager and older computer 'hackers' gaining illegal access into the computer system of financial institutions and destroying important data and/or defrauding them. Problems of this nature have led scientists to experiment with techniques such as using fingerprints and scanning an eye of customers in order to grant them access to their bank account, other information and/or locations.

There have also been experiments to engrave the code of the account on the body of the customer which will be electronically identified when that part of the body is scanned by the decoding device at the financial institution. Many Christians believe this innovation is too similar, for comfort, to the 'mark of the beast' as highlighted in Revelation 13:16-18. Persons who are found to have the mark of the beast would not be joining Christ in the Rapture but instead are doomed for hell. There is overwhelming evidence on scientific and other forms of advancements which are being made towards the fulfillment of this prophecy in our world today which should propel Christians not to sit idly by and accept every financial and other innovation, particularly if it is contrary to the Word of God and it is in fulfillment of 'end-time prophecies''.

The Internet, E-mail and World Wide Webb (WWW) are also viewed as major sources of unifying world financial and information systems, as predicted before the second coming of Christ. Although they offer many significant benefits, there are also many negative consequences such as easy access to pornography by children and adults, stalking and the promotion of homosexuality, cults and other undesirable elements on the Internet.

Some Christians, because of their educational background, financial position, sociological upbringing and/or other factors, may prefer not to deal with commercial banks and other formal financial institutions. Instead, they resort to saving their money under their mattress, in a hole in the ground or with traditional savings institutions. *Although saving small amounts of money at home is usually legal, saving large amount of money at home is unprofitable and often unwise, unless one is engaged in a business which demands this practice (even so one must compare the level of profit gained, versus the security threat of it being stolen or destroyed in a fire, for example). In doing this one would forego the interest which would accumulate if it were saved on an interest-bearing account. This practice is similar to that of the foolish servant who buried his talent (Luke 19:11-27) and was sternly rebuked by his master since he did not invest the money which was entrusted to him and his attitude towards his master. If money is not saved or invested in an account or activity which at least generates interest or other returns to cover the rate of inflation in that economy, the real value of the money will be decreased by inflation.* Believers will obviously not be expected to use devious measures such as concealing correct accounting data in an attempt to defraud the Inland Revenue, or be involved in money laundering or illegal drug trafficking.

The threat of loss due to the theft of their money, jewelry and other assets, possible destruction by fire have caused many persons and institutions to secure a safety deposit box at a financial institution or to purchase a fire proof 'heavy duty' safe to store these items. However, saving money in a financial institution such as a bank has several advantages other than merely the security which it offers. Two of them are:

1. If an interest bearing account is used, they may at least be able to earn some interest as a counter against the loss of the real value of their money due to inflation. (If inflation is 1%, at the end of this year, the real value of $100.00 which is not saved on an interest bearing account or invested in a business venture which generated a net income of at least 99 cents. If the $100.00 is saved for the year on a savings account which pays interest of 3% per annum, the real value of the saving is *$100.00 – 1 + 3 = $102.00*).

2. For a person who is seeking a loan, there is a record with the financial institution on how the customer was managing his cash flow over a given period. This information is usually crucial to support the request of the applicant for a loan to finance a business venture.

Christians are therefore encouraged to operate a saving and other accounts with an established financial institution or to save at a secure and trustworthy traditional financial institution such as a 'village bank' if formal financial institutions are absent in their community.

Methods of raising capital

"What are some of the methods which can be used to raise capital to finance the establishment or expansion of a business?"

There are several methods which entrepreneurs use to secure capital for investment activities. They include:

1. Using their own savings and/or borrowing from relatives and friends,
2. Forming a partnership and pooling their individual resources,
3. Utilizing funds from retained earnings (profit from the business which is not distributed to shareholders [the owners of the business]),
4. Securing capital from a bank and/or other financial institutions,
5. Privately offering for sale their stocks and/or shares or floating them publicly on the stock exchange.

It might be relatively easy for small entrepreneurs to use their own capital to finance business ventures. There are also many small and medium size businesses which have operated successfully without financial assistance from external agencies. This feature becomes more difficult for large businesses to raise capital primarily from the equity injection by shareholders and from their retained earnings. External funding from a financial institution and/or the stock exchange usually has to be secured.

In developing countries in particular, a company which floats its securities on the stock exchange is usually able to raise a large amount of capital easily, depending on the price of its shares and the attractiveness of the impending returns from the shares to perspective shareholders. Nevertheless, while it may be relatively easy for a small company, particularly if it is not well known, to secure capital from a bank, it is usually very difficult for smaller companies to successfully float their securities on the stock exchange.

Christians and investing on the stock exchange

"Should Christian invest in the stock exchange, even though we are aware that the management of many companies whose stocks are traded on the stock exchange are possibly engaging in accounting and other

practices which cause the price of their shares to be overvalued?"

Church officials usually do not have objections to Christians investing on the stock market, although some financial analysts contend that trading on the stock exchange is tantamount to gambling. It is true that **naïve traders**, that is, persons who do not use scientific methods such as Fundamental and Technical Analysis (two methods of financial analysis) when deciding whether or not to purchase or sell securities; therefore, they engage in gambling. However, the average trader on the stock exchange carefully analyzes market trends of the commodity, dividend reports and other issues that influence the movement of the price of the shares of a company before investing in the company. This is not gambling, even though an investor may make a 'well calculated' guess and make a profit or loss.

Stock markets such as those in Japan, the USA and the UK are classified as 'efficient capital markets'. These markets are supposed to be endowed with efficient methods of communicating the prices of securities, takeovers, mergers, the selling and bankruptcy of companies, for example, to players in the market without giving an unfair advantage to one or a few investors over others. In addition, private knowledge of such information by an individual or restricted group of investors should not put other investors at a serious advantage over others.

Many companies offer the employees stocks of the company instead (in lieu) of a bonus. There may also be offers such as special credit arrangements to purchase the shares of a company which is going public or expanding its capital base. These are often golden opportunities for employees to have part ownership of the company for which they are working. However, investing much money in one company, even if you are employed by the company, should be done only after much prayer and advice from competent financial planners. The principle of not 'putting all of our eggs in one basket,' also applies to making prudent investment decisions.

As Christians, we must pay heed to such guidelines, unless of course, the Lord instructs us otherwise. This statement is made in view of the fact that the Holy Spirit does not operate in a pattern which can be predetermined by man. His operations are dynamic and we must follow His directions or we would lose our blessings and breakthroughs. For the 'foolishness' of God far exceeds the greatest wisdom of man. A good illustration of this principle is the incident of the widow who was in serious financial difficulties and Elisha instructed her to borrow oil jars from her neighbors and to fill them from the little oil which she had remaining in her last oil jar. To the natural mind, this seem to be a foolish instruction, and Elisha may have been branded a heretic and/or an exploiter if she had publicized what he had told her, before she obeyed his instruction and saw the result.

The choice of a broker, financial planner or other investment advisor should be determined by reviewing the track record of the individual/s and the institutions which they represent. It is also recommended that such issues are discussed, even though the exact details do not necessarily have to be revealed, with other relatives, close friends and members of the church who may be knowledgeable in these areas. For this reason a potential investor must shop around until the best person or agency is secured who would be able to provide prudent financial advice.

A stockbroker once told me that he would ask a potential client how much he could lose without costing a night sleep before deciding how much to invest for the client. He would use that as the threshold of how much he advises the client to invest. If the portfolio were even to fall to that level he would advise the client to discontinue the investment scheme. As the portfolio grows, he would advise on alternative investment or to place the profit in a less risky investment. Even though this is not a universal strategy, it highlights the possible reality that persons can lose a significant amount of their investment while trading on the stock exchange. A trader in shares or manager of an investment portfolio would identify the point at which he would purchase or sell the share/s. Similarly, if an investor is speculating whether or not to purchase shares from a company and the price fells to a level which he feels is attractive and indications are that it would continue to rise, the risk taker may decide to purchase a large amount of that share.

The stock exchange is a safe place for Christians to invest in directly, once they have the necessary financial resources, are knowledgeable in this area and have enough time and resources to study market trends and other related issues in order to make prudent investment decisions. It has the potential to generate high returns and is a relatively safe financial market to invest in. Persons who do not have the necessary prerequisites to be successful and engage in direct trading can still derive some of the high returns by investing in mutual and trust funds and other financial instruments which derive their returns from stock market related investments.

Investing in pension plans

"What are some of the pension plans which are available to employees?"

There are several pension plans which a person can adopt to make a positive impact on their retirement. It is always advantageous if many of these programs commenced early in the working life of a person so that the greatest benefits can be derived. There is, for example, several retirement programs in many countries where the government offers special guarantees that their contributions will be payable to them irrespective of the financial situation of the country. This commitment is usually honored upon the retirement of the person. Many of these programs offer participants special tax incentives if they are disciplined enough to leave their savings until retirement. The government would be able to invest the money which is deposited in this fund in long term investment since it is anticipated that a large percentage of the population would attain the retirement age and the average payment per month can be computed and made payable to the retirees.

The USA has several bonds and other investment programs which self-employed persons and even employees can choose to participate in. A popular one is the **Serial I Bond** (**I**, is the abbreviation for inflation). This bond currently pays 5.92% per annum, which is tax deferred, in that the income which is contributed to this bond is not taxed from the inception, however, the payment on maturity is subject to taxation. The US Treasury declares a fixed interest rate and adds an adjustment every six months to protect the savings against inflation. The current interest rate is 3% and 2.92% is added because that is the level of inflation currently. This adjustment guarantees that the real rate of return on the investment, as far as is possible, is not adversely affected by inflation. This is very attractive to many small and large investors. These bonds can be purchased from commercial banks and on the web from as little as fifty dollars.

A popular retirement saving program in Barbados is the Registered Retirement Savings Plan (RRSP). Persons who earn a consistently good salary and who are disciplined enough can benefit tremendously from such a plan. It offers tax savings as well as a challenge to inculcate a saving program which will generate high dividends after retirement. Because of the high income tax in the country (in many instances over 30% of the gross salary of persons beyond the minimum wage) of a person's assessable income or $4,000.00, whichever is smaller, a person who is desirous of saving $333.00 from his/her income, by placing it in a bank account would not be able to benefit from the income tax concession associated with the RRSP. On the contrary, if that person participated in the RRSP he could contribute $333.00 per month from his gross income (before tax) directly to this scheme. In 33 years under this program, assuming a fixed rate of interest of 10%, the contributor would have accumulated Barbados $1 million (approximately US$500,000.00). (This is a highly hypothetical scenario, since it assumes that interest rates will remain constant at 10% over the thirty three years of the chart. In actual fact the savings interest rates for Barbados is currently under 5% per annum).

There are several **Retirement Plan Options** which some companies offer their employees. Two retirement plan options (the proceeds of both of which are usually taxable) are:

1. **A lump sum** – where the company pays the retired employee the entire pension at one time and he is allowed to spend it as he pleases. Persons who take this option would have the responsibility and challenge of budgeting wisely and spending, saving and investing parts of the pension in such a way that it would enable them to live comfortably for the remainder of their lives and if they so desire and can afford to, leave some of it for their dependants and for other causes. This is a tremendous challenge particularly for persons who are accustomed to a lifestyle which is commensurate with their salary. For many persons this amount only lasts a few years and they may have to resort to some form of employment such as a man working as a security guard and a woman working as a maid in order to cater for the financial needs of the family.

2. **Annuity** – this is where the retiree is paid a fixed amount per year over a given number of years. The **one-life annuity** will only pay the former employee a fixed amount until he dies, while the **two-life annuity** will pay the same amount to the spouse of the former employee in the event that he/she dies before his wife/husband. Many persons choose the latter option since it provides financial security for both spouses. However, the amount provided per year is usually less than if the retiree were to take the lump sum and even place it on a fixed deposit, for example.

Many countries have investment accounts such as the **Individual Retirement Account (IRA)** where government grants income tax concessions on a special amount, say $2,000.00. In some countries an employee has the option to inform one's employer of the amount that one will be saving monthly on such an account and the employer will have to send the

Insurance Coverage

INTRODUCTION

Many Christians do not 'believe' in purchasing particularly life insurance cover since they are of the opinion that the Lord will heal them when they are ill and many of them cannot afford to consistently pay the monthly premium payment. While payment to National Insurance and motor vehicle insurance is compulsory, for life insurance policies, payment is usually made independently. In this section we will be reviewing some of the negatives and positives of insurance cover.

The importance of life insurance cover

"Is it unacceptable for Christians to purchase life insurance when we have a heavenly Father who cares for us far more than the flowers and lower animals?"

There are several critical issues which Christians must take note of, they include the fact that:

1. We are in this world; we have an obligation to take advantage of the things around us to bring glory to the Lord in areas such as spiritual matters, enhancing our career, material resources and to care for our family.
2. We are exposed to disasters, sickness, the inevitability of death, and other adverse situations which affect the unrighteous also, until Christ returns, – the rain falls on the just and the unjust.
3. We have a Heavenly Father who has given us wisdom, the Holy Spirit, prayer, the Bible and other mechanisms to enable us to live successful lives.

Insurance coverage is one form of investment which offers us some form of comfort and assurance of financial and other forms of support in the event of unfortunate circumstances which may affect us and/or our assets in the future.

Examples of Insurance Policies

Life Policies:	Non-Life Policies:
- Whole of Life,	- Motor insurance,
- Endowment,	- Property – fire, theft and/or damage,
- Medical,	- Marine, air and road transportation,

A scripture verse which relates at least one important element of life insurance coverage, that is, of **planning for possible future eventualities** based on the likely impact of present or future activities on our lives and that of others, is Proverbs 13:22[a] which state that: "[22(a)]**The good leave an inheritance to their children's children.**"

Since Christian parents should be categorized as 'good' we have an obligation to leave an inheritance for our grandchildren. In the example of material assets, the inheritance might be durable enough that our children can, with proper care, deliver it to the true inheritors when they are old enough to enjoy and/or manage it. This creates a precedent where each generation is a custodian of the assets for the next generation. It is a reality that **the rich usually leave financial and other material assets for their children** (who they have not disinherited). Very often this inheritance is not durable enough to be passed down to a second generation. However, when Christians leave an 'intangible' inheritance such as the blessing of their Lord which extends from one generation to another, the inheritors usually receive special favors which often results in spiritual, material and other blessings.

The principle of material inheritance is evident in several successful family businesses and even professions. Inheritance can be in the form of:

1. A person bequeathing their property, business, liquid cash, money held in trust, and other forms of assets, to their heir/s.
2. Secular or religious titles, a good name, goodwill or other intangible assets can be inherited from predecessors.
3. Spiritual titles such as High Priest (the Levites, for example) are handed down from one generation to

other. Some types of spiritual anointing or blessing and also curses can also be inherited.

4. Life insurance coverage can be classified as a form of inheritance for the beneficiary of the policy.

The above verse has stirred up much controversy as persons seek to interpret it. A point to note is that **it is the good, and not necessarily the rich** that leaves the inheritance for the second and even subsequent generations. The truth of this statement is possibly due to the fact that if the blessing was merely financial, then the rich unrighteous persons may be able to reproduce this feature easily. This inheritance is more likely to be in the form of a blessing where the Lord blesses a child, grandchild and subsequent generations on account of the righteousness of their parents, grandparents and other relatives. This is similar to the relationship which the Lord granted Solomon and other persons in the lineage of David, on account of His relationship with David.

Insurance policies are generally divided into life and non-life policies. Among the common features of these two types of coverage is that the higher the probability of the insurance company being exposed to liability as a result of a claim, there will be an increase in the cost of the policy to reflect the perceived risk of the insured person and/or asset. A summary of some non-life policies are:

1. **Marine insurance** policies offer insurance coverage for the motor vessel, crew and/or cargo of the marine vessel in the event of extensive damage or the sinking of the vessel.

2. **Property insurance** is the provision of insurance coverage to assets such as homes and other buildings, goods in trade and household effects. Property insurance pays the sum insured or a specified percentage, on successful claim for the partially or complete destruction, or damaged due to fire, theft and/or other perils. Some insurance companies do not pay claims on buildings destroyed in a riot or natural disaster such as a flood, hurricane or earthquake.

3. **Motor insurance** coverage for most categories of motor vehicles which drive on public roads is a legal requirement in most countries. There are several types of motor insurance coverage such as:

   a. **Motor fire insurance**, which compensates the owner of the motor vehicle in the event of the motor vehicle being partially or fully destroyed by fire (that was not an act of arson during a riot, for example). If it is found that arson was conducted, the onus may be on the owner to pursue private litigation for compensation for the act.

b. **Insurance against theft;** which compensates the owner of the motor vehicle in the event of the motor vehicle being stolen or damaged as a result of theft. Two types of motor insurance policies are:

I. Some **third-party policies** only cover the medical expenses and/or repairs to the vehicle/s of the other party when the driver who is insured by their company was responsible for causing the road accident.

II. Coverage offered under the **comprehensive insurance policy** usually includes repairs to, or replacement of a motor vehicle (if it is damaged beyond repairs, or stolen, for example). If there is a road accident both parties are usually compensated once the court and/or the insurance company conclude that the insured person was responsible for causing the accident. A full comprehensive insurance policy usually includes coverage for fire and theft. Therefore, the policy is usually the most expensive since it offers the most extensive coverage. Some insurance companies stipulate that the vehicle should not be more than 10 years old and that it must be in excellent condition before the policy is granted.

There are several types of life insurance policies. They include:

1. **Medical insurance** which has features such as the payment of medical consultation fees, the cost of medication, outpatient and/or hospitalization expenses. The management of established institutions are usually compelled by law to provide adequate medical, and in some instances, on and off-the-job accident insurance coverage for employees. Private medical insurance policies can also be purchased by such persons. A sad reality for many persons who do not have medical insurance is that statistically they are more likely not to undergo even routine annual medical examinations which may identify current or potential complications which may develop later in life. Therefore, when they begin to experience the

symptoms of a serious illness, it may be very expensive to treat it or it may be too advanced to save their lives. For this reason Christian are encouraged to secure some form of medical insurance which affords them access to sound preventative medical examination and secure advise and treatment which will enhance their state of the health and wellbeing. This insurance coverage also reduces their medical expenses when they have to seek medical attention in the event of an accident or other forms of illnesses.

Well established healing ministries, such as Benny Hinn's encourages persons to visit their physician to ascertain the state of their health, to use any medication which is prescribed and undergo any treatment recommended. When we are aware of any specific ailment which we are suffering from our prayers can be more focused into believing God for the specific healing. Even after a person has received a healing from the Lord they are usually encouraged to return to their physician to be certified that they have been physically cured and that they were not 'merely believing God' for the fulfillment of His promises in this area, even though it has not been manifested physically.

2. **Whole of life insurance policies** are designed to provide the beneficiary/ies with the face value, and sometimes an additional sum, in the event of the death or incapacitation of the insured person. The insured person may also be paid a given percentage of the face value of the policy in the event of some form of physical incapacitation such as the loss of a limb and/or other parts of the body (which are stipulated in the contract) due to an accident.

3. **Endowment insurance policies** are primarily designed for persons who are interested in compulsory savings, while at the same time enjoying insurance coverage. These policies usually stipulate that the beneficiaries will receive the face value of the policy in the event of the death or incapacitation of the insured person.

4. **Term Insurance** – this is very often one of the cheapest types of insurance and it can usually be bought for a fixed period of time. A common purpose for which term insurance is purchased is to cover the life of the borrower over the duration of the credit facility. This

policy is usually assigned to the financial institution issuing the credit, so that in the event that the person dies or becomes incapacitated before the loan is repaid, the insurance company will pay the financial institution the outstanding balance owed on the loan.

5. **Care Insurance** – in the US and several other countries, when a person needs special care, such as the elderly or persons suffering from serious illness or are seriously incapacitated, the state may supplement a part of the cost, but the patient or their relatives will have to contribute towards the remainder of the cost. This may even entail the sale of the patient's home and other assets by the government in order to meet the additional expense. Even though the spouse or other beneficiaries would be entitled to withhold a part of the assets of the family, it can be very experience. For this reason, the elderly, who can afford to and where it is available, are encouraged to secure care insurance with a large enough benefit to cover such an eventuality. If a person becomes ill and one does not have adequate care insurance or financial resources to pay for the medical and other facilities needed, the state may bear the cost of the medical and other expenses of the victim but the standard of service provided may not be of the quality which the patient may prefer.

6. **Liability Insurance** - many insurance companies offer liability insurance which provides insurance cover for the medical expenses and other costs associated with a road accident, professional liability and other costs for which the insured person incurs due to negligence or for some other reason. The persons who was adversely affected or their representative can file a claim or even law suit and if their claim is successful, they may be awarded a financial or other award which the doctor or the hospital would have to settle.

7. **Group insurance** coverage which may include medical expenses, disability insurance and other forms of coverage to the employee and any of their dependants is normally provided by the employers and other agencies and is usually cheaper; than an individual policy. It also usually offers superior benefits to the unit cost of individual coverage. Whatever the

type of life insurance coverage desired, it should be a healthy balanced between security and affordability.

Many Christians do not purchase a life insurance policy for themselves and children since they are of the opinion that they are 'richer than a king' since their 'Heavenly Father has everything, and He has a million mansions in the sky.' Then again, since He provides adequately for the needs of the birds and the bees, for example, surely He will cater much more for His children. While it is also true that our Heavenly Father owns the world and all that is in it, He has allocated several responsibilities to us such as parents providing for their young children and children caring for their elderly parents. He has also given us hands to work, brains to think, the Holy Spirit to guide us, priests and pastors and other persons to provide spiritual counsel, prayer and other support mechanisms to enable us to succeed at our endeavors. The onus is therefore on us to be responsible and 'render unto Caesar the things which are Caesar's, to God the things which are His and to our families what rightfully belongs to them.' Parents have a responsibility to provide their children with facets such as love, spiritual guidance and material security.

There are many instances where Christian parents can hardly provide the basic necessities such as food, clothing and an acceptable standard of education for their families, to even seriously consider securing facilities such as insurance coverage for them. In reflecting on this predicament, reference can be made to the incident recorded in 2 King 4, when a prophet died and his children were saved from being enslaved by his creditor by Jehovah performing a miracle through the prophet Elijah. Even though there were no established insurance companies at that time, the accumulation of material and other assets such as a house, a business and money often serves the same functions as an insurance policy. A part of, or the entire assets left as an inheritance may be sold or retained and provide some form of material support for the other members of the family.

I can recall a Christian man who once said that he would not secure an insurance policy and leave the proceeds for his family when he dies since cash is too easily squandered and they would soon be destitute. Instead he would leave real estate for them since that is more difficult to dispose of. I was happy when he informed me a few years later that in addition to the properties, he had also taken out a life insurance policy, of which his family members were the beneficiaries.

A serious thought of the inevitability of death (unless Christ returns before we die) should challenge Christian parents to seek to adequately provide for their families. This should go a long way in reducing the financial difficulties of the family in the event of the death or serious incapacitation of one or both parents. An unrighteous man may contend that if he dies before his wife, she may marry another man who will have to take care of her and his children. If she is not already a salary earner, she may also become more industrious and secure a secular job. On the other hand, if he has an insurance policy and he dies, then another man may marry her and enjoy the money that he sweated for and may have even died in attempting to adequately provide for his family. We also hear of instances where the beneficiary of an insurance policy kills the insured person in order to collect the proceeds from the insurance policy. Such abnormalities are not consistent with Christian principles since we are more caring and loving and the fear of the Lord is in us. These are not considerations which Christians should harbor. Whether or not we acquire insurance coverage should not be based on a presumption of evil. Rather, it should be because we cannot predict every event which will come to our lives and attempt to provide some degree of comfort to in some way cushion the impact of negative events on our lives and that of our loved ones.

For many persons who are in favor of this investment and who can comfortably afford to pay the premiums, securing adequate medical, life and other forms of insurance coverage is categorized as a basic need. Medical insurance is often a great help in emergencies when the financial resources which is needed to pay for medical attention and/or other services may not be readily available. Very often we can pay very low medical insurance premiums that provide coverage of high value should a situation demanding medical attention occur. Once it can be afforded, parent/s, in particular the breadwinner of the family should secure adequate insurance cover for the entire family, if possible. This facility at least provides the family, with some form of financial security in the event of serious incapacitation or death of the insured person. It is important that Christians have some form of medical and hospitalization insurance if their motor insurance policy does not cover these eventualities. For these and other reasons, most persons who are aware of the benefits which can be derived from having adequate insurance coverage and who can comfortably afford to pay the premiums, categorizes adequate life insurance coverage for each member of the family as a basic need. It is a fact, however, that many families cannot afford this facility because of financial and other constraints.

Many parents enjoy the privilege of living for at least three score and ten (seventy years). As Christians we have the right to this age. However, many persons are not so privileged. The result is that when a parent, in particular the breadwinner, dies, the children may have to shorten their education while the family attempts to adjust their lifestyle to accommodate the seriously reduced standard of living. This situation could have at least been less severe if the parents were prudent enough and/or able to purchase and consistently pay for adequate insurance coverage.

An endowment insurance policy is an investment that Christian parents who are financially secure should be encouraged to purchase for their children at an early age. Some insurance companies would not insure children who are less than two years old because of the high incidents of infant mortality and serious illness among infants under that age, especially in developing countries.

Many parents believe that if they insure a child and God forbid, the child died, and they received the payment from the insurance company this act can be deemed as receiving 'blood-money.' Of course, this should not be a deterrent for embarking on such an important venture, for if the child lives, the payment from the insurance policy would at least provide a good start to his/her financial endeavors. If on the other hand, the child dies, if the parents so desire, the proceeds from the insurance policy could be used to establish a trust in the name of the child or it can be given to a worthy charity from which others can benefit.

An endowment life insurance policy that matures when the young person is about eighteen years and is about to enter university, embark on marriage and/or is desirous of securing a mortgage to purchase or build one's home, or using it as equity to inject into a business, for example, will be of significant benefit to the young adult. A friend once related that the reason he struggled to complete his secondary and tertiary education was that his father, although he secured a whole-of-life insurance policy, failed to pay the premiums, and his policy lapsed shortly before his unfortunate death. The result was that the insurance company could not honor the claim presented by his mother. We should learn from occurrences such as this, to be careful parents in every respect.

Many children would be thankful that their parents were thoughtful, and financially secured enough to purchase adequate insurance coverage that they benefited from in later years. Of course we have to consider the adverse effect of inflation and devaluation, for example, on the sum insured, for what is a substantial sum today, might become a pittance in fifteen years time. One can increase the sum insured over time to cushion the adverse effect of inflation, devaluation and other factors that may otherwise reduce the real value of the policy.

There are several scripture verses which admonish us not to 'take any thoughts of tomorrow, for tomorrow will take care of itself.' The key principles among these verses is that the Lord does not want us to worry and do things which are inconsistent to His Word such as visiting fortunetellers in an attempt to know what will happen to us in the future.

Mention was already made of several scripture verses which admonish us to plan, to write down our vision and other actions which demonstrates forward planning. Some of the ways of 'hiding from impending danger' as illustrated in Proverbs 22:3 in relation to our financial resources, include budgeting wisely, saving and investing prudently and consistently. These processes do not have to be stressful and worrisome, even as we inculcate the discipline and the joy of doing so and the joy when we achieve success. The disciplined persons are usually challenged to increase their savings and investment as they see their returns grow. Even as we engage in these practices, we have to leave room for the Holy Spirit to fulfill His promises and bless us with abundance beyond our natural capabilities 'even more than we can ever think of or imagine.'

> Purchasing **insurance policies should not** only **be seen as an investment per sé but as a form of protection for several reasons:**
> - **A loan on the face value of the policy for actually paying an interest for using one's own money.**
> - **The interest rate paid on most policies is among the lowest in the market.**
> - **The premium paid and the compound interest on the premium would have covered the face value of the premium on its maturity.**
>
> **However, if the insured person dies before the policy matures, the beneficiaries will benefit from funds which he did not invest in the scheme.**

The purchase of life insurance versus saving

"Are there advantages in purchasing life insurance rather than saving on an interest bearing deposit account, for example?"

In many respects it is better if parents secure an insurance policy rather than to hold a large deposit on a bank account for a child, if the primary focus is on acquiring long term funds. This is so because it is obligatory to pay the premium, monthly, half-yearly or annually, as agreed. Once the correct insurance policy is selected, the child can benefit from payments or the settlement of medical bills that may result from a serious accident, for example. The policyholder may also be able to use the face value of an insurance policy as collateral for a credit facility. Should the parent who pays the policy die or become financially incapacitated, that may not jeopardize the insurance coverage of the child.

There are usually clauses in some insurance policies where, if the person contributing to the scheme for a dependant becomes incapacitated or dies, then the insurance coverage of the beneficiary will continue until the policy matures. A possible disadvantage of an insurance policy to that of a bank account for the child is that one may only be able to withdraw the cash surrender value on the premium (which may include return on the investment on the insurance premium which is invested by the insurance company). The cash surrender value on a policy is usually minimal in the early years of the policy and increases over the life of the policy. This restriction may, nevertheless, be advantageous since a parent who is undisciplined, may withdraw funds in the short run and jeopardize the accumulated higher returns which would be realized if it is left over the long run.

It is advisable that every Christian adult who can afford to, should purchase an adequate amount of insurance coverage for one's self, where applicable and possible, and for the members of one's family. At least the breadwinners of the family should be insured in order to avoid a major catastrophe for the family in the event of the death or serious incapacitation of the breadwinner/s. A good starting point is an endowment policy with a face value of at least four times the annual salary of each breadwinner. Therefore, in the event of a tragedy, the family has some financial support to rely on, where with careful budgeting would tie them through a number of years by which time they should be able to better their circumstances. A person who is desirous of securing insurance coverage should shop around and seek honest advice from insurance brokers (this service is usually free even on the internet) and other persons/agencies to ensure that the policy purchased is best suited for their insurance requirements and that the premium selected can be maintained comfortably.

> **Insurance coverage attached to another financial instrument V/S pure insurance coverage**
>
> Very often it is cheaper to invest in a Mutual Fund, units in a Credit Union or other financial instrument which has an element of insurance coverage which would provide coverage such as reimbursement in the event of loss of income, rather than to purchase an insurance policy. Usually the dollar amount of the premium offers a higher face value of insurance coverage than it would cost to purchase insurance coverage solely from an insurance company.

Financial Management and the Golden Old Age

INTRODUCTION

Many persons from an early age seek to make adequate material provision for their old age, only to find that high inflation, high cost of living, medical and other challenges, cause them to live in poverty. The elderly are also particularly vulnerable to being targeted by robbers and confidence tricksters and other unscrupulous persons who seek to exploit them. The elderly are also frequently neglected by their children and other relatives after they spent years supporting their offspring and providing assistants to relatives and other persons. In view of these and other reasons, the church is often called upon to seek to assist this and other vulnerable groups in our communities and beyond.

Material obligation of children to their parents

"Do parents have a spiritual obligation to make financial provision for their loved ones before they die?"

Some Christians misguidedly emulate the attitude of the 'Rich Fool' (Luke 12) who at the end of his life offended the Lord by the disrespectful way in which he managed his material possessions. Even though he may have left much material resources for his family, he most likely was not a good spiritual example for them to follow. There are many factors which cause a large percentage of elderly persons to spend the latter part of their lives in a state of perpetual poverty and much unhappiness. They include:

1. **Many persons were not diligent enough to save and invest wisely,** therefore, they do not have enough savings to supplement whatever pension and other support they may be receiving from the government, their gratuity and from relatives and well wishers,

2. **Severe sickness and other disasters which affects them,**

3. **Neglect by children and other relatives,** who they might have spent much of their money to educate and care for but who did not feel it was their responsibility to care for their elderly relative,

4. **Poor state of the community and/or the economy,**

5. **After living a life of righteousness, many Christians leave this world without fulfilling their penultimate responsibilities of being good stewards.** The word penultimate is used since even though a Christian leaves a will or at least his assets are left for his family, there is still the responsibility to 'leave an inheritance' which may not necessarily be material in nature but his life should be a blessing to future generations since he is classified as being 'good.' Factors such as the following are prudent financial management strategies which will assist us to make a good end to the stewardship of God's material resources which He entrusted to us to manage while we lived on the earth:

   a. **Leave a part of his inheritance for the spreading of the work of the Lord. This is a prudent way for a Christian to end his days on earth knowing that one is going to spend eternity with the Father,**

   b. **A person should not go on a spending spree and live a lavish lifestyle merely to spend it all since he earned it,**

   c. **Have enough saved to cater for funeral, the settling of your estate and other expenses to ease the financial burden on relatives,**

d. *Similar to when they were alive, parents should not use their finances and other resources to fuel division among their children. This may be done in the form of leaving a part of their inheritance to a married child and debarring the spouse from partaking in it, particularly since there are no scriptural reasons for this practice.* There are other circumstances where, for example, a person is not as prudent at managing their finance, or is too young; it may be wise to leave the inheritance in a trust where the spending is supervised by at least one competent person.

It is important that *mature persons* **make a will,** detailing how we want our resources to be distributed at least after we die. It is always better when we have enough so that we can distribute it to our loved ones, the needy and to other areas of the work of the Lord. When we distribute our resources before we die, we will be afforded the opportunity of seeing the joy expressed in the lives of persons who benefited from our blessing. Hopefully, the allocation of the inheritance would not discriminate to the extent where there will be much strife in the family. Some persons make their final will on their death bed and it is honored by the court. There are many examples, however, where persons contest the fact the deceased may have been senile, or may have been coerced into leaving assets for a particular person.

It should be noted that it is enshrined in the statutes of the laws of many countries that the court will not approve any part of a will which had been allocated to the person who signs as a witness to the preparation of the will. **A holographic will** is one which has been written on an ordinary piece of paper dated and signed by the person making the will, even on one's 'death bed' and without the guidance of an attorney. In order to execute this will it is often necessary to probate the will, which may involve the sanctioning of a judge to verify the authenticity of the document.

Computation of the price of shares

"What are some of the factors which determine the price of shares?"

The price of the shares of a company is dependent on factors such as:

1. The supply and demand for the products and/or services of the company locally and/or internationally,
2. The profitability of the company, the amount of

dividends management can pay shareholders,

3. The success of the economic policies of the country and the effect of political and social activities on the economy,

No human financial system is perfect, and the stock markets of most countries have been exposed to several scandals which have led to the closure of trading and/or the rapid decline of the prices of securities and hence frantic efforts by shareholders to sell their shares. Companies with securities on the stock exchange and investors holding securities suffer from the sudden depreciation of the value of the securities that they hold. The Big Bang, the name given to the 1985 collapse of the London Stock Exchange, resulted in the loss of millions of pounds sterling by companies with shares on the stock exchange and companies and individuals who traded in securities. Adverse publicity in the early 1990's also affected the Indian Stock Exchange when several racketeers were accused of insider trading and other malpractices. This does not infer, however, that we should not invest in the stock exchange since the regulatory authority of most stock exchanges has implemented systems which discourages dishonest practices and to convict persons who perpetuate them.

Investment in government securities such as debentures and treasury bills are classified as 'risk-free investment'. This is so because the government of the country concerned usually guarantees the payment of the specified interest rate upon the maturity of the certificate. This agreement is usually honored unless there are extreme circumstances such as a military coup or the government is bankrupt.

Investment on the stock market has a propensity to generate a higher rate of return than investing in the banking and non-banking system. This is so because a correspondingly high level of return usually compensates a high level of risk of possible loss; *inter aliea* (all things being equal). In other words, since there is a high probability that investors will lose a part of or their entire investment on the stock market, the company issuing the security has to offer a lucrative incentive in an attempt to attract investors.

Many investors on the stock market do not have the time or knowledge of how to optimize their returns from direct investment (that is, trading through brokers and dealers who invest for clients) and would thus indulge in indirect investment instead. This is done by investing through intermediaries such as trust funds and investment companies.

The risks of borrowing from retirement account

"My family has exhausted all other options to secure finances for an emergency and the only one which seems available is to borrow from my husband's retirement plan. Is this a wise financial decision?"

Many countries and even legislation of some countries prohibit employers from lending directly from the pension of an employee. Where such restrictions exist, an employer may approve a staff loan using the accumulated pension as surety, or at least allow the employee to borrow an amount proportional to the accumulated pension. Failure to repay may result in the reduction of the amount of money payable to the employee or his dependents in the event of his death.

In the US, for example, an employee is usually allowed to borrow from his/her **Retirement Plan or 401 K**. The rate of interest on such a loan is usually high and there are many conditions which have to be satisfied in an attempt to discourage employees from borrowing from this fund. If the borrower is unable to repay it, it reduces the amount of money available to them at retirement. In some instances an employee is restricted to borrowing only to the extent of his contribution to the scheme and not the amount contributed by his employer. In effect, the employee is borrowing 'his' money and at the same time paying an interest for using it since this is a deviation from the primary purpose of the fund. Most employers would not seek to derive a profit from this loan but merely to cover the interest which would have accumulate if the money had remained in the fund and the cost of administering the credit facility.

In many countries an employee is not allowed to borrow from his pension plan or to use the amount accumulated as security for a credit facility. The primary reason for this is that the fund is designed to be used when the employee retires. There are several instances where employees are allowed to borrow against this fund and they are unable to repay, resulting in a low balance when the employee retires. There were several instances of this in the US where persons were allowed to invest a part of their retirement fund and the scheme failed. The result was that on retirement their pension was very small. Many such persons have to continue working or receive Social Security benefits in order to survive. For this and other prudent reasons, it is important that even when we have access to borrowing from the pension plan, we should as far as possible avoid using it. In instances when this is a last resort, we should endeavor to repay the amount borrowed as soon as possible.

Prudent management of retirement financial

"I have received a gratuity of $250,000.00, what is the best way of utilizing this fund?"

It is commendable that you have been a conscientious employee and are able to be employed by your company for a number of years to be able to earn a gratuity of that magnitude. The first consideration should be the fact that the first 10% is the Lord's tithes and you should also donate a portion as offering. In order to arrive at the best strategy, it is important to know of your temperament when it comes to consumption, savings and investment. You may want to allocate the gratuity as follows:

Items	Allocation
Tithes	$25,000
Offering	5,000
Fixed Deposit	50,000
Savings	30,000
Purchase of shares	40,000
Business investment	30,000
Investment in real estate	60,000
Repair and maintained[1]	5,000
Insurance coverage[2]	5,000
Total	**$250,000**

Notes: 1. Repair and maintenance include existing property, motor vehicle/s and other assets.
2. The insurance coverage includes life and property insurance.

Table 4.2 Example of a Personal/Family Budget

For the more affluent persons and families, placing at least $50,000.00 on a fixed deposit account, purchase treasury bills or debenture which generates at least 5% interest per year, guarantees a source of interest income which may be payable half yearly. While the fixed deposit is generating interest, it can also be used as collateral for a credit facility which is invested to generate additional income. Even though $250,000.00 may seem much initially, if it is not managed, it would be depleted within five years and there may not be any substantial evidence that it has been put to good use. I have included investments in shares, business ventures and also real estate to inject the importance of diversifying one's portfolio. The purchase of a house primarily for rental is usually a lucrative investment, once care is taken to secure or build a property which is in very good condition and which can be rented. This list is not static, since it may be more lucrative to place a higher percentage of the money in a particular area since another may be nonessential or not as profitable in a particular society.

Similar to any other investment, even though we receive counsel, the final decision of the best strategy to implement rests on a Christian's personal relationship with the Lord, where He directs us into making the best choice. When we have a close relationship with Him, we will know when He is giving us the nudge to make a particular decision, for even though the above, or another financial plan may be acceptable for one person who may turn out to be a millionaire from it, it may ruin the life of another person. The Lord may for example instruct one believer to give it all away. This may seem as an irrational decision for some of us. However, obedience to His direction may realize so many financial other blessings which is far more than if they had invested all of it in the highest yielding investment.

CONCLUSION

Moving from a debt ridden state to one of abundance is often fraught with many challenges. Unless we succeed during the testing period, we would live a life of defeat at a suboptimal level, when the Lord has abundance in store for us. Unless we deliberately choose to live a life of financial humility, we should be educated on the Biblical strategies which are at our disposal in order to overcome financial lack. Even though there are several scriptures which tells us that we will suffer for the gospel on account of us being followers of Christ, we are still reminded that we have an obligation to ensure that our family is well taken care of, least we be classified as being worse than infidels. The financing of the gospel has a very heavy price tag which we as Christians are obligated to provide. As the light of the world and salt of the earth our ministry is not limited to spiritual matters but we also have the solemn responsibility to demonstrate our love by showing others how to manage their affairs prudently. It is true that all of us will not receive 'five talents' but even if we receive one, we are expected to optimism the return on it. Our Heavenly Father created the world and all the wealth that is in it; surely a larger percentage of Christians should claim this inheritance and apply it to our lives and benefit from the manifestation of material and other blessings.

NOTES

****

Chapter 5
FINANCIAL MANAGEMENT AND THE FAMILY

INTRODUCTION

It was highlighted in Chapter 1 that as Christians, we are expected to be prudent in the use of our time, talent, and treasury which are at our disposal. The Lord has also placed around us persons and institutions which are designated to be instrumental in nurturing us into fulfilling the purpose for which we were created. The Lord has also placed His Manual, the Holy Bible; the Holy Spirit, prayer through which we can communicate with Him, holy angels to watch over us, the weapons of our warfare and other tools to enable us to live successful lives. *It should be noted that success for Christians, can be summarized as being in the right place, doing the right things which Jehovah decreed for one's life. This does not translate in much materially wealthy for all of us, however, it does generate a high sense of satisfaction in knowing that one is fulfilling one's destiny.*

Even with all of these resources at our disposal, sadly, many of us still live defeated lives not only in the spiritual realm but also in being able to meet even our basic material needs, that of our family and the wider society. It is not only persons who live in countries which are constantly ravished by famine, drought and other natural and man-made disasters who suffer want. Many Christians in developed countries also suffer serious financial lack because of their inability to earn enough money to meet their daily expenditure, debt payments and other financial needs. The result is seen in the high incidence of divorce even among Christians, where one of the primary reasons is dissatisfaction in the area of finances. In the light of this and other essential occurrences, **this chapter reviews some of the strategies which we can use to enable us to set the correct principles in motion to enable us to be able to secure the necessary financial and other resources which are needed** *to enable us to secure, manage and expand our financial and other resources.*

Managing Personal Finances

Jesus spent much of His ministry teaching the principles of the management personal finance. The importance of these principles are just as relevant today, for the management of personal finance is magnified to corporate, national and global finance. The fact of this principle was recently demonstrated in the 2000 global financial crisis, where the financial institutions which duped gullible mortgagees to secure mortgages which they could not adequately service, which resulted in massive foreclosures, the failure of several financial institutions and instability in the local financial system in several counties and internationally.

> *The fundamental principle of lasting spiritual and material prosperity is to give our lives to the Lord. We then have to observe ALL of His decrees including the giving of our tithes and offering, time, talents, and assisting the poor and needy; so that He can give us more to give to others. 'Our gifts will make room for us'.*

Overcoming the debt trap

"What are some of the principles which would enable us to get out and stay out of the poverty trap?"

Relying on the wisdom and direction of the Lord is the primary method which would enable us to emerge from poverty. This statement is actualized in several practical ways. Christians are expected to use their talents to earn a living for themselves and family, and to make a positive contribution towards the economic development of the society in which they live. This may include engaging in activities such as managing a cottage industry such as farming, selling of fruits and vegetable and animals, where possible or even establishing a large business. They can also engage in small ventures such as the rearing of poultry and farming where the produce is consumed by the family. Many of these activities can blossom into lucrative business ventures or at least a secured additional source of income for the family. Many persons apart from holding a 'day/night job', may also participate in other income generating activities such as commercial art, writing, singing, engage in a professional sport and/or playing a musical instrument professionally.

There are several examples in the Bible of persons who 'sowed' their way out of a financial and other difficult situation. They include:

1. As a consequence of their kindness, the husband and wife who did not conceive before they met the prophet Elijah, who built a room and furnishing it for him, and were blessed by the Lord with a child,

2. The widow who was obedient to Elijah and prepared a meal for him, he advised her to borrow oil jars from her neighbors and the Lord performed a miracle and they were all filled as she poured from one jar. She sold the oil and repaid her debt.

Many of us have had the experience of reading a Biblical passage and nothing seem to register in our spirit. This may be as a result of how receptive our spirit is to hear and apply the principles of the Word of God to our lives, our physical state, since tiredness and other distractions could cause us to miss what the Lord is saying in a particular passage. Then there are times when a passage and even a word has such a profound impact on us that it wakes us up even if we were physically tired. The latter experience occurred as I read Matthew 11: 4 and 5: "*4Jesus answered and said to them, "Go and tell John the things which you hear and see: 5The blind see and the lame walk; the leapers are cleansed and the deaf hear; the dead are risen up and the poor have the gospel preached to them.*"

What is evident in the first five examples was that Jesus provided the solution to the grave problems which these persons were suffering. Then Jesus tells us that the He preached to the poor. Of what significance is preaching to enable the poor to emerge from their state of impoverishment, you may ask? It must have been that the application of the principles taught by Jesus caused them to emerge from poverty. Even though there is also a spiritual aspect of the emergence from poverty; it is evident that the theme of verse 5 was that there were physical manifestations of the solution to the undesirable physical condition which the various categories of person suffered. We can therefore return to the earlier statement that indeed **the righteousness of God empowers us to emerge from poverty**. This occurs since we are now able to tap into the 'Source' of all wealth. As our minds are transformed, He equips us to access the avenues which would enable us to acquire, accumulate and expand our material resources. It we attempt to 'spiritualize' the implication that the preaching of the gospel by Jesus to the poor only pertained to the salvation of their souls and provide them a place in eternity, we have to answer the question of why Jesus should make an exception of a physical manifestation only on this issue.

Every spiritual act has natural and/or spiritual implications and *visé versa*. It is for the benefit of our physical existence that the spirit quickens the body. Similarly, spiritual transformation leads to physical success. An example of this phenomenon was shown where Joshua's success as a mighty warrior was manifested after he received the commission by the Lord (in his spirit) to be strong and courageous, Joshua 1:6. We are spirit, soul and body; hence, if we succeed only in one sphere but is a failure in the others, we would be incomplete as Christians.

> *As our minds are transformed, He equips us to access the avenues which would enable us to acquire, accumulate and expand our spiritual, material and other resources which are needed to fulfill our purpose. It we attempt to 'spiritualize' the implication that the preaching of the gospel by Jesus to the poor only pertained to the salvation of their souls and provide them a place in eternity, we have to answer the question on why Jesus should make an exception of a physical manifestation only of this issue. The liberating power of the gospel is for our spirit, soul and body.*

There are several things which are at the disposal of persons who desire to get out and stay out of poverty. They include:

1. ***Our minds must be renewed in Christ***. We become righteous through faith in Jesus Christ (Romans 3:22, 4:13, 5:17, 10:4 etc.) and thus derive all the prerequisite benefits. We can do all things through Christ who strengthens us.

2. ***Consistently make positive confession of our renewed state and 'act out' our confession***. Simple confessions such as "I am no longer poor, but I have the riches which are in my Heavenly Father" and "I can do all things through Christ who strengthens me" should be made. We have to confess prosperity, eat, sleep, dress and in other ways live in prosperity. This does not mean that we 'put-on' a foreign accent or copy the lifestyle of the rich and famous. Rather, it means that we should, as it were, discard the trapping of the 'grave clothes'. It may entail investing some of the little which we have into upgrading our appearance, home and other aspects of our lives.

3. ***Renounce generational curses*** since they will hinder us from coming into the full extent of our blessings. These include misfortunes, sins, and/or illnesses which seem to occur over and over again in our families. We have to denounce these curses and call forth the blessings of the Lord to fill the place of these curses.

4. ***Surround ourselves with persons who would assist us in realizing the liberty which we have already received.*** This does not infer that you will not associate with persons who are poor, for very often as we assist others we receive the manifestation of the liberation which we desire.

5. ***It may require that we go back to school, learn another language and/or engage in other activities in order to acquire the competence to enable us to tap into the resources which God has already made available to us.***

> **As we do our best (providing it is in keeping with the will of the Lord for our lives), the Lord will do the rest.**

There is no one formula which can unilaterally be applied by every person, family and/or corporate entity which would provide them the level of financial success which they desire. We all have different personalities, temperaments, spiritual and other callings on our lives. There are, however, several Biblical principles which we can apply which would guarantee the desired effect, providing we adhere to the conditions which must be met and maintained. For this reason what may constitute success for one person may be deemed as failure to another. Similarly, while one path may result in financial success in one person it may result in failure by another. The financial goals and the path to achieve these objectives differ among persons and institutions. What may constitute financial success is usually dependent on the goals which they establish and where on the scale of financial ability they fall. That is, do they have the capacity, ability and other attributes to continually strive to attain their goal of financial success and increase, or at least strive to maintain that level of success throughout the life or the existence of the institution? It is not possible that every person on earth will be a millionaire and live a life of luxury. Jesus confirmed that there will be poor among us always. Recognizing this, it is important for each of us to attempt to maximize the returns which are at our disposal.

For one person the Biblical concept of having 'more than enough' entails being able to build a mud hut, have a number of cows which can provide enough milk which can be sold and provide enough money for the family to live on. For another person it is being able to earn enough money to build a comfortable house and have it furnished modestly and be able to finance the education of all of the children, earn enough money to meet daily expenses and have enough saved to meet their financial needs when they retire. For another person it entails living in a mansion, having several villas in different countries, having a private jet and other luxuries. What is yours?

Many persons fail to achieve their desired level of financial success since they fail to recognize that they may be trying to achieve a level which may not be consistent with the will of the Lord for their life. This statement is made with reference to Jesus' parable in Matthew 25:14-30. *It should be noted that the master allocated the talents most likely in accordance with his perception of the ability of the respective servants. In the same way the Lord expects us to maximize the returns on the assets which He has placed at our disposal and to successfully accomplish the tasks which He has given us the ability to achieve. The servants who were given five and two talents and who generated 100% return were commended by the master.*

The servant who hid his talent and accused the master of impropriety was punished and his talent was given to the servant who was given five talents. We must recognize the level of return which the Lord expects to generate. Every Christian is expected to operate either at the level of the servant who was given five or two talents. Deviations from this principle leads to much frustration. A person who has the ability to operate at the five-talent level and fails to do so would suffer much frustration over the fact that he/she has underachieved. If the Lord has ordained that a person operates at the level of the two-talent servant and one strive to be a five talent achiever, it may also lead to much frustration since one may achieve financial success at the expense of other important areas of one's life.

We often find persons who earn a high salary and attain a high level of formal education, yet they are unable to amass as much wealth over their life time as a person who may not have acquired much formal education and who started a business venture with a smaller amount of capital, yet was able to acquire much material wealth. This is an illustration that it is not only the assets which we have at our disposal but more importantly how we use them and the amount of money we are able to save and invest prudently and consistently over an extended period. There are several other factors which determine the level of financial success which a person acquires. They include:

1. **The empowerment to prosper**, of the Lord on the life of a person. It should be noted that blessing is determined by character, faith and knowledge. Some of the characteristics which attributes specific types of blessings are highlighted in the 'Be-attitude' which link various character traits to specific types of blessings.
2. **A passion to achieve success,**
3. **The willingness to learn and apply the principles learnt to generate the required level of returns,**
4. **The ability to harness and utilize effectively and efficiently the resources necessary to achieve the desired level of financial success,**
5. **The ability to work with others and/or have others work for you to generate the level of financial success required,**

For many persons, the journey from where we are to where God wants us to be is quite a distance. Similar to the persons who accomplished great exploits in the Bible, it often entails an almost total transformation of who we perceive ourselves to be to what God has already invested in us, to enable us to received 'more than enough.' Many Christians will never be able to say at the end of our lives that we have truly enjoyed the abundance of material blessings which the Lord has promised the righteous since they have not correctly applied the Biblical principles of managing finances as directed in the Word.

It is important to identify what can be classified as being in a state of enjoying 'more than enough.' Most persons at the lower end of the income scale, whose primary source of income is from a **salary, will not enjoy a very high standard of living unless they have mastered the art of managing their net income.** Most persons in this category are primarily living from paycheck to paycheck, living on credit and are trying to 'keep their head above the water' or living above their means. Their home may be poorly built and/or heavily mortgaged and their lifestyle may also be one of impoverishment or a little above the poverty level. Many such persons may engage in some other form of income generating activity in an attempt to service. Many Christians in this category do not enjoy the state of abundance of financial status, even though they may be quite happy and live a contented life.

It is more risky to invest in maintaining job security and depending on a pension than to be adventurous and to generate at least passive income (along with one's main stream of income) from investing on the stock exchange, investing in real estate and other business ventures. It is true that inflation and other external factors can render our investment unprofitable, but it is at lease more secure than going to work one day only to be fired because one's services is replaced by a younger and more energetic employee, or one's pension is mismanaged by a crocked pension plan manager, as is so common today.

The financial status of the majority of persons can be classified into one or more of the following segments:

1. Unemployed/ Poverty stricken	2. Salaried earners	3. Self employed
4. Entrepreneurs		5. Investors

Diagram 6.1 Five Levels of Financial Status

1. **Unemployed/poverty stricken;** classified as persons who are not gainfully employed, living on handout, depending on handouts from relatives, friends, the church, government (such as social security benefits and medical and/or old age pension), NGOs, persons in refugee camps and/or depending on other support groups in order to survive. Many persons use such support as a stepping-stone to assist them to emerge from this state.

2. **The salaried earner;** persons who survive primarily on the salary which they earn from working for someone else or a corporate, government or other agencies. Such persons, particularly those at the lower end of the salary range, engage in meager amounts of savings and investment.

3. **Self Employed;** persons who earn an income from utilizing skills which they have acquired and/or by using the skills and assets to generate their income. Persons who are self-employed usually have better command over their income than a person who is a mere

employee, even though they may not have the cushion of a contributory pension from an employer and other fringe benefits. Among the advantages of this category of income earners over the salaried earner are:

a. They often have excess cash flow which they can save and invest. This often leads to the position where they expand to hire additional employees and/or invest in real estate, stocks and other areas.

b. Persons in this category have the advantage of maximizing their returns and the benefits of their input accruing directly to them,

c. Very often such persons maintain customer loyalty because of the high standard of service which they provide to their customers,

Among the primary disadvantage of this category are:

4. If there are major problems in their operations, they will also directly suffer from the negative effect of low income or their service may become obsolete,

5. Their operations may be closed or at least their income stream may cease when they are ill or go on a vacation,

6. It is often difficult for such persons to expand since finding another person to provide the same or higher level of service may be difficult and expensive. Even when an apprentice is hired, he may be there primarily to master the skill then to start his own business. This feature is common in professions such as mechanical engineering, joinery, carpentry and other skilled labor techniques. In many instances the self-employed persons have to revert to seeking employment if their business fails.

Entrepreneurs are persons who own one or several business entities from which their primary source of income is derived.

Contrary to the gambler who invests his money in a game of chance, an investor invests his money, time and other assets in mastering an activity where his skill in making prudent business decisions determines the level of his success.

Investors are classified as persons who invest their assets independently or with the assistance of professionals in a particular area of expertise and generate returns from their investment. Investors include persons who undertake trading in stocks and shares, property developers, money lenders, and investors in government securities such as debentures and treasury bills. They also include the 'mega-rich' who may have even inherited assets which are generating returns which is sufficient for them and their family to live on and to keep expanding their investment.

This list is not exhausted, since there are many persons who do not fit any of these categories exactly but may be operating in one or more of them. There are also the mega-rich persons, who have received a very large inheritance, who won a lottery or receive a large payment from a law suit, who may have so much money at their disposal that they may not even have to invest it but they have enough money to live on the principal amount, or even the interest for the remainder of their lives and a substantial amount will also be left for their inheritors.

One of the primary secrets of achieving financial success is investing in one, or a small number of business opportunities and/or financial instruments which consistently generate lucrative returns. This is usually not a story of overnight success, but as we are instructed in the Bible, we have to diligently nurture the resources which God has placed at our disposal so that His blessings will overshadow them.

Two popular maxims states that:

"Success comes when preparation (working smartly) meets opportunity".

"Winners see an opportunity in every risk, while losers see risks in every opportunity."

Each sphere of financial state, as highlighted in Diagram 6.1, has unique characteristics and ***it is often difficult to move from one category to another unless one is prepared to effect major changes in one's lifestyle (unless of course a miracle occurs, and even so, unless one maintains or retains the conditions which would enable us to 'keep the miracle,' even that can be lost)***. For most persons the change is gradual, as they increase their investments and make us of other opportunities and are able to realize more and more positive returns.

Most persons fall into the category of being an income earner. They include many farmer workers, domestic and factory workers, civil servants and member of the arm forces.

Salaried earners are persons who are employed by another person or institution and are paid for the level of service provided as governed by the policy of the employer. They range from non-skilled, semi-skilled to skilled persons. This category is generally classified as the poorest of the self-employed entrepreneurs and investors since a high level of performance is demanded for as little pay as the employee can afford, or is forced by government and other statutory bodies to pay. There are many persons at the top end of the salary scale such as Chief Executive Officers for some companies and other professions who earn very large wages and are able to live a very affluent lifestyle.

Some of the common traits of persons at the higher end of the bracket of income earner are that they acquire a 'good' academic education, technical and other skills and secured a job which they feel comfortable with, marry, purchase a home, acquire some means of transportation and save for old age. However, along the way they are acquiring more and more debt to the point where unless they work harder they will lose much of what they had acquired.

All of us are not born to be entrepreneurs and expert financial investors, nor are we all able, or prepared to acquire the necessary skills, financial and other resources which would enable us to become mega rich. It is thus important for us to identify where we are, what we are desirous of achieving and what we have to do to get there. Even though we are all leaders in some area of our lives, not all of us have the necessary ability to manage people and financial and other assets which would lead to much wealth. Therefore, most of us are satisfied to work for others, earn a pension, where possible, retire and hope that there is enough pension and other resources to enable us to have a relatively comfortable old age. Sadly, this is not a reality for most persons since old age is often plagued with sickness resulting in huge medical bills, and other disasters which cause many persons to have to depend on governmental and other support systems.

Similar to Jacob in Laban's household (Genesis 30:27), the blessings of the Lord accrues directly to you. They include persons who choose to, or who are unable to, secure income in any other way. It is important that persons who are able to do so prudently, should create an income stream whereby the blessings of the Lord come directly to them. They include:

1. Professionals who use their skills to earn money independently, under a business name or as a company. This category of employers has the advantage of managing their time and resources and they derive the level of returns as they inject into it and demand for their services and/or product increases. This category includes medical doctors, lawyers, dentists, taxi drivers, mechanical engineers, various categories of consultants, and independent farmers who choose to work independently. Even though the attributes of the blessing may come directly to the entrepreneur, their income stream is dependent primarily on their ability. Thus, even though their level of independence is usually greater than the self-employed, they may still be restricted in their scope of operations.

> *Many persons become materially rich not necessarily by working hard, but by strategizing and pursuing a highly successful business venture, acquire the franchise of one or several lines of business and/or product, and/or by investing wisely in one or small number of financial instruments.*

2. **The entrepreneur,** owns his own business and employs the service of others to work with and/or for him. The advantage of this category of persons is that the returns which they derive are not only dependant on their own level of output but also on that of others and on the returns from the capital invested. There are generally three types of businesses:

3. **The traditional business** where one or several persons and/or agencies pool their resources to form and manage a business venture,

4. **A person or company purchases the franchise of a business** operation and operates within the framework of the system established by the franchise owner. (A franchise is the system whereby the owner of a patent allows another person or organization to duplicate the product, production process or system which was invented, designed or created by the owner).

5. *A network operation* where one or several products are supplied by the controlling body. In this system the business owner secures a profit from the sale of the product and also a commission for the sale made by others whom he recruited to market the products of the organization.

6. *The entrepreneur enjoys the privilege where he may not necessarily be working with the institution, yet he enjoys the profit and other benefits from the business,*

7. *The ownership, management and the assets of the company can be passed down from one generation to another,*

8. *The Investor;* utilizes his personal and/or corporate resources to generate additional returns. He does not necessarily have to work for the institution but his investments generate revenue for him. This is the category where most rich persons, successful businesses and other entities are operating in. The responsibility of the investor is to ensure that he has enough personal and/or corporate finance or access to it, effect the investment and enjoy the net income from his investment. The investments can be from areas such as real estate, natural resources and financial instruments. Most successful investors tend to derive more than 70% of their income from their investments and even if they are salaried earners it is usually from managing their own businesses. Most persons do not just awake one day and become successful investors. The transaction is usually from a high earning salaried employee, a self employed or business owner who accumulates much positive cash flow over a number of years. Most investors start from a small beginning and expand their investment as they become proficient in one or several areas of investment.

Successful investors usually have a large amount of capital to invest and competent financial advisors who assist them to channel their investment into one or a small number of investment opportunities which generate high returns. Eventually, they should be able to master the art of making prudent investment decisions independently. Contrary to the gambler who invests his money in a game of chance, an investor invests his money, time and other assets in mastering an activity where his skill in making prudent business decisions determines the level of his success.

> *Becoming a successful investor usually require more than merely managing money. One must develop the knack to differentiate between a good investment from one which is merely appealing to the eye, emotion or where a good sales person or even financial advisor is not telling the whole truth. Even though having formal training in financial management and other academic disciplines usually aid the process, this awareness usually comes after undergoing a number of failed or not so successful investment deals.*

The four aspects of the investment system can be summarized as follows:

1. **Employee** works for the system,
2. **The self employed** creates parts of the system,
3. **Entrepreneur** manages and may even own a part of the system,
4. **Investors** invest capital into creating parts of the system without necessarily working in the system,

One of the primary reasons why many Christians remain poor all of the days of their lives is because of the fear of losing money if they invest. This fear often begins when parents inject negative thought in their children. Many parents and other adults are poor role models for others to follow since they are poor financial managers of personal finances and other resources. Some of these negative thoughts may include:

1. **They emphasize on the importance of their children obtaining a 'good education' in order to find a secure job that provides a pension, medical insurance and other 'comforts.'** Unless a person can be at the top of the income bracket and are paid a large salary and receives other lucrative fringe benefits, one is likely to be poor, or at the most, a at the middle income level of society.
2. **They do not set good investment examples for their children to follow since they are burdened with debt,**
3. **Children see so many persons fail in business ventures that they are afraid to get involved in business and investment,**

4. *We feel that it is too risky to invest and one or both spouses may not support the idea that they can do more than merely earn a salary,*

5. *The failure to identify an area in which one is comfortable to invest.* It is true that there are not many high return investment opportunities available to small investors in many societies. Even so, if a number of small investors are able to pool their resources they can benefit from the returns on their investment.

6. *They rigidly hold on to investment funds which are earmarked for the education of the children and/or other long term plans, instead of investing and generating higher returns in the near future to meet these and other financial demands,*

7. *We are not educated in the management of investment and feel insecure to trust even professionals in these areas to guide us along these paths,*

8. *The fear of failure in this vital area, which can dramatically transform the life and that of members of the family and larger community.* It is sad that many of us take serious risks which cause disaster, rather than to invest in a business venture which has a higher probability of generating substantial returns thereafter, adding quality to our standard of living. One of the most common mistakes is to secure large amounts of credit primarily for consumer items when we have little control of what may happen to us in the future. Very often we allow our emotions to take us deeper into debt rather than invest in a viable business which may give us the ability to pay cash for the item in a year or so and still continue to generate profit in the future. This principle is tantamount to a farmer eating all of the seeds instead of planting them and reaping a bountiful harvest.

Another way of reviewing the categories of persons is to identify their relationship to financial returns depending on their access to capital, their level of education on investment strategies and their attitude towards investment. Some of these activities may overlap. They include:

1. *A survivor* who has little resources and has little access to high earning investments,

2. *A saver* who accumulates small amounts of money over time and would invest in 'safe' opportunities which they can afford as they arise,

3. **A borrower** who accesses money from moneylenders, financial institutions and other sources to invest. Even though his return may be high, the high interest rate which he usually has to pay would absorb much of his profit.

4. **A partnership** where two or more persons pool their financial and/or other resources in order to generate higher returns from their higher combined resources,

5. **The rich may employ the services of a number of** financial advisors to invest on their behalf and/or master the art of investing on their own. Because of their wealth and affluence they are usually able to negotiate deals which generate returns in excess of 50% of their input.

6. **The mega-rich** can be classified as the few investors who have the capacity to generate huge profit from their investments because of the magnitude of their investment. Such persons are usually at the upper 5% of the economic system of a country. Their investment may be so large that the stock market of the country, and even the foreign exchange position of the country, may be affected by their investment. They include oil barons, majority shareholders in multinational corporations, and persons who may have inherited a huge fortune from their ancestors.

A person can be operating in two or more of these financial levels at the same time. He may be a salaried earner, for example, but is investing his surplus cash flow into a private business venture and/or in financial instruments. Similarly, a professional may have established a business of which he is also practicing his professional skills. He is therefore earning a salary while he is benefiting from the Net Income after Interest and Tax of the business as a result of employing other persons to manage other aspects of the business. Unfortunately, most persons fall into the category of salary earners.

The table below summarizes some of the generalities which separate the rich from the poor. Account is not taken of factors such as persons who may have become rich because of winning the lottery or other games of chance and those who may have acquired a large inheritance which they are merely managing. Even so, unless it is an extraordinarily large inheritance, if it is not managed, it could also be lost because of poor investment and/or spending habits.

No.	Indicators	Poor	Rich

1	Source of wealth	Primarily from income earned	Primarily returns from investment.
2	Attitude towards money	Earn to live	Their money and other assets and employees work for them.
3	Percentage of salary retained	Low	High
4	Percentage of taxes paid	High	Low
5	Payment of taxes	Deducted before salary is received	Determines how much is paid
6	Management of workload	More time spent working as salary increases	More time for leisure and other non-work related activities as returns on investment increases.
7	Attitude towards financial risks	Avoids risks. Hence, they are unable to retain financial and other assets during their working life to be able to enjoy a high standard of living after retirement.	Risk takers, and usually have enough money and other assets to enjoy a comfortable retirement.
8	Management of one's career path	Other persons determine promotions, salary, working hours etc.	Manages the level of success and returns achieved.
9	Management of debt	Increases as salary increases	Decreases as returns increases
10	Life style	Live above their means	Live below their means
11	Accumulation of pension	Limited access to manage personal contribution and that of employer which keeps declining after retirement.	Increased returns on assets continue to grow even after 'official' retirement.
12	Ability to leave an inheritance	Achieves very little surplus and may only leave a small amount of assets for future generations.	The assets invested continue to generate returns, possibly for several generations, once they are managed.
13	Relationship with laws such as taxation and other business related issues.	They are unable to take full advantage of the statutes of the law in order to increase their salary.	Uses the statutes of the law to their advantage.
14	Management of Cash Flow	Decreases, even when salary increases, as a result of poor cash flow management strategies.	Increases astronomically as net income increases.

Table 6.1 Comparison of the Life Style of the Poor and the Rich

Many persons are desirous of being at the point where they have enough money at home, saved at a financial institution and enough income that they will be able to meet their financial needs without undue worry. In order to enjoy financial freedom, we have to be prepared to maximize our returns in whatever area the Lord has blessed us. It is not automatic that because a person is desirous of becoming wealthy and he begins to invest that his returns will automatically be one hundred fold.

> - **Winners see opportunities in risks.**
> - **Losers see risks in opportunities.**

Prudent investments in opportunities such as the following have enabled millions of persons to achieve financial success:

1. **The acquisition of academic, technical and other forms of education**, even though many persons who are educated are able to utilize the skills which they acquire to earn enough money to live a comfortable life, the reality is that very often an entrepreneur who is far less educated than they are, hires the academic and technically qualified person and uses their expertise to amass a huge amount of wealth. Even persons who graduate in disciplines such as financial management and marketing, often do not apply their knowledge for the maximization of their personal returns but that of an institution for which they may not even be a shareholder. It is true that many persons who are not academically qualified in a specific discipline use what they may classify as a 'gut feeling' about a business decision and earn lucrative returns as a result of their decision. For the Christian who is 'in tune with the Father,' this is usually the Holy Spirit nudging them on to make a wise financial decision.

2. **Owning their own business**; the reality is that many persons do not take the time to study what they are getting into before starting a business. It is not a good enough reason that merely because a person is a good cook or loves to style hair, and/or is desirous of becoming wealthy, for example, that the person should establish a business. It is first important to study what one is getting into, acquire the managerial skill, finances, employees, large enough market and other

prerequisites needed to ensure its success, before commencing the operation.

3. *Investing in securities, mutual funds and other financial instruments which generate high returns*; it is important to be conversant with the intricacies surrounding the financial instruments which one is desirous of investing in before engaging in the investment.

4. *Investing in real estate is an excellent form of investment in most countries*; many persons and businesses purchase old buildings and rebuild or repair them and/or purchase a plot of land and build one or several houses and sell them or rent them at a handsome profit.

5. *The production of a commodity and/or the provision of one or several types of services.*

It is important to establish and expand our cash flow and utilize this excess to invest in areas which generate lucrative financial returns. It would not be long before we begin to realize significant expansion over a short time. As a person begins to reduce unnecessary expenditure and expand his investment he may be termed as being mean, a miser and other derogatory terms by those who are observing him. One also has to guard against persons who would seek to provide misguided advice and make offers which would result in a loss or minimal financial returns. They are also robbers and tricksters who are intent on depleting us of our hard earned assets.

We have seen from Chapter 3 that categories of investors are:

1. *Risk adverse investors,* whose desire is to take on as little risk as possible. As a result they save their money and may only engage in investments where they are sure that they will receive at least their full capital back.

> Similar to other areas of life, persons who are not prepared to take advantage of well calculated risks, usually achieve very little financial successes. *People who take risks create change;* sadly, this is not always for the better.

2. *Cautious investors* who employ the service of investment managers such as brokers and/or financial advisors who, independently or with the consent of the investors, allocate the investment. Unless the amounts invested are very large and the returns very high, such investors do not maximize their returns as if they were

knowledgeable enough to invest on their own. This is because they have to pay commission to the fund manager and the investment might be on a diversified portfolio rather than on a single or a few high earning securities.

3. **Gamblers** have the disadvantage of 'investing' in activities where the probability of securing high returns from this game of chance is disproportionately high against them. It is true that some gamblers do 'strike it rich' and they may be rich for the remainder of their lives and have enough money remaining for future generations. Gambling is also a sinful activity.

4. *Investors who study the market in which they are investing, wise financial and other business decisions, which generate lucrative returns,*

> For the unwise, money is like an addictive drug; they are happy when they have much of it, sad when they are broke, and would figuratively and literally kill themselves and others if necessary, to have more of it. As Christians, we should not allow our material things to dictate our lives. Our Source, Provider and Sustainer is Jehovah.

Most persons do not have the financial resources, managerial skills and other prerequisites to operate a successful-large business. Therefore, it is usually better to start on a small scale and expand under favorable conditions. Before expansion is undertaken conditions such as the following should be present:

1. Management should become proficient or able to acquire the increase inputs to manage at that expanded level,

2. The profitability of the business should increase as the efficiency in the production and delivery process of the product and/or service increases,

3. Demand for the product and/or service of the business should be increased in proportion with the desired level of expansion,

Many persons who are desirous of starting a business on their own and do not have the necessary inputs to do so, choose the option of forging **an alliance with other person/s to form a business entity**. This is the major system used by corporate entities where a small number of persons purchase the shares of a company or they are sold to the public. Another option which is used by some persons is to **secure the franchise, and/or become an agent for an established entity**. Established companies such as McDonald's, Kentucky Fried Chicken, Hilti, Pepsi and Coke would authorize other business entities to lease their franchise where they agree to adhere to the system which the parent body established. This would include building the restaurant or other entity the same way, using the same system of preparation of their product and/or implementing the management and other systems as the terms and conditions as stipulated by the franchise. It is usually very expensive to secure permission to use the patent of an established product and the parent body would send inspectors on a regular basis to ensure that their systems are being maintained. In this way, they secure the methodology and other prerequisites which have already been successfully used by the parent body. After overseeing the success of the management of a franchise, some entrepreneurs may establish similar systems on their own and/or increase the number of franchise holdings which they have.

Millions of persons have also invested into an existing **network marketing** system where they receive items from an established agency such as Amway Inc., and Avon, and sell the items on a commission. This system is used by millions of persons who sell toiletries, pharmaceuticals, groceries and other items in a small way or on a large scale. This is often done in a small way by persons who sell items to colleagues at work and to neighbors during their spare time. As their profitability increases, many persons incorporate the assistance of other family members and even hire the services of other persons and expand their operations. Many persons and companies conduct telemarketing and other methods to advertise their services and organize an effective delivery system. This system has assisted many persons to develop their marketing, managerial and other skills to expand their operations and/or establish other methods of conducting business as their capital increases.

Many persons are **wealthy** from the stand point that the returns from their savings and investments would ensure that they do not have to worry about being able to meet their financial and other material needs for a number of months or even years. Yet, they may be burdened with the responsibility of having to work very hard in a stressful environment in order to maintain it. The **financially successful** person on the other hand, has the benefit of having enough financial and other resources to meet their needs but without the worry and pressure to achieve and/or maintain them.

In some ways we have to learn the techniques which are needed to guide us in making wise financial and other decisions and apply them prudently. The failure to take well-guided risks is a primary reason why many persons remain poor financially and otherwise and do not achieve their full potential in this and other areas of their lives. There are several things which we usually have to do before we can move to the path of the financial abundance which God has already decreed for us. They include:

1. *Be in the place where you can hear from God as to what area/s He wants you to invest in*. We must be in the place where we are committed to give of our time, talent and treasury to see the fulfillment of His will in our lives. We should also recognize that the level of abundance which He has for each of us would be dependent on His purpose for our lives; some one hundred fold, some sixty fold etc. Similar to King Solomon, once we are committed to 'building the tabernacle' then He will also provide abundant resources to enable us to 'build our own palace'' 1 Kings Chapters One to Ten describe the blessings which Solomon received even as he was willing to follow Jehovah and to build the temple of the Lord. We are also instructed in Proverbs 3: 5, 6 as follows: "*5Trust in the Lord with all of your heart, and do not rely on your own insight. 6In all of your ways acknowledge Him, and He will make straight your paths*."

2. ***Be educated in the area where He directs you to invest in.*** Areas where we can be educated to achieve financial success include academic qualifications and technical training which would enable us to secure the desired job, be competent in managing our business, and make prudent investment decisions. It is also useful to attend trade fairs and seminars on leadership, marketing, human resources and other disciplines relevant to the success of our business. Also subscribe to magazines and other literature which provide information on the local and international market in which you operate and align yourself to persons who can be a mentor in various aspects of the investment program. It is important to keep abreast with events surrounding the activities which you are desirous of investing in.

3. ***Formulate and keep abreast with the personal vision of the owner/s or the corporate entity.*** It is also important that even small investors are conversant with issues such as the preparation and interpretation of financial statements such as the income statement, balance sheet and cash flow statements. This knowledge is useful for an investor to know where he is, where he desires to be and how to achieve his goals.

4. ***Secure the necessary finance needed to undertake the desired level of investment.*** A good way to commence this process is to adopt a disciplined lifestyle including budgeting wisely and to consistently increase the amount of money we can save from our salary and other sources of income. This process may entail one or more activities such as avoiding unnecessary debt, investing in high return projects, forming a partnership or other forms of business alliances, and where necessary, securing credit from a financial institution and/or other sources. When the amount of capital cannot be raised privately, external funding must be sought. The ability to access an adequate amount of cheap capital at the time when it is needed and other factors of production are basic ingredients to help one achieve the desired level of financial success. Too little, and too expensive, factors of production as well as the unavailability of essential inputs when needed are classic causes of the failure for many businesses.

5. **Harness the necessary skills needed to take you to where you are desirous of being.** As we progress up the road to financial success, it usually demands that we are better able to manage people, systems and other assets, in order to achieve the desired level of success. It is a fact that many persons can prepare more tasty food items than many of the popular successful eating-houses. However, unless they are able to access the level of capital and operate better systems than these institutions, they will not be able to generate the level of profits as these established agencies. This includes the location of the factory, distribution center and/or other buildings, the deportment of staff towards management and customers, the standardization of the output and the image projected in the advertisement of the product and/or service provided.

6. **Accept change and be adequately prepared to take advantage of the benefits which change creates.** If we review the number of areas which we have seen significant changes over our lifetime alone, we will recognize several significant changes which have occurred. Many persons who are creative are able to invent, design or produce items, patent them and derive much financial and other forms of success from the sale and/or rental of the patent, franchise, brand name or other systems and/or from marketing the product or services. Other persons are able to create new products, improve on the efficient use of various items, and/or production processes, improve the efficiency of a system and in other ways are able to benefit from the introduction of new and improved products and services. Bill Gates, the Rockefeller family and other famous entrepreneurs have been able to take advantage of increased demand for cheaper, faster, and more efficient products and services provided.

7. **You must be prepared to take well-calculated risks.** The maxim which states "**nothing ventured, nothing gained**' must be heeded. It is often useful to start on a small scale and expand as management fully equips to optimize returns.

8. **In order to optimize sales, steps must be taken to ensure that factors such as the quality of the product, the cost, standardization, efficiency of the supply system, packaging, advertising and other market**

related issues are managed. It is important to market the concept that *good things are usually not cheap and cheap things are usually not good. Thus the selling price must be reflective of the quality and other prerequisites of the product.*

9. *Equip yourself with the necessary resources needed to enable you to maximize your returns.* This is essential since many persons accept mediocrity simply because they do not take time to acquire the necessary knowledge to empower them to succeed. This may also entail seeking prudent advice from financial planners, consultants and other knowledgeable persons in a specific field. Depending on the type of investment, many successful investors generate huge profit since they are able to benefit from economies of scale, tax and other advantages, by operating on a large scale.

10. *The necessary infrastructure must be in place to take full advantage of the financial, human and other resources which are needed to achieve the desired objectives.* It is important to master the system which would enable you to utilize the resources available in an efficient way to generate the desired level of returns. The investors must have mastered the art of generating the desired level of returns in that particular endeavor independently or with the assistance of other persons who are knowledgeable and are committed to inject the necessary inputs to make the investment a reality. This may include other investors, financial advisors, employees and/or other persons and institutions.

11. *Even if a person feels secure as an employee, his income should be complemented with interest from saving in high yielding financial instruments such as mutual funds, dividends from shares, rental income from real estate, profit from investment in business venture and other returns on their investment.* At the same time, they should seek to abstain from, or incur as little additional debt as possible while they are controlling unnecessary spending, increasing their income and expanding their saving and investment thrust.

12. *Entrepreneurs and other investors have to take advantage of business opportunities, information and other benefits which are available on the internet.* It is

increasingly being recognized that the new frontier of 'offshore' business is in cyberspace. Billions of dollars change hands each day on the internet. Many of these transactions are far cheaper than purchasing from 'regular' stores, since they often do not attract the high taxes and other charges.

13. **We must secure the necessary advice from persons who are experts in the desired area of investment.** They may include stock brokers, financial planners, real estate agents and other professionals who would at least assist us to understand the intricacies of the business and guide us to master them. Depending on the nature of the advice it may be necessary to befriend such persons or where possible to hire their service at least until we become competent in managing the operation independently.

14. **It is important to be prepared for disappointment.** Many persons are so scared of being disappointed that they would stay in a dead-end job since they are afraid of being exposed to financial and other losses when a better opportunity materializes. Weak managers often avoid making important decisions as they are afraid of facing the consequences of failure. Some other reasons why we experience failure are due to ignorance, or not being diligent enough to apply the correct Biblical principles in the execution of a particular task and/or not listening to the wise council. Once our ways are committed to the Lord and He is directing our path, even if He allows us to fail in a particular area it is only for our betterment in some way. We should be diligent and committed enough to learn from our mistakes and to use failure as a stepping stone for success.

15. **Specialize in one or a small number of areas of investment.** Most persons derive more profit from investing in areas in which they are knowledgeable and for which they have a love and a passion, instead of merely doing it for the sake of accumulating riches. The concept of diversification is usually not as profitable as specializing in an area which one is knowledgeable of and/or is able to employ other persons to assist in the process. This may include hiring specialist advisors and other categories of persons. In many instances a decision has to be arrived at on whether the emphasis of the business would be

operating on a low markup but with a high level of turnover as is common in supermarkets and the sale of non-luxury items, as against a high mark-up on a slow moving item such as the sale of jewelry, and luxury cars. Failure to manage sales is a primary reason why a large percentage of businesses fail.

16. **Master the art of managing people**. Most persons who achieve financial success have done so by utilizing the services of others such as employees, and professional advisors. Unless such persons are stimulated by factors such as their job security, financial rewards and a conducive working environment, then they may not provide the service to cover their cost of working and generate the required level of returns for the investor. Some persons use force, bribery and other unscriptural methods to achieve their financial success. The result of such actions may be that their operations are adversely affected by strikes and other industrial actions by employees and court actions by the state since their practices may be investigated for illegal activities.

17. **Patent inventions, musical and other recordings, books and other items.** This would result in the accumulation of royalties and other fees when persons use the item for commercial purposes. It is true that many items which are patented are used without the users even paying the necessary royalties. A common example of this is persons and companies who download music from websites on the internet, burn CDs and record audio and video cassettes without the permission of the holder of the copyright for these recordings. The legislation to prosecute such persons is not well defined in many countries, while they are not rigidly enforced in many others.

18. **Ensure that you are living within your means and not merely living in an illusion**. Many persons are of the opinion that earning more money would solve their financial problems, only to find out that as they earn more, their expenses are still more than their income since their consumption pattern increases more than their income can afford. (The economic jargon which is used to describe this phenomenon is that 'the propensity to consume is a function of your income.' As the average person receives an increase in income, they very often increase their purchase of

consumer items and live a lifestyle which is beyond the level of increase in their income). The answer to this problem is usually to first learn to manage your cash flow and ensure that you have a positive cash flow each month, which would enable you to save and invest the difference. This principle is needed by the owners of businesses and investors who live a lavish lifestyle, instead of investing their retain earnings until they can really afford to live at the desired standard of living.

If, for example, a farmer eats the seeds instead of planting them, then he would not have the desired harvest. It may be necessary to spend a part of the profit from one's salary or net income from a business venture. At the same time, a prudent person would seek to save and invest/reinvest a part of the earning in order to generate higher returns in the future. Similarly, if a person perpetually spends as much or even more than he earns, he will not be able to save and invest as much as he would have if he had managed his cash flow. This would have disastrous consequences when an emergency arises. As a person masters the art of managing his cash flow, and as returns from investments increase, he would be able to gradually increase his affluence, consistent with his true level of financial freedom. This process is facilitated by reducing personal and/or corporate debt, emphasizing on saving and investing in areas which generate high returns, and require planning and executing long term goals.

> *We should not only seek to live within our means, but also to increase our means to enable us to enjoy a comfortable standard of living, not in the sense of being complacent, but being able to fulfil our personal, spiritual and other responsibilities.*

19. **Do not quit when the goal is just around the other corner.** This issue goes back to the mindset of the investor. We are reminded of the maxim which states that; **quitters never win and winners never quit.** This is

not suggesting that we should jump around like 'three blind mice,' for a similar fault would result when a poor investment decision is made and because of pride, we would not abandon it.

An investor with a sound business and/or investment concept, which has been ratified by the experts in the area of their investment, must have the strength of character or obtain the necessary assistance to see it through to a successful completion. There are, however, circumstances where we have to allow an undertaking to 'die a natural death.' This may be when we encounter challenges such as the following:

1. 'Everything' gone severely wrong even though one has done all that is within ones control in an attempt achieve success and the task is still unsalvageable,

2. After consulting competent advisors and the Lord we are not given the clearance to continue,

3. The cost of implementing and maintaining the project far exceeds the benefits usually occurs when exogenous factors (which are beyond the control of management) have a negative effect on the projects.

Other important considerations in fostering long term success in financial management and other areas of our lives include:

1. **Avoid the quest for instant gratification and instead pursue long-term objectives.** As we focus on the long term, we will be challenged to make wise decisions over the short and medium terms in order to fully achieve the abundance which we expect from the execution of our long-term goals. *A vital part of this process is benefiting from the principle of compounding when saving at a commercial bank, which generates interest on the principle and interest accumulated, instead of losing when the money is kept at home in a safe or hidden somewhere else.*

2. *Particularly at the initial stage of the investment, our priority should be in the area of investing rather than merely providing financial security.* Persons with their house and/or car as their largest 'investment' are usually not prepared or able to invest in income generating activities which have a significant effect in taking them to the desired level of financial liberation.

3. **We should seek positive role models from persons who have achieved success in the endeavor in which we are pursuing, and in other positive areas.** This does not infer that we should shun even persons who are

financial failures, for even they can be an impetus to challenge us to succeed. However, we should seek mentors who would guide us to achieve financial and other forms of success.

4. **Take control of the aspects of your life which the Lord has entrusted into your care.** Even when you fail, do not blame others for failures which were due to your ignorance, incompetence and/or other defects. Failures should be used as an educational experience which should encourage you to rethink your strategy and propel you to retool and overcome these challenges. There are times, however, with the prompting of the Holy Spirit and advice from genuine persons when you are directed to chart a new course.

5. **Invest in a business venture and/or investment opportunity in which you have a passion**. One of the primary reasons many businesses fail is that the owner/s is not committed to its success. Even if a project is generating high returns and management does not have the passion to see it grow to its full potential, there is a high probability that it would fail. For this reason it is important to know what the Lord wants us to be and the investment area that He wants us to be involved in.

6. **You have to acquire the necessary knowledge to equip you to take advantage of prudent investment opportunities**. Focus on the area which you desire to invest in and acquire the knowledge necessary to execute it successfully. If you are desirous of purchasing property, and renovating it for resale, for example, you must be knowledgeable of factors such as being able to secure the best:
   a. Purchase arrangement, such as a low purchase price and being able to negotiate the most advantageous mortgage package. The legal and other costs associated with closing a mortgage are very high at some financial institutions.
   b. Contractors who would provide the required level of renovation to the property or construction of the building within your budget.

If we cannot manage our cash flow by budgeting wisely, increasing our income, decrease expenditure and/or apply other prudent methods, then we may have to pay others to do so in the form of interest on credit, tax penalties and other cash outflows; and the loss of investment opportunities, for example.

Millions of persons are mislead into believing that pursuing an academic career, securing a job which has benefits such as a pension upon retirement and medical insurance and other forms of job security is the panacea to achieving financial success. An increasing number of such persons are being forced to recognize that this path often leads to frustration and a life of mediocrity in terms of the quality of life they can afford to live. *Financial freedom from a secular perspective is primarily achieved by a person or corporate entity owning and successfully managing one or several business ventures.* Even though this is a satisfactory state, it is important that we ensure that this and every other aspect of our lives are in keeping with the will of the Lord. The latter principle is highlighted in the parable of the 'Widow's Mite,' where the widow experienced financial freedom in that among other things she recognized that Jehovah was her source, and even if she gave all the money that she had to Him, He would have provided for her in ways which far surpassed the value of the coin which she gave to His work.

> *Financial freedom from a secular perspective is being in the state where a person can enjoy the desired standard of living when his money is working for him rather than him merely working for money. This is limiting in comparison to the spiritual connotation of financial freedom, which entails having enough financial resources to enables a person to fulfill the will of the Lord for his ministry; personally, the family, and further a field.*

Accumulating the necessary capital to be able to invest at the level required: For many persons this is accumulated as they purpose to live within their means and increase their savings. The strategy of consistently saving, even a little each month over a number of years is often successfully used by many persons to accumulate much money. The money accumulated over time often provides them the opportunity to acquire the necessary knowledge and expertise to enable them to be successful when they decide to invest. This process is usually more promising when they begin to save a little at a time and are challenged as they realize how much their financial resources have grown, to increase their savings and investments.

Many persons who are in the coveted position of enjoying financial prosperity, are individuals or families who have their own business, private owners of large corporate entities and persons who are generating huge returns from personal and/or corporate investments. One of the significant benefits from a corporate entity is the tax concessions which can be derived.

The disposable income of the **salaried employee** is shown as follows:

SALARY $\Longrightarrow$ **TAX** $\Longrightarrow$ **DISPOSABLE INCOME**

The disposable income of the **business or corporate** entity is shown as follows:

DISPOSABLE INCOME $\Longrightarrow$ **SPENDING** $\Longrightarrow$ **TAX**

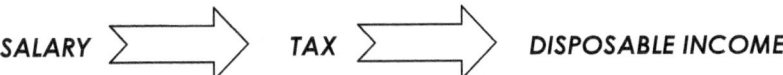

Diagram 6.2 A Comparison of the Disposable Income of the Salaried Earner and the Owner of a Business.

It is interesting to note that some of the expenses which are normally borne personally by the Manager/Owner and other employees can legally be included as part of the expenses of the company. Among the benefits which can be derived from this practice are:

1. Expenditure such as the purchase and maintenance of the car used by the Manager/owner and other senior staff, can be incorporated into the expenses of the business,

2. The home in which the family lives can be bought in the name of the company. Vacations, which the family goes on can also be expensed to the company as benefits for the Manager and other senior staff.

3. In some countries even items such as the education of the children may be expensed as contribution made by the company or included under other categories, and expensed before the taxable income of the company,

Persons who are salaried earners and those who are self employed are often subjected to racial, sexual and other types of prejudices much more than entrepreneurs and investors. In addition, the higher up persons are in the social ladder, the more their money and position will 'speak' for them and the less their presence as individuals is felt.

> **Salaried workers and the self employed** earn most of their money from their income. They usually pay in excess of 30% of their gross salary as income tax in many countries. **Business owners and investors** earn most of their money from their assets and pay little or no income tax on their earnings. It is no wonder that persons from the latter group are richer. Which group would you prefer to be in?

The balance sheet and income statement of a person or organization with a managed portfolio verses one which is unmanaged as follows:

Balance Sheet

| Savings, Investments & Other Assets |
| Liabilities |
| Positive Net Worth |

Income Statement

| Income |
| Expenditure |

Diagram 5.3.1 Showing a Schematic Balance Sheet and Income Statement of a Managed Portfolio

Balance Sheet

| Assets |

Income Statement

| Income |

Debt	**Expenditure**
Negative Net Worth	

Notes: A person or company with a negative net worth is generally classified as bankrupt

Diagram 5.3.2 Showing the Schematic Balance Sheet and Income Statement of an Unmanaged Portfolio

Many persons take advantage of establishing a business venture while the company which they worked for decides to outsource specific arms of their operations, in an attempt to cut cost. Such persons may have been employees of the organization who settle for a retirement package which they can invest to purchase the equipment, rent factory space or secure other assets to conduct their operations. Depending on the type of operation it may be possible to convert one or several rooms of their home into office space or workshop to conduct their business.

If a person attempts to lie to himself and to others that he can live comfortably at a certain standard of lifestyle when in fact he is living on excessive amount of credit which he cannot afford, for example, then it is only a matter of time before he will become bankrupt or have to engage in dishonest practices in an attempt to maintain his inflated lifestyle. Many persons secure loans and run up huge credit card and other debt primarily in an attempt to maintain a standard of living which they cannot afford. The result is that the obligation to meet the loan payments results in many persons living from one paycheck to another and even being in poverty. Truth on the other hand creates wealth. Some of the areas where this principle is manifested are:

1. Recognizing that Jehovah is the source of all true wealth and that we can achieve all that He has already provided for us, and applying this fundamental principle to every area of our lives,
2. Even though 'manna still falls from heaven,' from the perspective that God often performs miracles to

enable us to achieve financial and other forms of success, He has also provided us with the principles in His word which we can use to guide us along the path of success in our financial and every other area of our lives.

3. We have to learn the necessary techniques and apply them in the correct way to enable us to achieve success,

4. Once we manage the resources needed for success, unless we allow the 'cankerworm' (which may include inflation, theft, and a net loss) to eat away at our investments by not guarding them with faith, prayer and other instruments which the Lord has placed at our disposal, then we will achieve financial success.

A person who lives a lie, be it living above their means in order to impress others, and believing that their wealth provides ultimate happiness, will end in poverty. Even if it is not material poverty it will be spiritual poverty, that is, separation from Jehovah in this life and in eternity.

It is important to note that the blessings of the Lord go beyond our capabilities and what we can achieve on our own. Biblical examples of this include:

1. The Lord revealed to Jacob a creative method to multiply livestock.

2. The favor of the Lord on the lives of the Hebrews caused the Egyptians to give jewelry and other gifts to the Children of Israel as they left Egypt.

3. The Lord granted success and much spoil to King David and other leaders in many battles even when their armies were outnumbered.

4. Even though Peter and the other disciples toiled the whole night they did not catch any fish. When they obeyed the Lord, they caught so much fish that their boat was almost sunk and they had to solicit the assistance of other fishermen to help them to collect the abundance of fish which they had caught. This is an indication that the blessing of the Lord in financial and other areas of our lives goes beyond our abilities. Miracles are common in the lives of Christians and even non-Christians since Jehovah is a God of love and mercy.

We are reminded of Psalm 49:10 which states: "**¹⁰When we look at the wise, they die; fool and dolt perish together and leave their wealth to others."**

This is a confirmation that Christians often receive inheritance and other favor from being in the will of the Lord.

> **Lies** create poverty, while **truth** enables persons to take advantage of opportunities which would enable them to secure wealth. Why lie to yourself that you can live a lavish lifestyle when you know that you are deep over your head in debt which you cannot even pay. Isn't it better to be truthful and live on a budget which you can afford comfortably? In this way, over the medium and long run you would have achieved far more than you ever can hope to achieve if you remain in perpetual debt.

One of the important financial choices which each of us has to make is whether or not we are prepared to enjoy financial security or financial freedom. Persons who are desirous of enjoying financial security would usually be a salaried earner in a 'secure job.' Such persons are usually scared and/or unable to invest much money and other assets and thus, remain very poor. On the contrary persons in pursuit of financial freedom would acquire the knowledge, financial and other prerequisites, start their own business utilizing their skills, finances and other inputs, invest wisely, enabling them to generate the desired high returns on their investments. The level of success begins with the mindset of the investor/s. The way we think will challenge us to make the required preparation. We are reminded of the maxim which states that 'as a man thinks, so is he.'

Many persons have the misconception that buying a large house, fancy car and other trappings of the rich would make them rich, only to find that these things only make life more difficult since they have to do several jobs and may even engage in dishonest practices in order to survive. It is better to implement the principles of the Bible in order to achieve success in financial and other forms of success which last, and which they can enjoy. That includes living on a well structured budget, executing long term plans, saving and investing prudently and increase their affluence gradually at the level they can comfortably afford and which is consistent with their long term success. Throughout the process we have to rely on the Lord for wisdom, strength, favor and other blessings which are needed to execute these mandates, while we are fulfilling our responsibilities in areas such as giving of our tithes and offering, and assisting the poor, for example.

The path to Biblical success as experienced by many persons can be summarized as follows:

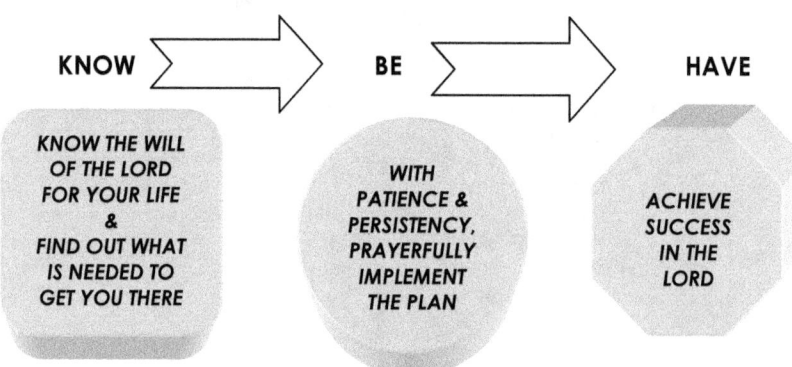

KNOW → **BE** → **HAVE**

KNOW THE WILL OF THE LORD FOR YOUR LIFE & FIND OUT WHAT IS NEEDED TO GET YOU THERE

WITH PATIENCE & PERSISTENCY, PRAYERFULLY IMPLEMENT THE PLAN

ACHIEVE SUCCESS IN THE LORD

Diagram 6.4 Illustration of the Road to Biblical Success

The following table presents hypothetical examples of the application of the above principles:

Know	Be	Have
To be the head of an international missionary body.	Attend Bible school, affiliate yourself to, or establish a local church and train, become a missionary and establish affiliation with other missionary bodies.	Send missionaries to other countries and also finance missionaries from other church bodies willing to work with your ministry.
Accumulate a million dollars before age fifty.	Secure a high paying job and save and invest prudently. Establish a viable business entity within two years of employment. Invest in property development and on the stock exchange.	A significantly growing cash flow and new worth.
Have a happy family life.	Seek the Lord for His will on whom to marry. Spend quality time nurturing a loving relationship	A stable and loving family where each member of the family is fulfilling the calling of

| with your wife and children. | the Lord on their lives. |

Table 5.5 Strategies to Achieve Goals

The above table provides some broad parameters which can be used to guide us along the path of achieving our goals in life.

Managing the Family Budget

INTRODUCTION

The mismanagement of finance is one of the primary reasons for the high percentage of divorce, even among Christians. Many families also experience financial lack since parents have not mastered the important art of budgeting wisely and as far as possible, implement the plans of the budget. This is also the reason why many persons who work very hard at their career, find it difficult to live comfortably shortly after retirement, they have depleted most of their gratuity and savings. In view of these and other important factors, this section is very important.

The application of prudent financial management strategies

"As a married couple, what are some financial strategies which we can employ in order to manage our financial resources?"

When planning financial matters, as in most other areas, it is important that the family is conversant with alternative options which are available to them. For example:

1. ***Invest in real estate.*** This may take the form of investing in a private dwelling house and/or in commercial properties such as an office complex, apartment buildings, condominium, or building or purchasing one or several houses, and/or other properties. Some couples take the option of securing the land, and building as they accumulate money, build their home over a number of months or years instead of securing a mortgage. This method is advantageous to many persons in that it avoids the high mortgage rate which financial institutions usually charge, legal and other expenses associated in securing a mortgage. However,

this has to be weighed against considerations such as the amount of rent which they would have to pay while their house is being built. In addition, it might not be cost effective to utilize the large cash outlay required to build a house over a short time, versus borrowing and investing one's cash in a lucrative investment which would generate a far higher rate of return than the cost of repaying the mortgage.

Some couples avoid paying rent at least at the initial stage of their marriage by living with their relatives. This of course has it own problems such as conflict with in-laws and the infringement of their privacy. Many couples have been divorced since they were unable to cope with these difficulties or they had a negative impact on the marriage over a number of years. These possibilities must be weighed against the amount of money that they would save during this period.

2. *Invest in financial instruments such as* treasury bills, debentures, shares which may be particularly profitable if they are held for a number of years and possibly sold when they mature or the price is very high.

3. *Purchase jewelry, exotic art, antiques, vintage items such as cars and other assets whose prices increases over time*.

4. *Investing in their children.* This includes purchasing books, computer and accessories, ensuring that they receive the best private or at least the best form of education which is available, ensuring that they eat a balanced diet and engage in other healthy practices. Many parents do the best they could, yet their children do not achieve the level of prominence which their parents desired. In such circumstances the parents should take solace in the fact that at least they have done their best, given their limited financial and other resources. It is also important that parents be aware of God's calling on the lives of their children so that the children can be encouraged to pursue that path.

5. *Obtain a 'good' education* from which one can secure a good paying job from which one can enjoy the standard of living which one desires, including that of benefiting from medical insurance coverage, and pension. Some organizations also provide employees with the option of securing shares from the company from which they will derive dividends and they also

have the option of selling the shares, if they so desire. *A very strong word of caution must be injected on this issue since, as presented later in this chapter, a balanced view is important in highlighting pros and cons of being employed verses being an employee and also the advantage of being an investor. It is a fact that high academic success does not guarantee professional success in our society, nor is it the panacea for material success. It is a fact that the majority of materially wealthy persons in the world have not achieved high academic success. Nevertheless, it is necessary that they have a high degree of business accruement or at least be able to harness those qualities from employees and/or other persons.*

Another fact of life is that some of the highest paid persons are sports men, actors, models, and other professions which often do not necessitate that the person must attain high academic achievement. It is often said that the more academically qualified a person is, one is often more cautious to take some of the chances which entrepreneurs often take. We should not decry academics, for many of them have used their professional training and channel it into highly successful business and other endeavors. This feature is common among highly skilled cosmetic and brain surgeons, heart specialist, researches and publications of medical books and famous writers, for example.

6. *Starting or securing a business* which is managed, and hence generates lucrative financial returns. The business may be passed on to children and/or other relatives, or it may be sold and the proceeds used as a comfortable retirement nest-egg or invested in another venture.

Each method has advantages and disadvantages. Investing in real estate, for example, can be profitable. However, the value of property may decline if a new low income housing project is established or a 'slum' area emerges in close proximity to the property.

> *A popular maxim states that a fool and his money are soon parted. This is possible by methods such as:*
> - *He would not be able to detect the cunning devices of persons who are merely out to fleece him.*
> - *He spends his money foolishly and before he knows it, the money is finished.*
> - *He is robbed, since he did not take adequate precautions to protect his wealth.*

Wealth can also be stored as jewelry, providing there is adequate provision to guarantee its safety. Business people often have a fire proof safe in their office or at home, or they may store in a safety deposit box in their bank or other financial institution, usually at a small fee.

Even though financial planning for the family is absolutely necessary, these plans can be temporarily or permanently interrupted by factors such as loss of the net worth of assets, sickness and/or the death of a spouse. As stated in Chapter 4, where possible, insurance coverage should be obtained to provide some form of financial security for member of a family. More importantly, we have to consistently exercise faith in the blessings from the Lord of good health, protection from robbers or fire and other incidents which can create disaster for our families. The inevitability of death, unless the Lord returns before one's appointed time, cannot be avoided, even though one's life span can be extended with healthy living, medical intervention, and the grace of God.

Managing daily expenditure

"What are some of the methods which we can use to reduce our daily expenditure?"

There are several methods which we can use to reduce our expenditure and increase our disposable income. They include:

1. *Taking lunch to work* saves money as well as serves as an impetus to promote the eating of a more nutritious diet. This is of course conditioned on whether the person who prepares the meal has the time, and knowledge, to prepare a nutritious meal, usually the wife of a married couple has the time and energy to do so. Some men are reluctant to take the meals prepared by their wife to work since she may not be a good cook or they merely prefer to eat fast food. Many of these men end up being overweight and unhealthy as a result of their poor eating habit.

2. **Car pooling** is an effective method which some persons who attend the same church, good friends or relatives can form, where they rotate the day when a particular member of the group picks up the others and they go to work, church and other places. This method reduces the cost of petrol, as well as the wear and tear of the motor vehicles of members of the group. It also reduces the traffic congestion and pollution. This method demands a high level of cooperation between members of the group, where punctuality, and the proper coordination of their activities are essential to cause minimum delays to the group.

3. **Benefiting from coupons** where persons accumulate coupons from newspapers or, magazines produced by the store for items which are on sale and other forms of sales promotion.

4. **Benefiting from rebates from stores which provide customers with electronic or manual recording cards from which points are accumulated for purchases above a given amount.** Customers usually have to register for these cards and points accumulate with every purchase from stores and other businesses which participate in the scheme. In some instances petrol stations, banks, wholesale and retail stores participate in this scheme. The points are accumulated and translated into dollar value, which customers can redeem when purchases are made from designated outlets.

5. **The sale of glass and plastic bottles, egg trays and other items which are recycled.** It is beneficial to recycle these items which accumulating cash in return. There are many disturbing pictures of poor adults and children scavenging dump heaps and garbage bins in search of these and other items which are sold or consumed by them. This is often their only source of income. Such persons are exposed to a high risk of infection from contagious diseases and other harm as a result of visiting such sites. It is important that we not only pray for such persons but that we support charitable and other organizations which are seeking to irradiate poverty and improve their standard of living.

6. **Purchasing cost effective gifts** which are within the budget at Christmas time, for birthdays and other

special occasions. It is often better to send a card or visit someone who is living close by to show your affection and appreciation for the person, rather than to overspend to purchase a gift which the recipient may not even use.

7. Use **energy saving appliances and methods.** By using fluorescent rather than other bulbs which us much electricity, for example, saves much money, even though the initial cost of installing them may be higher. In the long-run they are far more cost effective and also better for our eyes when we are reading.

8. Purchase **items which are on sale,**

9. Purchase **items wholesale**, where possible, even in a group and dividing them among individual members in accordance with the order,

10. **Purchase items which are in season or** when **there is a glut on the market since the price will be lower than normal,**

11. **Purchase local items which are good substitutes for imported items**. This not only supports local businesses but items such as local fruits are usually fresher than imported ones.

12. **Spending more time in fasting and praying** - many persons would spend at least one day per week fasting and in prayer. This is a healthy practice, of course after the approval from the family physician that their body will not be adversely affected by the fast. Persons suffering from diabetes, for example, may have to undertake a partial fast while using their medication and the necessary dietary intake. Even so, some persons would trust the Lord to protect them from any adverse effect on their body.

We are reminded of Proverbs 13:18 which states: "[18]**Poverty and disgrace are for the one who ignores instruction (discipline), but the one who heeds reproof is honored**."

If I spend $5.00 per day purchasing sweets for my children, I would have spent not only $5.00 × 365 = $1,825.00 per year on sweets, but would also forgo the interest which I may have been able to accumulate had that amount been saved, or even a higher return if it were invested in a high yielding financial instrument or business venture, for example. I could have also contributed it as a part of my tithe and/or offering and would have reaped the highest dividend possibly, from the Lord. This principle is referred to as the **time value of money**, since the difference in the amount spent and the accumulated interest and/or profit, represents the amount which could have been earned from saving or investing the $5.00 per day.

Formulating of the family budget

"What are some of the important considerations necessary when formulating a family budget?"

Most of the above issues focused on financial management from a macro perspective as they affect the Christian family. The first part of this section discusses various aspects of financial management that the family has to consider when preparing their budget. A vital part of a couple becoming one-flesh is that they must **plan together and execute their plans together**. Even if a Christian husband is the sole breadwinner of the family, he is not expected to practice the outmoded dogma that he has the right to plan the family budget and forcefully control spending.

It is important that in instances where both parents are working, that the **correct disclosure** is made of each spouse's income, so that the budget is based on honesty. When a couple has not mastered the spiritual principle of cleaving (where the couple is united in body, soul and spirit; where they plan together and execute their plans in unison), the budget is one area where there will be much deception. In some instances one partner may believe that the other is a lavish spender, or may not be as prudent as is expected when it comes to saving. **Wives are particularly noted for hiding money in secret places**, which they may use in the event of an emergency. The effect of this principle may be positive or negative, depending on several mitigating circumstances. Some benefits which may be derived when one spouse saves (a small amount of money) in secret include:

1. It often comes in handy in an emergency, when all other avenues of meeting the financial demands of a situation may have failed,
2. It may force the other partner to rethink their attitude towards saving and encourage thriftiness,

There are also many disadvantages which are associated with saving in secret, including:

1. It may harbor suspicion from the other partner that the secret saver is possibly having an extramarital relationship from which financial support is being

received,

2. The partner who is not saving may feel inadequate in not being as prudent as the saver. This sense of inadequacy could challenge the non-saver to improve in this area, or it could fuel further disillusion in a spouse who finds it difficult to be disciplined in this area.

3. Both partners may become very cagey about their finances in an attempt to 'out-save' the other,

4. The saver may become frustrated by the undisciplined nature of the other in this area and resort to lavish spending,

The system of undisclosed savings between spouses does not promote cleaving in their marriage since one or both partners may not be committed to working as a team. However, there are instances where one partner is really not as conscientious as the other in managing finance, despite genuine efforts made by the other to promote this discipline. Christians are not expected to be inconsiderate. However, unless a spouse is mature in spirit, soul and body, they are likely to show weakness in these and other vital areas of the marriage. With encouragement, prayer and loving guidance from each other, the church council and even professional help where necessary, each partner will achieve the correct discipline in financial management.

> Make your plans so big that you would fail if God is not in them. Dr. Robert Schuler, Sr.

Forward financial planning during courtship

"What are some of the financial considerations which a courting couple should take into account even before they are married?"

There is hardly a sane adult who enters marriage with the preconception that throughout their marriage they will live in abject poverty with no likelihood of dramatically improving their standard of living. Even though the initial stage of the marriage may not be as the couple may have desired, the most ambitious couples would consistently work arduously at improving their standard of living. The financial position of the family would improve substantially as the couple prayerfully plans and executes their plans in unison. For this reason many couples are willing to forgo even the high standard of living which they may have been accustomed to prior to their marriage, in order to acquire their own material possessions as a family.

The Christian couple who is embarking on marriage would usually be asked by the Marriage Counselor how ready they are to manage the financial responsibilities of marriage. A review may be made of the assets which they are taking into marriage. These may include:

1. The amount of salary earned by one or both of them, and the potential for and efforts which are being made to improve their financial position. This would include if they are engaging in, or embarking on a program to improve the standard of their education, acquiring other skills to enable them to command a higher salary and/or engaging in other activities which have the potential to improve their standard of living.

2. If they are involved in any business ventures, they may be asked whether or not they are implementing a strategy to increase the net income of the business by expanding the current operation and/or introducing new product lines, for example.

3. The likelihood of their parents or other relatives leaving an inheritance for them. The option of winning the pools, national bingo or lottery or other forms of gambling obviously would not be considered, since Christians are not expected to engage in these activities. However, Christians are expected to use their talents to earn a living for themselves and family. This may include establishing commercial ventures such as a cottage industry, farming, selling of fruits and vegetable and animals, where possible, even if it is on a small scale. They may also engage in the rearing of poultry and other farming activities even if the produce is consumed by the family, relatives and other close associates.

Many of these activities can blossom into lucrative business ventures or at least to secure an additional source of income for the family and/or reduce their expenditure. Farming is also an activity which can be a source of relaxation while flowers will beautify the home and its environment. The more talented among us, may be involved in commercial art, writing, singing and/or playing a musical instrument professionally, for example.

The fundamental principle of lasting spiritual and material prosperity is to give our lives to the Lord. We then have to observe all of His decrees and commands including the paying of our tithes and the giving of our offering, time, talents, and assisting the poor and needy; so that He can give us more to give to others.

As outlined earlier, it is important that we have a vision of what we are desirous of achieving as individuals and also as a family, and in other areas of our lives such as our business activities. The following principles are reiterated in Habakkuk 2:2, 3: "*2And the Lord answered me and said, write the vision and engrave it so plainly upon tablets that everyone who passes may (be able to) read (it easily and quickly) as he hastens by. 3For the vision is yet for an appointed time and it hastens the end (fulfillment); it will not deceive or disappoint. Though it tarry, wait (earnestly) for it, because it will surely come, it will not be behind hand on its appointed day.*"

It is important to have a macro vision with regards to one's whole life as a guidepost, and as a source of inspiration and a reminder of what one's objectives are. In the same way there can also be micro-visions for individual areas of one's life such as what one expects to achieve from a business venture and the material possessions which the family is aspiring to achieve over a given time period. The projections are usually based on what the couple has brought into the marriage and what is realistically within their ability to achieve, and what they believe God will provide. The projections can be subdivided into short, medium and long-term goals. The priority and composition of such a statement will be based on the projected earning capacity of the family and projected expenditure.

Material security should not be the main criteria for a woman to agree to marry her suitor. However, it is at least important that a responsible suitor be in a position to show that he is well able to adequately provide for his future family. The questions which is often asked in this area is; What about Christians living in poorer communities or where one is called to serve in poorer communities, where it may be necessary to take one's entire family to live in such communities? It should be noted that the Lord has promised to satisfy all of our needs and not our wants, once we are walking in His ways. There are occasions when the Lord, being the epitome of an ideal parent, will 'spoil' us and meet even our wants. However, we should be like Job and be prepared to serve Him even if He chooses not to deliver us from a life of material want. Our love for and service to Him should be premised primarily on who He is and not merely the benefits which we derive from serving Him.

After attaining, by God's grace, a significant target, a couple often reminisces on the struggles which they went through and how the Lord gave them the inspiration, encouragement, grace and strength to successfully achieve their objectives. As mile stones are achieved, the couple will be encouraged to launch out for bigger ones. It is wise that the couple should strive to enjoy a period of rest, usually during their formative years when they can sit back and enjoy the fruits of their labor. Some of the excitement of pushing to attain targets would have been lost during the period of rest. It does not infer that life loses its meaning after this stage for there are always targets to be achieved in areas of our lives as individuals and as a family.

In the process of attempting to achieve targets, unless a couple has really mastered the process of cleaving, their marriage can be plagued with much tension from attempting to conserve on spending even in vital areas. For this reason it is important that both spouses are fully committed to budget wisely and execute their plan in the best possible way and is not merely one superimposing their will on the other. There is also the need to consistently assure each other that they are working for the common good of the family, and that the intensive sacrifice at least at the initial stage of their marriage will go a long way to enhance the quality of their marriage. It is also vital that such projections take into account the needs for periods of relaxation and review of plans to assess whether or not the period of sacrifice is having any serious negative effects on any member of the family.

A wife who enters marriage with just about all of the material amenities already provided for by her husband, according to the norms of the society, would have failed to experience the very unique experience of building together. Of course many couples would be more at peace if they do not have to struggle together, for a period of struggle can create much tension and dissatisfaction, depending on how intense the process is and also the disposition of the couple.

There are several advantages which the couple who marries into a financially comfortable standard of living experiences. Since the couple does not have to bother about acquiring the basic amenities, they will be in a better position to concentrate more on investments, as illustrated by the household of the virtuous wife. The couple will be in a better position to plan on how to expand their material resources, of course taking care in avoiding the pitfall as depicted in the parable of the rich fool as Jesus told in Luke 12:16- 21. (The rich fool was making plans to build bigger barns to store the abundance of grains which his fields had produced so that he can relax, eat drink and be merry. He neglected important principles such as giving thanks to God for his abundance and he was not contemplating assisting the needy from his wealth). Instead they have the unique opportunity to seek ways of giving more of their finance, time and other resources towards the spreading of the Gospel.

> Most persons can transform some activity which they conduct into an income generating business venture. Even if it is a small project, it can grow to the extent where it reduces our expenditure and may even complement our income. The more entrepreneurial persons may be able to expand to the extent where the project grows into a full time business even and employ others.

Saving practices of married couples

"Is there an ideal method of saving for a married couple?"

An area that tests how much cleaving exists in a marriage is how a couple manages their savings. Several methods are available to save with a financial institution, including:

1. All savings are made in the name of one spouse. It is usually the husband who does this in several traditional societies. This may be because the wife is illiterate, she may not have identification documents, and/or she may feel that her husband can better manage situations such as banking, or he may be domineering. In this situation it is advisable that the wife is kept abreast of all major financial transactions. She should also be encouraged to correct any deficiency which may prevent her from being involved in banking, for she should be an equal partner in this and every aspect of the marriage.
2. In some instances a couple maintains specific accounts to finance individual projects such as to purchase a house and to educate the children.
3. The couple has individual savings, current and/or other

accounts and also one or several joint account/s.

4. The couple has separate bank accounts.

It should be noted that any one of the above methods is not necessarily superior to the others, for the strategy employed in saving is usually primarily influenced by the individual circumstances of the couple. In some instances it would be imperative that a couple have separate checking accounts, for example, unless it is stipulated that either of them can be the sole signature to the account. At the same time, if the couple has a high level of understanding and commitment, they may find it useful to save in the name of one spouse who is responsible for accounting and for all major transactions, yet wholly accountable to the other partner.

The system of saving which has promoted much unity in many marriages involves the couple having a joint account into which they channel their savings. Once there is accurate disclosure of the income and expenditure of the family, funds budgeted for savings can be deposited there. The discussion of the bank statements will enable the couple to keep abreast of all transactions on the account. Among the disadvantages of having a joint account, particularly if the couple agrees that both of them should have to authorize withdrawals, is that in any emergency one spouse may not be available to sign the check, or may be indisposed to make the withdrawal.

The common system of saving, particularly, in affluent societies, is that even if the couple has a joint account, each spouse may also have individual accounts for personal transactions. On occasions, such as when a spouse is traveling on an extended journey, the need for one to make individual financial decisions will be necessary. The joint account may be used for the main savings of the family, while the individual account may be used to finance the individual expenditure of each spouse during the month.

> The family budget should be prayerfully formulated since our plans should be consistent with the will of God for the lives of each member of the family.

Pros and cons of couples saving and investing

"Are there distinct financial advantages in a married couple saving and investing collectively, rather than individually?"

Deuteronomy 32:30 states: *"³⁰How could one have routed a thousand, and two put a myriad (ten thousand) to flight unless their Rock had sold them, the Lord has given them up."*

This verse is often used when referring to the compounded strength which unity produces. A couple who is united in Christ will be able to achieve ten times more than if they operate independently. This law is demonstrated naturally in several ways. It is stated, for example, that two horses which are able to synchronize their efforts, will be able to pull as much as seven times more weight than they would have been able to pull independently.

Married couple can also apply the principle of collectivity and reap substantial benefits. For this reason, a family who budget together and pool their financial and other resources will be able to achieve substantially more than if they are doing so independently. When spouses save independently, and are very cagy about disclosing their financial plans and resources, it leads to much distrust and disharmony. Such couples may only be collective in emergencies and even then, they may still be apprehensive about disclosing the full extent of their resources and what they can do to assist. Therefore, they conduct independent financial and other transactions and they may actually be competing to out-save each other or to secure various assets. The devil obviously delights in such situation, for there will be so many avenues for him to create distrust and animosity in such a family.

When a couple pools their financial and other resources, they will be able to purchase items cash, for example, instead of one spouse paying the huge hire purchase interest when purchasing an item on hire purchase. Collectively, they could have purchased the item cash and use the saving from the transaction to invest in a venture which realizes significant returns. The couple will also be able to save and invest far more and generate higher levels of return together than if they were doing so independently. Very often the return from the accumulated resources of the couple would be compounded and generate a far higher return than that of the individuals.

Methods of budgeting for the family

"Is it necessarily wrong for one spouse to budget for the family?"

An elderly friend related to me that from the time he was married he has always given his wife his entire salary for her to formulate the budget. This he contends saves him from the tedious process of looking into minute details of the daily expenditure of the family. Since she does not have a secular job, she is more familiar with the detailed financial requirements of the family. It also saves him, he contends, from the possibility of her blaming him when there is a shortfall of finance before the end of the month. In addition, since she is familiar with his average daily financial requirements, unless a major financial demand occurs, she places in his pants pocket each morning the amount she feels he would need to spend on that day.

Some persons would find this system commendable and would congratulate him on his confidence in his wife's judgment and her prudence. In addition, this system must have been successful for them, since they have their own home, which is well furnished and they have a good car and several other major assets. This system obviously works for many other couples for there is a strong cultural and spiritual unity that fosters this level of commitment. On the contrary, some persons, particularly those who view the role of the husband as that of the 'boss,' would deem this practice of the husband as irresponsible, since he is not taking full responsibility in assisting in the planning and implementation of the family budget. Many persons today in the light of the high divorce rate (even among Christians), see the need to maintain personal standards, and/or to continue a certain level of personal autonomy, would also see this practice as an endangerment of welfare of the husband. The converse scenario may occur where a wife willingly, or by force, gives her husband her entire salary and the two of them, or he alone plans the budget of the family.

In some wealthier families, a husband may decide that his wife should use her entire salary for her personal expenditure. This may be because he is well able to support his family. There is wisdom in the couple implementing the system which is best suited to the unique situation of their family. It is important that the couple is at peace with the budget and that they are committed to ensuring that it is successfully implemented as far as possible. Despite how systematic the budget is, provision has to be made for changes to the forecast. Therefore, contingency funds should be in place where necessary and/or possible, to cater for financial demands which were not budgeted for.

Whose money is it?

Is the salary which I earn mine, that of my family or is it the Lord's?

Christians must recognize that the salary which they earn is in fact the Lord's money, since we are His, and everything which we have belongs to Him. Therefore, what we are budgeting on is in fact God's money. We should thus be committed to being good stewards of God's property. We should seek His guidance to enable us to formulate the best possible budget and to implement it with diligence and in love.

> Since God owns the earth and everything that is in it, every financial decision is spiritual in nature.

Financial planning for engaged couple

"We are about to be married, what are some of the more important challenges which we can expect in managing our finances when we marry?"

It is important to recognize from the onset that we all have different historical experiences of the way our parents and other close associates manages/ed money, our individual way of managing money, our values, perceptions, plans for the future, our ability to reason, and just about everything about us. Jehovah has presented these differences, yet He has decreed that 'the two shall become one' in the marriage covenant. For this reason it is essential that from the early stage of the relationship of the couple that engage in practices such as that they:

1. Fully disclose their indebtedness, if any,
2. Disclose their attitude in managing money and assets in general,
3. Agree on issues such as budgeting, spending, saving, and investment,

Some of the influences of in the way we manage finances include:

1. **The way our parents manage/ed their finances and the impact that it has had on our lives.** The impact of parental influence on our lives can be positive or negative. A person coming from a poor background may be very conservative in the way they manage finance. Some persons may be very conservative in the spending, save and invest wisely and generally have a

positive outlook in managing their financial and other resources. Conversely, many such persons are lavish spenders in an attempt to compensate for the deprivation which they have suffered when they were younger. On the other side of the spectrum, a person from a wealthy family may have been exposed to the 'power' which persons who are perceived to have much money have on the poorer segment of society. Such persons may be arrogant and resentful to a partner who attempts to curb excessive spending in areas which he/she deems as non-essential. There are, however, persons who irrespective of their upbringing, are prepared to work with their spouse to foster the best financial and other management strategies for the common good of the family.

2. **One or both spouses may value themselves and the other based on their earning power, background and other material standards.** For this reason a spouse who is earning more than the other may be very demanding and arrogant. A husband who is the sole breadwinner of the family, for example, may demand that his wife be at his 'beck and call' even at the expense of more important personal and family needs. Similarly, a wife who is earning more than her husband may despise him for not being more resourceful in meeting the financial demands of the family. This may also have a negative effect on their sexual relationship and other areas of the marriage where she demands to be the 'boss'. The husband in such a relationship may become resentful of his inability to meet the financial needs of the family and may retaliate by becoming resentful and even abusive to his wife and children.

3. **One spouse may place a higher premium on the value of money than the other.** This may result in one spouse being conservative while the other is lavish in their spending habits.

4. **The spouse who contributes the higher percentage of income to the resources of the family may establish sole ownership over assets** which should rightfully belong **to the collective family.** Such behavior does not foster the unity, growth and development of the family.

From a legal perspective, most countries recognize the income of both spouses as a joint entity in a marriage framework. The rationale for this is that even though one spouse is earning more than the other, even if there was only one breadwinner in the family, the contribution of the other in terms of managing the wellbeing of the family is considered as being equally as important. The parameter of the law also recognizes that there is an emotional, spiritual and other contribution by spouses which may be just as important as the financial contribution of the other.

| Practical Methods for Managing Financial |

"What are some of the practical methods which I can employ to manage my material resources?"

There are several principles which we can implement in order to manage our financial resources and achieve the level of success which we desire. These include:

1. **Know who you are in Christ. This will be achieved as we apply the many promises which the Lord has given us in His word to our lives.**
2. **Formulate realistic** *individual* **financial goals and that of family, and write them down.** These should be for the short, medium and long-term.
3. **Seek to increase your income while reducing expenditure** will increase our cash flow and make more funds available for saving and investing.
4. **Establish a realistic budget which the family is comfortable living with.** This budget should place permanence on features such as:
   a. **The payment of the Lord's tithes and giving an offering in areas such as helping the poor, supporting a minister and/or ministry.**
   b. **Make our money work for us.** This may be achieved as we save and invest in excess of 20% of the disposable income of the family in high interest or income generating accounts or schemes. There are millions of persons who retire and have to depend on welfare or live in poverty due to improper budgeting sickness and/or other circumstances.
   c. **Get out of debt and avoid unnecessary debt particularly for consumer items.**
   d. **Do not be merely content to live within our means, based on the traditional concept that we seek to merely make out with what we have, rather, we should seek to improve our means, which entails budgeting wisely and saving and investing prudently.**

e. *Allocating* our resources prudently for short-term needs such as the payment of utility bills, food, clothing, to meet emergencies, and also to attain medium and long-term goals.

f. Avoid unnecessary spending in areas such as insurance coverage over our lives and assets.

♦ *Take advantage of tax and other concessions* which are available to enable us to increase our disposable income and/or increase our savings and investment. This includes the establishment of accounts such as the Individual Retirement Account, Mutual Funds and saving in a credit union.

♦ *Maintain a diversified investment portfolio* in an attempt to cushion a negative effect on one or more investments failing or not generate the projected level of returns.

♦ *Avoid overspending on the purchase of a house, motor car and other large expenditure by securing appropriate guidance and not seek to live above our means.*

♦ *We should not neglect our spiritual responsibility of leaving an inheritance for our 'children's children.'* The implication of a prudent estate plan will prevent waste of resources due to high estate tax, and avoid division in the family since a will was not made by the decrease and also allocate or resources in a manner which we desire before we are deceased.

Forward financial planning during courtship

"We are a mature couple who were both married before and both have children from our previous marriages and considerable amount of assets. Is it unscriptural for us to have a prenuptial agreement?"

The Bible clearly states that when two persons enter a marital covenant, the two of them should become one. There are circumstances outside of this relationship which should not be neglected since they may have a bearing on the marital relationship, particularly in circumstances as you have mentioned. In this instance, the assets which have been acquired in a previous marriages do not only belong to the adults but may have been awarded as a result of a divorce procedure, to the children of the previous marriage also and the parents may be custodians of these assets for the children. In such circumstances there must be a clear demarcation of what are legally the children's and what belongs to the new spouses. It may be necessary to seek advice from a Christian legal practitioner for further guidance on this issue.

There are circumstances such as when a spouse legally adopts the offspring of their spouse and thus becomes their joint custodian. Even so, the assets from their biological parent can be protected from any possibility of unfair or unwise practices of the adopted parent or new couple and especially in the unfortunate even of a divorce between the current couple.

Under a normal marital relationship, the principle of a prenuptial agreement contradicts the intent and spirit of the Biblical concept of 'one flesh.' However, there are peculiar circumstances where there is a legal obligation to separate assets acquired before the union, as mentioned in paragraphs one and two.

Precedent management of our financial resources

"What criteria can be used in deciding when we should consume, save or invest?"

Several times each day of our matured lives we are confronted with several basic financial decisions. They include:
1. Should we engage in a consumption or investment with money at our disposal?
2. What would be the implications of delaying the decision to consume and instead engage in a prudent investment program?

When the decision is to engage in consumption, we have to further consider whether or not the decision is based on a necessity or merely as a result of the quest to fulfill a want rather than a need. It should be noted that there is nothing inherently wrong in spending money in purchasing things which we just enjoy for the wholesome pleasure which we derive from the activity and/or item. The fact of the matter is that the Lord very often provides us with 'more than enough' for our pleasure. This principle can be supported by several passages in the Bible which attest to the fact that He is far more loving and caring than our earthly parents who delight in seeing their children enjoy themselves. The difference is usually in our attitude towards material and other resources at our disposal. Are we so greedy that we merely spend all of our resources on ourselves and family and are uncaring about assisting the poor, giving to the work of the Lord and other noble deeds? The reward of the contrasting groups can be seen in the life of the 'rich fool' who displeased the Lord and was put to death since he desired to build bigger barns and expand his affluence and did not acknowledge the Lord as the source of his wealth and give to the poor, for example. This contrasts with a person who gives to the Lord and assists the poor and needy and has blessings 'pressed down and running over'.

> A dollar spent on prudent investment has the capacity to generate additional dollars in the future. A dollar spent on consumption is very often a dollar which would not generate additional income, unless it is spent on items which would contribute to our wellbeing and that of others and would enable us to produce additional output.

Before embarking on the preparation of the budget, the couple must have preconceived objectives of what they intend to achieve in the short, medium and long-term as a family. They must be able to prioritize their expenditure, giving more weight to items which are important to them. At the early stage of their marriage their priority may be to acquire furnishings for the home, commence saving for the children's education, purchasing a house or a car, for example. They must be able to allocate enough funds in these areas while not neglecting important considerations such as the need for leisure, making provision for adequate health care and for personal development such as the payment of tuition for one or both of them as an investment to increase their income in the near future.

We all budget in one form or another even though we may not have a structured approach to allocate the money at our disposal. An incorrect way of budgeting is to spend all of the money we earn as soon as we are paid and have to live on a minimal amount for the remainder of the month, or rely on credit cards and other forms of credit to supplement the shortfall until the next payday. Sadly, this is the fate of most salary earners. I can recall the philosophy of a former colleague who would have a lavish meal at a restaurant the day after she received her salary. Her rationale was that after budgeting she would most likely not be able to spend so much on a meal for the remainder of the month. Of course with prudent budgeting, she may be able to enjoy at least another meal before the end of the month at a restaurant, even though it may have to be less expensive.

The philosophy of paying one's self first

"Is there necessarily anything wrong in the philosophy of financial advisors who contend that we should pay ourselves first before allocating to any other expenditure?"

Many financial counselors advocate that we should **pay ourselves** before allocating funds to any other source. For some persons this means spending ten percent, or more, on entertainment, since they feel that they have worked long and strenuous hours under difficult conditions. Therefore, it is only fair that they should enjoy a well deserved period of relaxation, involvement in sporting and other activities of one's choice. For others it infers engaging in saving and investing a given amount per month in preparation for retirement or to achieve other goals. Even though the latter strategy seems plausible, there are several possible flaws which must be considered, particularly for Christians. They include:

1. Our first consideration should be the tithes and offering which go towards the financing of the work of the Lord. Giving to the Lord is an act of obedience and love for Him. God considers anything less than our first ten percent as dishonor, and refusal to tithe and give of one's offering as robbery. Confessing our love for Him, without right actions which expressed that love, is similar to faith without works, dead!

2. As a rule, as far as possible, every dollar of the budget, particularly for a couple, should be spent on the collective needs of the family, and only a small amount should be unaccounted for. Even in allocating a percentage of the salary for personal expenditure, an account should be given to the other on how each person spent their allowance.

3. The richer segment of the population earns so much that they do not have to worry about overspending in any given month. However, even if they do not manage their resources, they will face financial difficulties in the long run. Thus, the more prudent will attempt to structure their spending to enable them to achieve the financial objectives which they are aiming for.

A common error which many persons make when they begin to work with a budget is that they expect to see an instant change in the amount of money they can save and in the reduction of the debt. The process of achieving the ultimate objective usually takes some time for most of us since there may also be bits of indiscipline by one or both spouses as well as other factors, such as the low level of income coming into the family (which is beyond one's immediate control).

As Christians our tithes should be our first expenditure. For this reason many Christians practice the principle of paying their tithes (10%) as a percentage of their gross income, that is, income before taxes, National Insurance Scheme contribution, medical, loan and other deductions, which may be deducted from their wages or salaries. They also deduct a percentage from the remaining 80% to contribute as their offering. Some persons deduct 10% or even more of their gross or net income, as they prefer, and would either save that amount and/or invest it in some high income generating activity, or at least long term investment. They would utilize the remaining 70% to meet their living expenses. It is a commendable practice if from very early in our working life we can develop and maintain the discipline of living off of less than 70% of our income. This would entail much sacrifice for most of us but as we see our savings grow and the interest, dividend and/or whatever form of return accumulate, many persons are encouraged to consume less and save and invest more of their income.

Managing excessive spending

"What are some methods which are commonly used to manage the spending of individuals or a family?"

Some persons, particularly those who are paid in cash, use the **envelope method** to assist them to achieve discipline in their spending. They would have several labeled envelopes in which they put in the amount of money budgeted for each of the major expenditures which has to be utilized over the period of the budget. As a part of the expenditure is paid, they would record on the envelope the amount spent and reduce the total amount of money recorded on the envelope by that amount. Categories such as **House Rent/Mortgage Payment, Car Expenses, Food, Transportation, Entertainment, Medical Expenses and other Emergencies would be recorded on the respective envelopes**. Some persons would have an envelope for contingency which they would retain during the month in the event that there is an emergency. Once they are able to maintain a balance in any envelope at the end of the month, they would save that amount. The disadvantage of the envelope method is that unless they are very disciplined, the additional amount of money could be a source of temptation to overspend, as opposed to saving in a bank account, where they would not have ready access to it. Money kept at home may also be stolen. Even in an emergency, once the money at the bank is in a checking account, or if they have a debit, credit or other plastic bank card, from which funds can be withdrawn, the bank account is easily accessible.

The application of wisdom is one of the best principles which cause persons to comply with the discipline of a well-structured budget. Some of the consequences of not formulating and consistently adhering to a well-structured budget include huge debt, the failure to attain realistic financial goals, disunity in the family and divorce. Many persons are encouraged when they realize how much they are able to save, the amount of debt they are able to pay off and other positive results achieved as they undertake the discipline of implementing the guidance of the budget. A parallel can be drawn between a budget and a well structured fitness program, which includes the adherence to a discipline spiritual life, a sensible diet program, exercise, right eating and other disciplines to reduce weight and maintain a healthy soul, spirit and body. Highly visible results may not be seen during the first month of the program. However, as the program is consistently maintained over a number of months, tangible evidence of the program becomes noticeable in ways such as a fit body, an alert mind and nicely fitted clothing. This discipline has to be continued over the greater part of a person's life time for it to achieve and maintain the best results.

> *A couple who consistently suffer from serous financial challenges usually experience other difficulties in areas of their marriage such as poor communication, commitment and cooperation, unless they have mastered the principles of trusting in the Lord to see them through every difficulty which they encounter.*

Celebrating the emergence from the debt

"Is it unreasonable to have a celebration of one's emergence from a string of debts with a reasonable amount of overspending during the following month?"

The question which is frequently asked is, "What should we do after we have been successful in getting out of debt and achieving other objectives of the budget over the short, medium and long-term?" Some of the prudent strategies are:

1. **Increase our giving to the Lord** since this will be a seed for financial and other blessings. We should not merely aspire and embark on a program to 'build bigger barns.' Instead, we should give back to Him a portion

of our earnings and other forms of thanksgiving and in acknowledging Him as the source of all blessings.

2. **Increase savings and investment** in mutual funds, certificates of deposit, shares and in one or several business ventures.

3. **Avoid getting into other unnecessary debt again.**

Challenges in formulating and implementing the family budget

"What are some of the common problems encountered by families in formulating and implementing a workable budget?"

There are several **difficulties associated with the budget** of some persons. They include:

1. **Budgeting on an irregular source of income** such as casual or seasonal workers, persons who are frequently ill or are not able to secure or maintain fulltime employment.

2. **Budgeting on a reduced income** such as instances when a person is demoted, loses his job or retires. This is usually a traumatic process as the family is forced to restructure their lifestyle to cope with the reduced income.

3. **One spouse, who opposed the discipline of the budget, refuses to assist in formulating and implementing the budget.** These are usually difficult situations to manage and can be overcome by prayer, counseling and by the partner, who is pro-budget, lovingly explaining and demonstrating the benefits which are derived from working with a budget.

4. **The process of preparing the budget is viewed by some opponents as being merely a futile period of worrying** before we do our own thing and spend the money as we please, since most of us do not earn enough to be able to afford a comfortable standard of living, at any rate.

A large number of individuals, families, corporate entities, governments, church councils and other agencies can attest to the significant achievements which are attained as a result of budgeting and executing the mandate of the budget.

It is amazing how many persons simple overspend, indulge in unnecessary purchases and literally 'waste money' because they cannot **balance a checkbook**. The process of balancing the checkbook includes subtracting bank charges due to the return of checks, service charge, overdraft fees and any other bank charges from the bank balance at a particular day. At the back of some check books there is a section where a number of items can be recorded. They include the check number, date of issue of the check, who the check was paid to, the amount of the check, deposits made on the account, and the running balance of the account.

Mastering this simple technique would prevent the wastage of money and much embarrassment when the bank has to return a check because of insufficient funds on the account. This damages the credit rating of the issuer with the person to whom the check was paid. Apart from having to pay the amount owed, plus the charge for the returned check, some suppliers would take the check to the police, where the issuer can be charged and prosecuted for conducting a fraudulent transaction.

A following table is an example of how the running balance on a check book is maintained:

No.	Date	Particulars	Checks		Deposits		Balance	
20	May 12/14	H. C Trading Inc. (fan)	240	20	500	-	3,542	58
21	May 14/14	The People's Cathedral (tithe)	300	00	-	-	3,242	58
22	May 20/14	Deposit - sales from garden project			150	-	3,392	58

Table 5.6 Running Balance Table on Check Book

In this way the holder of a checkbook can keep an accurate account of what is happening on the account. Deductions must be made of amounts withdrawn with an ABM card or other methods and any service or other charges deducted from the account. The process of balancing the checkbook is also assisted by the use of *tele-banking* services at some banks, where the account holders can have access to information on the account via the telephone at any time of the day and conduct transactions online. The bank statement which is usually posted to customers at the end of each month also assists in the process of managing the account.

Care has to be taken that there is no blatant discrimination in the allocation of the budget to the disadvantage of any members of the family. As far as possible each member of the family should have enough clothing and other essential items. When there is an acute shortfall in the budget, nonessential items and those which can be delayed may be omitted. Some of the methods which couples use to allocate the budget are:

1. *Ensuring that all of her financial needs are met*. Once there is agreement in a marriage where the wife is not working, or where she has a low income, an allowance may be allocated each month for her to take care of her personal effects and whatever else she chooses to use it for. This may be in keeping with the principle that the husband should be a better provider than his wife's father in that he has the solemn responsibility of providing for her material needs. This is a commendable gesture. Many husbands are unable to meet this criterion, at least in the initial stage of the marriage.

2. A man may still provide an allowance for his wife even though she is employed with a commercial entity, since he feels obligated to still provide for her beyond her earnings. It is particularly beneficial if the wife could become involved in some form of lucrative investment, and a part of the profit from such a venture is used to expand the investment and for the benefit of the family.

Proverbs 16:3 states: "[3]**Commit your works to the Lord, and your plans will be established**."

Whatever the method of budgeting and the system used for distributing the finances of the family, it is important that there is agreement between members of the family. It is commendable where each spouse has enough personal cash at their disposal where they can bless each other in purchasing, even if it is merely little gifts, for each other, as a demonstration of love and appreciation for each other. The sad thing is that far too many Christian couples cannot meet the basic necessities of life and the area of giving is often stifled. Even there, the couple should squeeze some money in the budget on leisure and on ensuring that the personal effects of each member of the family are met.

Some of the ways by which we can be guided on the correct budgetary and other decisions are by answering questions such as the following:

1. Is it consistent with the principles of the Bible?

2. Is one's conscience at peace with the decision? Care must be taken that one's conscience is in tune with spiritual matters and that one is not given over to a reprobate mind because of one's consistent disobedience.

3. As far as possible, there should be agreement between the spouses, where applicable, and other members of the family. Care must also be taken to ensure that when there are disagreements, that the decision which is adopted is consistent with the leadership of the Lord for the specific issue.

As far as possible, priority should be given to the fulfillment of long-term goals, particularly when it is possible to forgo some short-term, less important pleasures.

It is very important that we engage in saving and investing not only for the immediate future but **our planning should also be medium and long term**. For many persons the stages are 1 to 5, 5 to 10, and above 10 years, respectively. The emphasis which is placed on the various stages is usually dependent on factors such as the period of our lives, our financial strength and investment as well as the other opportunities which are available to us.

1. **Short-term goals** include having enough money to be able to finance our immediate consumption needs such as food, clothing, medical care, utilities, transportation and other expenses.
2. **Medium-term goals** for the newlywed, for example, may include saving to accumulate enough money for the down payment and closing expenses of a mortgage, the purchase of one or several motor vehicles, and the commencement of saving for the secondary and tertiary education of the children.
3. **Long-term** financial goals may include accumulating at least $500,000 for retirement, for having a debt free home, and for having enough capital to commence a well establish business.

It is not enough to have lofty ideas if we are not disciplined enough or willing to seek the counsel of the Lord and other believers and implement the best strategies at our disposal in order to achieve them. Planning without implementing the plan to realize the objectives is tantamount to building sand castles on the beach. They will either be washed away by the sea or destroyed by others, if we do not destroy them ourselves.

Another important area in financial planning is in **whose name items such as the house, car, furniture and other major assets will be bought.** This is another area which shows the level of cleaving in marriage, particularly in societies where the title of properties does not go automatically to the husband. Usually, it is better if major assets are purchased jointly in the name of both spouses to avoid complications that occur after the death of the spouse in whose name items were bought and where a will was not prepared, for example. If the motive for joint ownership, on the other hand is an insurance against loss of possession in the event of a divorce, the couple is standing on shaky grounds.

Wives should be familiar with items such as budgeting for the family, knowing where the title deeds for the property, the bank book, birth, academic and other certificates and other documents concerning the affairs of the family are stored for safe keeping. This is not only as a precaution for eventualities such as death of the husband, if indeed she outlives him, but rather she has the right to such important information since there is no such title as major and minor shareholders in marriage, but rather they are equal partners.

Even if the husband is classified as the Chief Executive Officer (CEO), it is noted that in most corporate organizations it is the Deputy CEO who manages the daily operations, while the CEO attends external meetings, much like the Virtuous Wife who was alluded to in Proverbs 31. This is not a dogmatic approach, since a husband may be forced to stay at home because he has been made redundant, or because of sickness, for example, while his wife pursues a secular career.

Proverbs 11:29 states: "[29]**Those who trouble their households will inherit wind, and fools will be servant to the wise**." There are so many examples in our societies of persons who deliberately promote disharmony in the home will be severely punished by the Lord, for the Lord places a high premium on the fostering of harmony in the home.

We have to be good stewards of the financial and other resources which God has placed at our disposal. When we master this principle, it will be transmitted to our children and to their children and to others. When parents fail to do their part in this and other important areas, it may hinder the fulfillment of the plan of God for future generations. Many parents believe the Biblical interpretation of training up a child in the way of the

Lord relates only to spiritual matters. The fact is that God is concerned that each child has a well-rounded personality. We have to be good mentors by leading with good examples to our children in the way we manage our financial and other resources. Instead of spending our income in attempting to maintain a lavish lifestyle and live above our means, care must be taken that we are prudent so that our children can learn from our success.

> *The family budget is the mechanism which highlights the financial resources which are available to execute particular aims and objectives of the planners. The budget may include the allocation of time, financial, personnel and other resources for the fulfillment of particular goals.*

The unmanaged family budget

"What are some of the common symptoms of an unmanaged family budget?"

It is remarkable how haphazard our control mechanism usually is when there is no clearly defined target which the family is pursuing. Manifestations of an unmanaged budget include:

1. Items which are not really important are purchased and investments which are not lucrative may be undertaken, simply because a person or family did not have a specific objective to attain. They seemingly may achieve many material and other forms of successes, but when they reflect on their achievements, they will realize that they would have been more successful had they planned and executed their plans in unity. In addition, many of the short-term successes do not provide them substantial long-term benefits.
2. There is much duplication in the items which the couple purchases, in some instances; very often in an attempt to outdo each other in what they purchase.
3. They save separately and are usually very cagey about disclosing the amount of their savings and spending.
4. One may try to persuade the other to take care of the major expenditures which will enable them to save more.
5. Major items are purchased in the name of the spouse who contributed most of the cash or who

will be paying the higher percentage of the higher purchase installment. There may also be bickering about who owns which items and therefore, should have exclusive or more use of it.

6. Short-term successes are sacrificed for more lucrative long-term ones.
7. The couple lives together for an extended number of years and yet does not have much evidence that they have attained many material possessions.

Guidelines on making prudent financial decisions

"What are some of the important guidelines which would assist us in arriving at prudent financial decisions?"

Some of the ways by which we are guided on the correct budgetary and other decisions include the following questions:

1. **Is it consistent with the principles of the Bible?**
2. **Are the members of the family who are in a position to understand the budget at peace with it, at least on the majority of occasions**? There may be occasions such as during a major budgetary shortfall when less essential items will have to be omitted from the budget. This may cause dissatisfaction to persons who have to undergo the period of deprivation. Even then, the need for effective communication to 'sell' the reason for the shortfall should be conducted. Care must be taken to ensure that when there are disagreements, that the decision which is adopted is consistent with the leadership of the Lord for that specific issue. Care must be taken that your conscience is in tune with spiritual matters and that you may not have been given up to a reprobate because your conscience was severed because of persistence disobedience.

It is important that a couple **plan their work and work their plan** in an effort to ensure that there is a high level of cohesion in their marriage. Failure to do this will result in a situation where at the end of their lives, as a matter of fact even before, they would realize that they are not achieving the high level of success which they would have as if they were united. Such a couple will be called unfaithful stewards in managing the financial, spiritual and other resources which the Lord has placed at their disposal.

The process of assessing the areas of success and failure during the execution of a plan is very important. Post budget evaluation is absolutely important at the end of the budget period so that an objective appraisal can be made of lessons which could be learnt from the last budget. A review of possible better alternatives of how this could have been achieved will enable us to better manage future budgets.

CONCLUSION

This chapter reviewed many of the fundamental issues which we have to focus on in managing our financial and other material resources. It is so sad to observe the large number of families which are destroyed because couples have not been able to collectively manage their financial and other resources. Most persons are of the opinion that the most important reason for their lack of financial success is that they do not earn enough. The reality is that in most instances the presence of an acute financial problem is primarily as a result of indiscipline in the way we mismanage the resources which we have at our disposal. When we play our part in giving to the Lord our very lives and commit all that we have to Him, He will direct our path. He gives us the ability to become wealthy. His desire is for us to have His best. If we put Him in the first place in our lives, surely He will direct our path.

It is a fact that there are millions of Christians who are poor. Many of us live in societies where there are limited resources to enable us to emerge from a state of poverty. We are also often limited by the lack of formal education, sickness, infirmity and other setbacks in life. Many persons also accept the defeat of poverty and feel that they cannot emerge from this trap. There are countless examples where the Lord has brought persons who have experienced even worst limitations to a state where they can at least live comfortably.

Many persons become disillusioned after the failure of 'get rich quick schemes' which are propagated even by Christians. This occurs when we ignore the fundamental principles of Biblical Finance, when we fail as we undergo the 'fire' of testing and trials that would enable us to succeed and to graduate to the abundance which the Lord has in store for us. If we cannot succeed at the little, how can we expect to graduate to the abundance which the Lord has in store for us? We have to be faithful in our tithes, offering and sowing other 'seeds' before we will `truly attain the state where we are not greedy, selfish and display other negative traits which hinders the flow of the abundance which the Lord has in store for us.

God does not need our money. As a matter of fact, Jesus, for example, stated that if we do not praise Him, the rocks will. The principle of giving is primarily for our benefit, for as we give, He blesses us. When we give, we set into motion God's principle of sowing and reaping. If the farmer eats the seed, there will be no harvest. Similarly, if we do not give, it hinders the fulfillment of the promise of the Lord to bless us in abundance, pressed down and running over.

Notes

****

Chapter 6: CAREER PATH AND PERSONAL DEVELOPMENT

INTRODUCTION

I t is a reality that many persons when they are old, would reflect on the number of things which they did not do even though they knew that they had the ability to accomplish them. The Lord knows the purpose which each person was created to fulfill. Once we live close to Him, like Samuel, He will reveal His purpose to us from an early age and once we are willing to accept His guidance and direction, He will enable us to fulfill our purpose.

Planning for the Future

INTRODUCTION

There are several sections of the Bible which admonish us to plan for the future, even though we must ensure that our plan much include provision for the leadership direction of the Lord. It is however, important to differentiate between planning and worrying, for in the latter we seek to infer that we are in control of our future.

Achieving prudent financial decisions

"How do I get from where I am to where I want to be?"

Many persons, even Christians, spend a lifetime not knowing the purpose for which they were created. As a result we waste valuable time and other resources attempting to find out what the Lord wants us to do. It is a basic part of the nature of a person who comes to know the Lord to attempt to find out what specific part we are to play in the kingdom of the Lord. This factor is illustrated in the lives of many persons in the Bible. The Apostle Paul, for example, in his spectacular encounter with the Lord on the road to Damascus, enquired of the Lord what He wanted him to do. Similarly, if we only find out specifically what the Lord requires of us to do, we would save valuable time and resources doing things which do not optimize our potential in Him.

> **Our attitude** in terms of savings, investments and our general financial discipline, **determines our altitude** in terms of our progress in academics, savings and investments, spiritual and other areas of our lives.

| **Making the best career** |

"What are some of the important considerations which should be taken into account when choosing a career?"

There are several implications in choosing a career path. There are usually financial implications in choosing a career since the process of training adequately to maximize one's return from the career usually involves the investment of finance, time and other valuable resources.

It is common to find parents who desire that their children be a medical doctor, a lawyer, a pilot, university professor, computer technician and other careers which generate lucrative financial returns and have some degree of respectability in the community, country and internationally. As a result many parents discourage their children from pursuing careers such as mechanical engineering, farming and other jobs where their clothing and skin are likely to be dirty, or at least untidy. Thankfully, this stigma is quickly losing its influence and most jobs are classified as important to the development of society. Many parents choose a career which they desire that a child should pursue even before they are born, and would from an early age groom the child into the desired career. As a matter of fact, they often act as God, who knew us before we were born, as highlighted in Jeremiah 1: 5: "*5Before I formed you in the womb I knew you, and before you were born I consecrated you. I appointed you a prophet to the nations.*"

There are several factors which may lead to a person pursuing a particular career. They include:

1. ***His parent/s and other elders in the family may have 'pushed' his into it***. This may be because the family has

a history where several members or close relatives are practicing a particular profession such as farmers, medical doctors, lawyers or entrepreneurs. Predecessors may have the necessary books, influence in society and other attributes which are admirable to younger generations who seek to emulate their elders. Conversely, parents and other members of the family may influence younger ones into pursuing a particular career path since it would be an asset to the family business.

2. **One has a 'natural' aptitude for a particular career.** Some persons have an innate liking for a particular career. It is common to find a person who may be struggling to attain academic pursuits, for example, if that person is placed in a kitchen, even without any formal training, that person would spend hours experimenting with various dishes and is an excellent chef or caterer. Even though a person may not be a 'born-genius,' for example, some persons seem to have an innate ability to excel in particular endeavors. It is common to find a child who from an early age declares that he wants to pursue a particular career and remain resolute in his choice and accomplishes it. Such an occurrence is usually appreciated by parents, which contrasts with other persons whose parents may be spending an enormous amount of money on them since they may change their career when they may be near to the completion of their training.

A person may, for example, decide to become a lawyer, early in life since one likes debating and admires the command which the lawyers seen on TV and other forums have over the courtroom and also their assisting in determining the fate of persons accused of committing various crimes. A person may choose to become a doctor, since he is desirous of caring for the medical needs of his parents and others who he has seen suffering from some ailment. It is common for some persons to change their career several times as their perception of life changes. This may be due to financial and other considerations and of course when one identifies the specific calling on one's life which may be different from one's personal choice. For this reason children and youths should learn what it is to hear from the Lord for His direction in vital areas such as their career.

3. **It offers lucrative financial returns**. This may include careers such as acting, modeling, computer science, medical science and business, masons, carpenters, mechanical, civil, aeronautical, and electrical engineering, banking and accounting.

4. *By divine intervention*; since nothing happens to a Christian who is consistently in communion with the Lord '**by accident**' or '**by chance**' in the true sense of this phenomenon. (Even in tragic events, as seen in the life of Job.) It is the experience of some persons that 'an opportunity seems to have appeared out of thin air' and they took advantage of it. Such a person may later discover that that career was financially rewarding and that it was not providing them with much job satisfaction, and also the opportunity to be an effective witness for the Lord. The Lord would usually '**point us to the right direction and opens doors of opportunities for us**'.

5. **They recognize that it has no authorized retirement age** and they can continue to perform their duties, or to functions in that office for as long as they live. There may also be spiritual considerations such as how long the Lord wants them to function in that office. Of course they have to take cognizance of the need to familiarize themselves with new developments in that and related areas and keep abreast with recent technology and other features which are introduced into the practice. This would include careers such as farming, engineering, teaching, nursing, legal practitioners, and medical doctors, entrepreneurs and preachers. Even if such persons retire from the public service, they may continue to work with a private institution or provide a consultancy service, for example.

Many persons operate as Justices of Peace or Notoriety Public and earn an income even after they may have retired from their official career. Even so, a person must recognize that there is a period of rest which the Lord expects each person to enjoy. For this reason we are instructed to 'work while it is day.' This statement is not only made from the perspective of a twenty-four hour day since many persons work during the evening also, but it refers to while we are young we should take advantage of the opportunities which are presented.

6. Old age should be primarily for relaxation and to guide the younger generation to take over and expand the dream which the Lord has so graciously allowed us to establish, or continue from the inputs of persons from previous generations. It is also a period for enjoying the fruits of our labor, which should include our well-placed children and their offspring.

7. **The fulfillment of the calling of the Lord on the person's life.** Some persons are pursuing spiritual offices or a secular career since they have received a personal revelation of a specific calling on their lives to pursue a particular career or vocation. A person who pursues a career as a medical doctor, for example, may be specially called by God to minister to the many terminally ill patients, whose last source of being ministered to and to accept Him as their Savior, is at the hospital. One may also serve as a missionary and render medical attention as an avenue to minister the gospel to the community in which one is serving.

Prudent parental guidelines

"What are some of the things parents can do to bring up a child in obedience to the Lord, such as in areas of Biblical financial management?"

We are admonished in 2 Timothy 2:15: "[15]**Do your best to present yourself to God as one approved by Him, a worker who has no need to be ashamed, rightly explaining the word of truth.**"

The importance of adopting the correct attitude in order to excel in academic pursuits, prudent financial management, maturing in the things of Christ and other aspects of life which constitutes a well-rounded personality, cannot be over emphasized. For this reason, parents have to begin planning for the upbringing of their children even before they are born. Important considerations when bringing up our children include:

1. Providing a stable home environment where the presence of the Lord dwells continually, where the spiritual, material and other aspects of the family's life are being adequately managed.

2. Providing the child with toys, books and other items which would stimulate his/her spiritual and intellectual development.

3. Increased emphasis is being focused on phonics and other principles which would challenge the child to learn to read. The importance of the principle of **'learning to read so that one can read to learn'** cannot be over-emphasized.

> Young people in particular should seek to conceptualize the importance of **studying and achieving excellence** in their academic, spiritual and other pursuits. If they could only shut themselves away from the distractions which could prevent them from achieving their goals, then their future can be dramatically transformed into that of great success. As we make the effort, the Lord will grant us the desires of our heart.

Knowing God's will for your life is of utmost importance to Christians. There are two aspects of the will of God. There is the **permissible will**, such as every Christian is instructed to do good deeds, make converts of men, carry out the mandates of the great commission, etc. However, as explained in the above scripture verse, there are duties which each of us were specifically created and saved to perform and thus, walk in His **perfect will**. Failure to perform that specific function would prevent us from saying like the Apostle Paul that we have 'fought the great fight and kept the faith.' The latter concept is the most important consideration for a Christian since only things which are done in conformity with the will of God have eternal significance. Our primary purpose as Christians should be to fulfill the purpose of God for our lives and to walk in His perfect will. For this reason as Christians we should not choose a career path merely because it offers high financial reward.

Most parents hope that their children would pursue financially rewarding careers, that they would be successful in their careers and that the child will be financially independent as early as possible. This would enable the parents to utilize their money to finance the education and other requirements of other siblings. In addition, more money would be available to go on vacations, invest and to save for their old age.

Every legitimate job has its place of importance. Thankfully, the services of persons who were previously classified as being a lower caste, second class citizens or by other derogatory terms because of their jobs, color of their skin, sex and other superficial stigmatizations are now being recognized.

The failure to do this in the past has resulted in chaos in many societies. (A person's sexual orientation which is not consistent to Biblical principles cannot be included in this class since the Bible only concedes to sexual intercourse between a husband and a wife, and does not condone homosexuality, lesbianism and other perverted sexual practices. Even though Jehovah hates the sin, He loves the sinner, and Jesus died so that everyone can be saved once we confess our sins, repent, accept His forgiveness and turn from our wicked ways, and receive Him as our Lord and Savior).

Discovering God's perfect will

"How can we discover God's perfect will for our lives; in our career path and other areas of our live?"

There are several methods which God may use to reveal His perfect will to a Christian. They include:

1. **Hear His voice**, that is, we must be in a close relationship with the Lord where we can consistently commune with Him. Biblical examples of persons who experienced this relationship include Adam and Eve, Moses, Samuel, Samson, Mary, Jesus' mother, and the Apostle Paul. We can recall that when the Lord spoke to Samuel on the first two occasions he did not recognize His voice. It took the wisdom of Eli to direct Samuel to this new relationship with Jehovah.

2. **Divine revelation** personally and/or through one or more Christians. Examples of this occurrence are the revelation of the part of the future life of David through Samuel and the disciples through Jesus. Jesus, for example, instructed his disciples to leave their secular jobs and to follow Him to be 'fishers of men.'

3. **Being** *in the right place at the right time*, where one realizes that this is the exact place which one's training and aptitude were designed to fulfill. Examples include Gideon and Moses in leading the Children of Israel. Moses was able to apply many of the principles of leadership which he had learnt when he was in Pharaoh's household. Nevertheless, he had to rely more on the Lord, who brought assistance such as the Midianite Priest to guide him in other systems of administration.

4. **One's innate or 'natural' ability**. For example, Queen Esther's beauty in securing her the position of queen,

was an opportunity which was used by the Lord to save His people from annihilation by the plot of Haman.

5. **God still appoints and anoints persons for a specific office or job.** Care must be taken that one has indeed 'heard the voice of the Lord' on the issue. There is usually confirmation of one's calling by others, such as a prophecy or word of wisdom, and circumstances such as 'doors' of opportunities opening up to channel one into the position.

Some of the important issues which should be considered when choosing a career path include:

1. **Being in the perfect will of the Lord**, as alluded to earlier.
2. *Achieving the prerequisite academic and/or vocation qualifications and/or other forms of training* to enable one to be well equipped to maximize one's competence to perform one's duties with excellence.
3. **'Selling one' self'** by convincing the prospective employers at the job interviews and other forums which are used to recruit employees, that one is the best person for the job.

Establishing & Accomplishing Goals

Planning ahead

"What are some of the benefits from formulating goals?"

There are several important issues which should be considered when formulating personal goals for individuals and also the corporate goals of the family. They include:

1. **Knowing God's will for one's life and the direction God is leading the family in**. This is important since it will assist in the prudent allocation of the budget to ensure that the essential expenditures are met.
2. **Formulating short, medium and long term goals for the family** after which they are prioritized.
3. **Allocating the tithes (10%) and offering (as the family chose)**.
4. **The budget should not be restricted to the earning capacity of the breadwinner/s** since provision should be made for the additional blessings which God provides for His people.

Developing Your God-Given Talents

Far too many persons spend most of their lives working for others, instead of at least spending time seeking the face of the Lord and securing direction to launch out into some enterprising activity on their own. When we are self employed and/or employ others to work for us, we will have the benefit of the blessing of the Lord in this area of our lives coming directly to us.

Living one's dream

"I am aware that I have a God-given talent, how do I take it from knowing, to fulfilling my dream of using it to bring glory to the Lord?"

It is vital that a person is resolute in their pursuit of a given objective, of course, providing it is consistent with the will of the Lord for their life. The importance of this thrust is confirmed by several scripture verses which condemn slothfulness, double mindedness and other negative attitudes and practices. Hebrews 6:11-12 states: *"¹¹And we want each of you to show the same diligence so as to realize the full assurance of hope to the very end. ¹²So that you may not become sluggish, but imitators of those who through faith and patience inherit the promises."*

There are a number of persons who are confined to mental institutions, made very bad decisions, destroyed the lives and souls of others and even their own. This may be because of their pursuit of aspirations which are inconsistent with the will of the Lord, because of selfish aspirations and even misguided methods of attaining material wealth even in areas such as one's spiritual calling.

I would hope that the contention that your talent is God-given is confirmed by the righteous works which your talent has enabled you to achieve for the Lord. It is important to test the fruits of your talent in order to conclude definitely that it is indeed God-given. In John 15:5, Jesus stated: *"⁵I am the true vine, you are the branches. Those who abide in me and I in them bear much fruit, because apart from Me you can do nothing."*

The spiritual gifts or talents which are deposited in our lives are usually confirmed by our spirit, even as the Lord reveals Himself in this area of our lives. There are however, examples when a person may have received a particular gift and it is recognized by someone during the operation of the spiritual gift of discernment, for example. Spiritual gifts may also be imparted through prophecy and by the laying on of hands by persons with the prerequisite spiritual authority to do so. 1Timothy 4: 14, for example states: ***"¹⁴Do not neglect the gift that is in you, which was given to you through the prophecy with the laying on of hands by the council of elders."***

It is important to consistently maintain a healthy balance between displaying your talent and flaunting it in an attempt to capitalize on possible favorable returns for selfish motives rather than as a means of spreading the gospel. Some persons are brilliant and achieve high grades at an entrance examination for an educational or another institution or achieve the necessary qualifications to enable them to enter a school, college, university or other academic or training institution of one's choice. Such persons should, however, not be boastful and convey the impression that the achievements were as a result of their superior ability. We must give honor to God for what He has imputed in us; all glory and honor belongs to Him. Persons are often misguided into relying on friends and other acquaintances in strategic positions to grant them special favors in opportunities to secure a particular opportunity. This method has proven successful for many persons to a certain extent. It is important to recognize that even if such a relationship is established the person is not the source of the blessing but it is the Lord. Our trust should never be in a person, for they may fail at a crucial moment.

Faith is a very important ingredient in every area of our lives. The great exploits which were achieved by men and women of God have the singular similarity of the exercise of faith. Other principles which would enable you to fulfill your mission include:

1. Maintaining rich fellowship with the Lord by engaging in praying, studying the Word and applying the principles to your life.
2. Seek the relevant training which would equip you to be able to present your talent in a manner which depicts maturity. This may include attending Bible school, an academic institution and/or other training forums.
3. Associate with persons with the similar gift and/or other persons who are desirous of promoting your area of

expertise. This may include attending conferences and workshops and other forums which your talent is being displayed.

4. Wait on the Lord for specific direction on how He is desirous for you to display your talent.

A large percentage of persons who achieve financial independence follow principles such as the following:

- **Put God first** – this includes the area of tithing (the first 10%), giving an offering, wowing into the lives of pastors and other believers, and assisting the poor and needy.
- **Paying yourself second** - this includes saving and investing prudently in excess of 20% of their income.
- **Endeavoring to accelerate the repayment of existing debts and avoiding new debt.**
- **Purchasing cash as far as possible**, since it often forces us to make wiser financial decision.

Fulfilling God's will for one's life

"What are some of the important steps which will enable me to fulfill the purpose for which I have been created?"

We have been created to fulfill several objectives. They include spiritual obligations, the management of material resources, to pursue a career, for most of us, to manage a family and to have a positive impact on our wider community. Some of us are given 'five talents' which if used efficiently will enable us to achieve a noble prize in a specific discipline, achieve prominence in sporting events, music, ministry and other endeavors. The majority of us would not achieve international prominence, yet we can be equally blessed once we fulfill our special purpose in the area which the Lord created us to achieve. This is similar to one of the principles of communism (which of course, cannot be attained with any earthly philosophy) where each person is required to be the best he can in the specific area which he is talented and which is beneficial to the society as a whole. The garbage collector, for example, is regarded as being equal to the most brilliant scientist, since they are both intertwined into contributing their best towards the growth and development of society.

Some of the important steps which we can take to fulfill the purpose for which we were created are:

1. **Recognize who we are in Christ.** This includes identifying and applying the principles in the Bible such as that we are more than conquerors through Christ Who strengthens us and that the Spirit of Excellence lives in us.

2. *We should recognize that we are who we are, and will be able to achieve what He said that we will achieve.* Our reliance should not be on our own strength and ability but on who we are in Christ, for we are nothing without Him.

3. *Irrespective of where we are, we can and have to change our mindset by relying on His promises.* It is true that many persons die without recognizing the purpose for which they were created and others do so when it is too late for them to achieve their best in life. For these reasons it is important that we come to the realization early in our life that we will only achieve our best by walking in His ways. Romans 12:1-3 declares that the act of presenting our bodies as daily sacrifices will enable us to *prove* the will of God. This promise goes beyond merely *knowing* it but to see it fulfilled in our life.

4. *Begin from where you are.* Too many of us sit idly by waiting for the 'the big event to come' for us to achieve instant international acclaim, without first starting to utilize the resources and opportunities which we have available to us right where we are. To get to where we want to often requires that we attend an educational institution or undertake the necessary training, acquire specialized qualifications, skills and other prerequisites to launch out into the desired area of specialization. As we put our resources, talents, financial and other assets to work, the Lord will expand our vision and our achievements.

5. *We should not lose sight of our spiritual obligations.* As our aspirations begin to come to fruition and our vision expands, we should not lose sight of important factors such as: God is our source; the importance of walking in honesty, integrity and keeping our way straight and established in order to keep the statutes of the Lord (Psalm 119:151). We have an obligation to use our experiences to minister to the lives of persons whom we come into contact with in our daily activities.

6. *Every stage of the success ladder demands faith and trust in the Lord.* It is true that God has given us spiritual and other gifts and talents and He expects us to use them instead of coming to Him for things which He has already placed at our disposal. However, as 'branches,' our nutrients and other substance come

from Him, the '**True Vine**.' Therefore, we have to abide in Him continually.

7. **The returns which we receive are not intended to be used only for our personal growth and development.** Many persons have the selfish attitude that after investing much of their time, talent, finance and other resources, the returns which they receive should be for their benefit and possibly to share with members of their immediate family. This should not be so, since our giving and other ministries are to 'the world,' that is, to our immediate and extended family, community, country, region, continents and other geographic locations.

8. **We should not allow our position and other achievements to distract us from serving the Lord.**

Many of the above factors are exhibited in the lives of Biblical characters such as Joseph, David and the Apostle Paul.

It is true that many persons are not adventurous and would not be able to manage a large business on their own. There are however, several business concepts which start in a small way at home or another location, which can be developed as much as the person managing it care or has the capacity to do. Some of the common enterprises which can be expanded into economic ventures are:

1. Making toys from cloth and other materials, sewing, making table and floor mats, decorations for the wall, ornamental flowers.
2. Farming, fishing, animal husbandry.
3. Retailing 'home-made' beverages, cakes, confectionaries and other items which can be sold to children during their lunch recess at school and/or to the wider community.
4. Projects such as pickling onions and other vegetables, making tomato ketchup, and exchanging them for other products from neighbors or sell them.
5. Selling barbecue, fried, baked and other types of meat along with other dishes.
6. Persons who are artistic can indulge in painting, carving, making pottery and other craft items which can be sold.
7. Skilled persons such as tradesmen can start by working from home during the evening and weekends and expand into a permanent self employed activity.
8. Many persons are engaging in web designing and other computer related activities from home.

9. Many persons are working from their homes and have lucrative contracts from organizations which out-source their work.

Deuteronomy 28:12, 13 states: *"12The Lord will open for you His rich storehouse, the heavens, to give the rain of your land in its season and to bless all your undertakings. You will lend to many nation, but you will not borrow. 13The Lord will make you the head, and not the tail, you shall be only at the top and not at the bottom – if you only obey the commandments of the Lord your God, when I am commanding you today, by diligently obeying them."*

Isaiah 45:2, 3 states: *"2I will go before you and level the mountains, I will break in pieces the doors of bronze and cut through the bars of iron. 3I will give you the treasures of darkness and riches hidden in secrete places, so that you may know that I, the Lord, the God of Israel, who call you by name."*

This passage is filled with promises which millions of Christians who trust in the Lord enjoy. He is reminding us that He has already given us dominion over all of the world and its treasures. He promised that He will take what may seem to us to be extreme measures to ensure that we achieve **success in all of our endeavors**. These promises are not restricted to the Children of Israel in the Old Testament but are also applicable to our lives today.

A scripture verse some persons view as controversial is Job 36:11 which states: *"11 If they listen, and serve Him, they complete their days in prosperity, and their years in pleasantness."*

Some of the interpretations of this verse are:

1. Job was relating his personal experience and not that of all the followers of Jehovah.
2. Prosperity and pleasantries do not apply only to material wealth but include features such as good health, happiness among members of our family, peace and progress in our communities and beyond.

It is true that not every Christian will be materially wealthy, however, it does not deny the fact that we have the Spirit of the Lord dwelling in us, and as we submit to Him and seek after wisdom, God will reveal His principles pertaining to the acquisition and expansion of our material and other resources. There are however, several requirements which we have to fulfill in order to receive these blessings. Once we fulfill these requirements, and it is in accordance with His will for our lives, there seems to be no reason why more of us cannot own a villa in a scenic location and enjoy other pleasantries of life, own multimillion dollar businesses and other substantial material resources and still serve Him.

The importance of Godly vision in realizing a successful business

"Is the principle of having a Godly vision important in investment decisions also?"

As outlined earlier, it is important that we have a Godly vision for every area of our lives as individuals and also as a family, and in other areas of our lives such as our business activities. The following principles are reiterated in Habakkuk 2:2, 3: "²*Then* **the Lord answered me and said: Write the vision; make it plain on tablets, so that a runner may read it. ³For there is still a vision for the appointed time; it speaks of the end, and does not lie**."

It is important to have a macro vision with regards to one's whole life as a guidepost, and as a source of inspiration and a reminder of what one's objectives are. In the same way there can also be micro-visions for individual areas of one's life such as what one expects to achieve from a business venture and the material possessions which the family is aspiring to achieve over a given time period. The projections are usually based on what the couple has brought into the marriage, what is realistically within their ability to achieve, and what the level of their faith in the Lord will enable them to achieve, and in accordance with His grace. The projections can be subdivided into short, medium and long-term goals. The priority and composition of such a statement will be based on the projected earning capacity of the family and projected expenditure.

After attaining, by God's grace, a significant target, a couple often reminisces on the struggles which they went through and how the Lord gave them the inspiration and encouragement, grace and strength to successfully achieve their objectives. As mile stones are achieved, the couple will be encouraged to launch out for bigger ones. It is wise that the couple should strive to enjoy a period of rest, such as during the annual vacation during their formative years, when they can sit back and enjoy the fruits of their labor. Some of the excitement of pushing to attain targets would have been lost during the period of rest. Nevertheless, this does not necessarily infer that life loses its meaning after this stage for there are always targets to be achieved in other areas of our lives as individuals and as a family.

In their quest to achieve targets, unless a couple has really mastered the process of cleaving, their marriage can be plagued with much tension because of attempting to conserve on spending even in vital areas. For this reason it is important that both spouses are fully committed to their plans and that it is not a program where merely one partner is superimposing his/her will on the other. There is also the need to consistently assure each other that they are working for the common good of the family, and that the intensive sacrifice will not be throughout the marriage. It is also vital that such projections take into account the need for periods of review of the level of success of the plan in an attempt to assess whether or not the period of sacrifice is having any serious negative effects on any member of the family or even other persons.

There are several advantages which the couple who marries into comfort would enjoy. Since the new bride does not have to bother about acquiring the basic amenities, she will be in a position to concentrate more on investments, as illustrated by the virtuous wife. The couple will be in a better position to plan on how to expand their material resources, of course taking care in avoiding the pitfall as depicted in the parable of the rich fool as Jesus told in Luke 12:16-21. They have the unique opportunity to seek ways of giving more of their finance, time and other resources towards the spreading of the Gospel. (The rich fool was making plans to build bigger barns to store the abundance of grains which his fields had produced so that he can relax, eat, drink and be merry. He neglected important principles such as giving thanks to God for his abundance and he was not contemplating how he could have assisted the needy from his wealth).

> *Many persons can transform some activity which they conduct into an income generating business venture. Even if it is a small project, it can complement our income or be the sole source of income which adequately covers our financial needs. The more entrepreneurial persons may be able to expand to the extent where the project grows into a full time business and even employ others.*

When planning financial matters, as in most other areas, it is important that the family is conversant with alternative options which are available to the couple. For example:

1. *Negotiate* **a mortgage** from a commercial bank, building society, insurance company or their place of employment, to build or purchase their home. Some couples have taken the option of securing the land and

building as they accumulate money instead of securing a mortgage. The latter method is advantageous in that it avoids the high interest rates which financial institutions usually charge. However, this has to be weighed against considerations such as the amount of rent which they may have to pay while their house is being built. In addition, it might not be cost effective to utilize the large cash outlay required to build a house over a short time, versus investing their money in a high yielding scheme which would generate a far higher rate of return than the cost of repaying the mortgage.

2. **Save their money in a bank, and/or invest in securities, purchase jewelry, exotic art, treasury bills, debentures, shares, invest in real estate, and/or other assets**. Each method has advantages and disadvantages. Investing in real estate is usually very profitable. However, the value of property may decline if, for example, a new low-cost housing project and/or a 'slum area' emerge in close proximity to one's property.

3. **Investing in their children**. This includes purchasing books, computer accessories, ensuring that the children receive the best form of education which they can afford, ensuring that they eat a balanced diet and engage in other healthy practices. It is also important that parents be aware of God's calling on the lives of their children so that the children can be encouraged to pursue that path. Many parents do the best they can, yet their children do not achieve the level of prominence which their parents aspired/s that they would. This issue must be analyzed carefully, since many parents seek to fashion their children into careers and other endeavors in an attempt to fulfill their own desires or because it is 'politically correct' for the child to pursue a given course. Many attributes in the life of Mary, Jesus' mother, attest to the fact that she had some degree of understanding of the calling on Jesus' life and encouraged Him to fulfill His calling.

Formulating and implementing goals

"What are some of the important principles which we should adhere to when formulating and implementing goals?"

It is very important that we formulate goals in every aspect of our lives. The sad thing is that many persons establish goals for the type of person they would like to marry, what career they would like to pursue, for example, but when it comes to financial goals we are often reluctant to establish goals which we work ardently to at least attain, but where possible, surpass. Very often the vision of the young when it comes to financial matters, stops at completing one's education, securing a well paying job, purchasing a home, car, living a 'good' life and traveling. Thankfully, as many persons mature and start a family they become more focused and begin to plan their life beyond living a flashy lifestyle and begin to plan for their future family.

Planning for retirement usually becomes a reality for most persons after their thirtieth birthday, or even later, possibly when they see their parents and other persons undergoing hardship when they retired, since they did not make adequate financial provision for the remainder of their lives and that of their loved ones.

It is important that we set realistic financial and other goals as individuals, a family and the wider community. If the question of what are some of our financial goals is posed to a young person it is common to hear responses such as:

1. The desire to be a millionaire before age twenty.
2. To have enough money to be able to purchase a home and furnish it before getting married.
3. Ownership of the latest model of the motor vehicle.

For the married couple it is customary to hear goals such as:

1. Being debt free within a year.
2. Having enough money to pay for the education of the children.
3. Owning one's own home, being able to adequately meet the monthly expenditure of the family and go on a holiday to another country at least once per year.
4. To be able to save enough so that they can enjoy a comfortable retirement, meet any medical and other expenses which may arise and to be able to travel and enjoy the many things which they were unable to afford, because of their schedule during the years of employment.

Proverbs 4:7 states: "⁷*Wisdom is the principal thing: therefore get wisdom and with all your getting, get understanding.*"

It is important that we 'study to show ourselves approved', be educated to accelerate at our chosen careers and be successful with whatever we undertake. As we pursue this course, it must be recognized that the tasks which Jehovah expects us to accomplish cannot be accomplished by relying only on our own abilities. We have to receive His favors, guidance, protection and other blessings. Other important considerations for formulating goals include the fact that they must be:

1. **Challenging,** in that they should take effort, discipline and other positive attributes to attain them. If important goals are not challenging, we tend to under-perform in this and other areas of our lives. On the other hand, if they are too demanding, they could result in much mental anguish, frustration and other negative effects on individuals and the family.
2. **Time specific**, where a realistic time-frame must be given by which time the goals should be achieved.
3. **Quantifiable,** in that one must be able to compute the amount of resources which would be needed to realistically attain the goals,
4. **Measurable,** in that it should be possible to ascertain the extent to which they are on, or off course towards attaining the goals over the time-frame allocated for their completion,
5. **Realistic,** in that they should be attainable given the time, finance and other resources which are at your disposal to achieve them,
6. **Specific,** where the persons conducting the activity would be aware of precisely what they are aiming to achieve, rather than merely working with no specific goal to direct them,

Since goals are not usually 'set in stone' there will be occasions when it may be necessary to adjust their parameters in order to arrive at a realistic outcome. Some of the long-term financial goals which are formulated by some Christian families are:

1. *The acquisition of their own home, furniture, car and other assets,*
2. *To have enough money saved to be able to finance the education of their children,*
3. *Investment and saving schemes which should realistically afford the family a comfortable standard of living.* Even if there are short term deviations from their plans due to unemployment, sickness or other deterrents, for which there is a reduction of income and/or increase in the expenditure.
4. *Saving and investment programs for their retirement,*

5. *Leaving an inheritance for their children, grand-children and other relatives and loved ones,*

There are several obstacles which can prevent us from attaining our objectives if we are not sensitive to the leading of the Lord. This may include the economic condition of the country, health and other personal issues in the lives of the couple and even the change in the direction which they have received from the Lord. *It is important that we remain 'connected to the True Vine' each step of the way as we seek to fulfill His calling on our lives. This is so because He may reveal the direction which we should go a little at a time, even as we trust Him and launch out into where He is leading us. Conversely, He may reveal the end, but we still have to trust Him each step of the way in order to get there.* A typical example of this fact was illustrated in the life of Abraham and Sarah, when God instructed Abraham to move his family and possessions on several occasions. If Abraham was unable to hear and understand the word of the Lord, and was not willing to move as He directed, his life would not have been fulfilled.

> *The parable of the three servants who were left with various amounts of money by their master, is an illustration that God does not expect all of us to perform at the same level. He allocates assignments in accordance with our ability. Once we fulfill our commission we will all be rewarded accordingly. There are however, extra rewards for persons who perform above the average.*

Some of the important reasons for setting realist goals are:
1. *They provide direction and purpose*: Even though we may not have all of the parameters in place to accomplish the goals, it at least identifies the necessary resources which are needed to enable us to attain them.
2. *It provides personnel and corporate motivation:* Once we are committed to the goal, it is usually a challenge to advance it from conception to fulfillment.

3. ***It challenges us to rely on Jehovah to sustain us and to provide mechanisms to achieve the goals.*** We know that our lives are not our own and once it is a Godly goal, we should recognize that He will enable us to as far as possible, complete the purpose which He birthed in our minds. A note of caution is interjected here, since it may not be the will of the Lord that the goal be expanded over time, so that even though the initial vision may be fulfilled, a greater need emerges over time. In other instances, the Lord may decree that the goal be fulfilled by another person or an organization. The Lord also surrounds us, or opens doors for us to contact other persons who would enable us to fulfill our calling. This fact is illustrated in the example of King David's desire to build the temple. The Lord decreed that his son Solomon should fulfill this vision which was birthed in David.

In Philippians 3:14, the Apostle Paul stated: ***"14I press towards the goal for the prize of the upward call of God in Christ Jesus."***

It is important to formulate short, medium and long term goals. Far too many persons only exist on short term goals, with only a vague idea of long term goals. It is a fact that we achieve far more when we have long term goals and when we are disciplined enough to ensure that the short and medium term goals fulfill the longer term goals.

Even so, we have to set goals and work ardently, relying of the direction and assistance of the Lord and the persons and resources which He places at our disposal in order to achieve the goals. The act of setting goals is an act of faith. If it is a goal which is not in conformity with the will of the Lord for our lives, or if we are relying on our own strength and ability to achieve it, this is a sinful act. Two important elements of setting goals and achieving them are **faith and work**. The importance of relying on the Lord is emphasized in Ephesians 3: 20: ***"20Now to Him who by the power at work within us is able to accomplish abundantly far more than we can ask or imagine."***

These goals are illustrated in the following diagram:

Diagram 2.1 Presentation of Objectives over the Short, Medium and Long-Term

---

Vision and financial projections

"Can the concept of a vision be related to financial issues?"

There are several attributes of a vision which have been popularized. They include the ability to:

1. **Think creatively**; this ability is not only limited to artists and entrepreneurs, but is found in the mind of every individual who is prepared to extend his life beyond merely existing. Persons use their immediate environment and the wider community and focus on

implementing strategies to improve their standard of living, making chores lighter, being more efficient at what they do and grapple with solving national and international issues. One of the fundamental principles for persons who have been successful in various aspects of life is identifying an important need that has to be met and implementing a system, or providing a product, to satisfy that need. This does not only apply to the invention of commercial ideas but is also the basis for many individuals, families and ministries achieving recognition in their community and beyond.

2. **Explore possibilities**; which include activities such as investigating, researching, and inventing different ways of doing things to find economic and efficient ways of performing a particular task. A famous maxim states that '**nothing ventured, nothing gained**'. We may also be familiar with the maxim which states that '**it is better to try and fail than to fail to try**', for in so doing, even if we fail, someone else may be able to improve on our strategy or product and be able to create a product and/or service which is in great demand or fulfills a particular need.

3. **Tap into potential**; God has created in each of us the unique ability to fulfill a specific task or tasks. The process of actualizing that potential requires that we undergo a period of preparation in areas such as academic training, physical and/or mental exercise. It may also require that we alienate ourselves at least initially with others, access funding and other resources to be able to put into effect that which the Lord has burdened our hearts to fulfill.

Vision is absolutely essential in order to foster progress. This is also the ingredient which causes persons to remain young even though they may be advanced in years. It is the vision of having an active body, and/or winning a sporting competition which propels athletes, as well as persons who use exercise as a leisure activity, to keep pounding their bodies to run or walk for a number of kilometers each week and indulge in weight training, aerobics and other exercise programs. This is also the concern which fuel students to spend years of their lives attending classes and studying. Inventors also extend hours each day to improve the standard of their product which transforms into huge profits as it is perfected.

There are several examples in the Bible and in our history where the fulfillment of a vision which may have been birthed a number of years, only became a reality after one or several major catastrophes. Examples in the Bible include the life of Samuel whose vision which the Lord revealed to him when he was a small boy only became a reality after God killed Eli's sons who were exploiting the people when they offered their sacrifices. Joseph's vision of royalty only came into fruition after we was sold into slavery, imprisoned and suffered other disasters. Even so, we should not be over anxious to fulfill our vision but instead wait on the perfect timing and the season which the Lord has established for its actualization.

Attributes of Godly visionaries

"What are some of the attributes of Godly visionaries?"

It is possible for a person to be saved and not be categorized as a 'Godly visionary'. Many Christians serve the Lord and do not seek or are not taught that there is more to their salvation than attending church and being labeled as a Christian. A simple definition of a Godly visionary is someone who has had a revelation that the Lord desires to have His will fulfilled in their life and one who is committed to fulfilling that calling. Some of the characteristics and mind set of Godly visionaries are that they:

1. **Have a humble, receptive and willing heart,** where they are prepared to wait on the Lord for Him to reveal His perfect will for their lives and be willing to do whatever it takes to carry the vision to fulfillment,

2. **Recognize that it is often a lonely and painful journey** which demands much sacrifice to carry the vision from conception to fulfillment,

3. **Are never satisfied with anything under the optimum fulfillment of the vision**,

4. **Are risk takers**, even as they encounter failures and disappointments and other challenges along the way. This does not include persons who foolishly take unnecessary risks or gambles, but persons who are diligent, and with the wisdom of the Lord operating in their lives, are willing to venture into areas even if they are un-chartered.

5. **Have a passion to fulfill their calling**; in that they never say that it is over until God says so and do whatever it takes to fulfill it, of course, within the limits of what is permissible scripturally,

6. **They prefer to suffer personal and other forms of deprivation, rather than to fail to fulfill their calling.** To

them, nothing else may as important, since they are committed to doing their best for the Lord. This single-mindedness may be criticized by others who do not share the vision or who may not deem it as being very important, at least not at the expense of other areas of their lives.

7. **Align themselves with the right person or persons** who would channel their potential or provide the necessary assistance needed to achieve the task ahead,

8. **Be position on a 'high place'** where they can see the extent of the 'land to be conquered' (Habakkuk 2: 1). We should, with the help of the Holy Spirit, have a clear picture of the challenges which lie ahead and be adequately equipped to maximize the opportunities which are available.

9. **Are at the 'right place at the right time'**. The Holy Spirit would lead the believer to where the opportunities are and also give them the wisdom on how to maximize benefits from it,

10. **Recognize that success comes after work** (the converse occurs only in the dictionary).

11. **It is often a lonely road to carry a vision to the stage where it becomes a reality**, others may not have the same vision, empathize with your vision, feel that you are the right person or qualified enough to fulfill such a vision.

12. **Adapt the mindset of living the life of the end product as the fulfillment of the vision progresses** so that by the time it is fulfilled, the magnitude of the success does not overwhelm you. (Not being prepared to manage the magnitude of the success of the achievement has caused many persons to mismanage funds, for example, when the blessing started coming, since they did not spend time to recognize that their success in a particular area is not an end in itself, but merely a means to graduate to a higher calling). It is possible for a person to be successful materially even though they are not serving the Lord. We can recall that the devil offered Jesus the material things of this world, which Jesus rejected. Similarly, a person may be wealthy without being in Christ.

13. **Recognize that it takes faith, patience and other Godly characteristics to fulfill the vision**,

14. ***Do not go around disclosing their vision to everyone they meet, particularly to persons who are jealous or not able to carry or support the vision.*** Such persons may even attempt to stifle the fulfillment of the vision or steal the idea from them. Destiny cannot be stolen, someone may try to duplicate it, but it can never be stolen.

15. ***Would accept God's rebuke, reproof and discipline.*** Since we are not perfect, He has to fashion us to the place where we can receive the tools in order to fulfill the vision,

> *We are what we are today because of what we believed in the past. We will become what we will be tomorrow because of what we believe today, and the extent to which we allow the Lord to work in our lives.*

Excellent Career Choices

INTRODUCION

Several studies have highlighted the fact that the pursuit of financial reward is not the most important factor which persons highlight when they indicate that they enjoy their job. It is a fact that financial security is very high on the metrics, however, persons who feel challenged to go to work daily knowing that they enjoy what they do, are usually more productive than the person who is working primarily 'for the money'. It is therefore important that we know God's will for our lives in this important area and vigorously pursue it.

Making the best career choices

"How do I motivate myself to pursue a goal or career which would generate the level of income which I desire to have?"

Many secular motivation speakers use principals which are found in the Bible to challenge their audience to 'reach deep within themselves' and to secure the impetus to challenge themselves to achieve goals which would transform their lives and significantly improve their standard of living. There are also other persons who use non-scriptural methods such as transcendental meditation, yoga and other methods to expand their 'minds' and motivate themselves to move to the 'next level' of achievements. It is true that many persons who have achieved financial, political and other forms of prominence, profess that these practices were instrumental in transforming their lives. Their success would not count for eternity, unless they give their lives to the Lord. Christians who study and live by the Word of God have found that there is a better way than these man-made and satanic philosophies and practices.

There are several scriptural methods of challenging ourselves to be the best we can be in this world. They include:

1. Implementing Biblical principles in our lives such as those outlined in Romans 8:38, which states: "**37No, in all these things we are more than conquerors through Him who loved us.**"

2. Acknowledging principles such as outlined in Proverbs 10:22: "**22The blessing of the Lord makes rich and He adds no sorrow it.**" Romans 8:28 also states: "**28We know that all things work together for good for those who love God, who are called according to His purpose.**"

3. We have the Holy Spirit living in us. Once we allow Him He will direct us to the correct investment and other decisions which we make. We are instructed in Romans 12:2 as follows: "**2Do not be conformed to this world, but be transformed by the renewing of your minds, so that you may discern what is the will of the God – what is good and acceptable and perfect.**"

4. We are presented with hundreds of promises in the Bible which the Lord decreed that we will inherit, once we walk in obedience to His words.

> *The returns of the three servants were 5:5, 3:3 and 1:1, respectively, yet they were all 100% returns. Even so, the Lord expects us to generate the level of return which is consistent to the abilities and other resources which He has given to us. It is thus important to find out where we fall on His measuring scale and perform at that level. A person, who is to serve at level 3, for example, should not envy a person who is to perform at level 5, or look down on another who is to serve at level 1. Once we fulfill our individual calling we will each receive equal rewards.*

Boosters to rapid job promotions

"What are some of the factors which hinder our promotion on the job and in other areas of our life?"

Many Christians are in organizations where they are not receiving any, or substantial promotion. Factors such as the following contribute to their stagnation:

1. They are not paying their tithes and giving their offerings, consistent with Biblical principles,
2. They may be in a job which is not consistent with the will of the Lord for their lives,
3. They may not be displaying the correct attitudes which are consistent with the culture of the organization. This may include:
   a. They are not adequately qualified or are not applying themselves to perform their duties at the required high standard,
   b. They may be consistently late, ill, not a conscientious worker and may disregard the dress code and other norms of the organization,
   c. They may have a poor attitude towards fellow employees and their customers. This may include an attitude of *disdain* towards others who are not Christians, therefore, not being a good witness in essential areas such as showing love and kindness.
   d. They may not be willing to 'work beyond the call of duty' when this is required. There is usually an unspecified clause in the job description where it is stated 'any other duties' as designated by one's supervisor or management. This clause is usually applied in a reasonable way to balance the smooth operation of the organization and job related and other activities of the employer. When this clause is applied to the detriment of the employee, there is usually a need to attempt to resolve the disagreement with management to be paid for the additional service or that for it to be done by another person. Failure to arrive at an amicable solution may result in the employee consulting the union, in a unionized workforce. For a non-unionized workforce the employee would have to weigh the severity of the dispute verses considerations such as their ability to secure another job.

There are many organizations which are not owned by or managed by Christians where there is a deliberate policy to employ a large number of Christians. This may be because it is felt that Christians are honest, conscientious workers and/or that they are less likely to be rebellious and stage industrial actions, for example. They may also be perceived as persons who are more likely to promote love and harmony among fellow employees. Conversely, Christians may be deliberately employed by some organizations since they may be perceived to be easier preys to be exploited, since they are perceived to be less rebellious and 'humble'. This is not so, since like Jesus who showed His distaste for unrighteousness by overturning the tables of the persons selling in the temple and wiped them, even so, we are to stand for the truth even in the area of upholding the rights of both employers and employees.

Many persons who have the prerequisite qualifications and working experience are unable to secure the job of their dreams primarily because they are unable to get past the preliminary stage of being selection for an interview. This is so because they were unable to 'sell' themselves to the selective panel since their résumé or curriculum vitae was not impressive enough to convince them that the applicant warranted being short-listed.

Most organization would request **a formal letter of application** and an attached résumé. The formal letter of application affords the applicant the opportunity to summarize why they may be the most suitable person to fill the vacancy. It would include one's full home or contact address, the name and address of the person (usually the Administrative Manager) of the organization, the body of the letter, and the salutation. Some organizations prefer if the email address of the applicant is included in both the covering letter and the résumé. Care must be taken that the covering letter highlights one's eligibility for the position and one's commitment to give of one's best to the organization. Some organizations request a hand written application since they will have a handwriting expert analyze the character of the applicants as depicted by their handwriting. In this scenario the applicant must be patient and form their letters correctly and that they write as neatly as they possibly can.

Effective résumé presentation

"What are some of the essential issues which should be included in a résumé?"

The résumé or curriculum vitae are usually structured in the following segments:

1. **Personal details** such as name, address, email address, contact telephone number/s, where applicable. Many specialists in this area advise that details such as marital status, ethnic origin and age should be omitted until the interview or unless the perspective employee specifically requests them.

2. **Academic qualifications.** Special training which one may have undergone and certificates, degrees and other qualifications gained which are relevant to the position. The name of the respective institutions, their addresses, the year the certificate was awarded and grade awarded should be included. Depending on the position, it may also be useful to list the major courses which constituted the program of training, particularly, if the request is for a detailed résumé.

3. **A summary of your area of specialization** which makes you suitable for the position. This may include details such as your experience in a similar position,

4. From the more senior applicants:

   a. **A list of the relevant positions at various organizations where one worked**, providing a brief outline of your job description, and your major achievements in the position, and your reason for leaving the organization,

   b. **A list of the papers, publications, books and other documents which highlight one's achievements in one's field of specialization.** For some positions one may be asked to include a copy of a recent publication as a testimonial of one's ability to present written reports and conduct independent research.

1. **Other related skills** which one possesses which would enhance one's performance on the new job. This could include computer skills, the mastery of a second language and professional bodies of which one may be a member.

2. **The list of two or three referee reports or testimonials (as requested) or the name, address, telephone, fax numbers and email address of the referees,** as detailed in the job advertisement. Care must be taken to select referees who are persons of high integrity and who are renowned. This is because when a person writes a referee report for someone else, the writer is placing their professional integrity on the line in making such a recommendation. It is also important that the referees

are consulted and agrees to submit the report on your behalf.

Getting past the selection panel and being called for an interview is a very big step towards being selected for the job since there may be many applicants for the job to whom the organization may not have replied because they were ruled out since these were deemed illegible. Usually, organizations do not shortlist a placebo, (a person, in this instant, who is used as a control mechanism, but is not considered as a serious prospect for the position) unless they are conducting a survey. Hence, it is important that if you are truly desirous of accepting the job that you are well prepared for the interview.

As Christians, we must recognize that the forces of darkness are unleashed in an attempt to frustrate us and even kill us. When we are consistently not being called for interviews and are turned down from job applications for which we felt confident of acquiring it is very frustrating. This is a sure way where some Christians turn away from serving God since they feel that He is not concerned about them and that He is not working on their behalf. It is thus important that we learn to take authority over the forces of darkness and see God work on our behalf. It is also important to be patient and to keep trusting that everything will work together for our good, as the Lord promised that it would.

Christians can therefore walk into an interview room with the foreknowledge and confirmation from the Word and/or a specific prophecy, for example, that God has already selected us for the job. However, we still have the responsibility of studying and showing ourselves approved and of convincing the interviewing panelist that we indeed have the correct aptitude and prerequisite skills and are the best person for the position. When a Christian is selected for an appointment, he has the obligation to confirm by his dedication, hard work, commitment and other positive attributes that he was indeed the best person to have been selected. With consistency in our outstanding performance, good stewardship and the manifestation of the Excellent Spirit which dwells in us, as was present in the life of Daniel, Jehovah will guarantee a promotion to a senior position within that organization or to another.

Some persons directly or indirectly contact members of the interviewing panel before the interview and try to find out what are some of the issues which will be highlighted at the interview. This is usually not a very good strtaegy and an applicant may be disqualified from the interview if he is found to be soliciting undue strategy, particularly, from members of the prospective interviewing panel. There may be no harm in finding out specifics such as the salary range of the position, for example. However, care must be taken that undue assistance and overtures are not made to representatives of the organization.

| Sourcing appropriate vacancies |

"What are some of the ways we can become aware of a vacancy in our career paths?"

There are several ways a person may learn of a vacancy which exists in an organization, such as:

1. A number of organizations publish vacancies in popular newspapers and/or magazines; advertise on radio stations and television channels and other news media. There are also several magazines which specialize in publishing vacancies. Persons who are desirous of securing local and international jobs can subscribe to such publications. The Financial Times, Wall Street Journal and News Week are popular publications where several local and international appointments are advertised. It is a law in some countries that senior positions in government corporations and publicly quoted organizations must be published in popular newspapers and the best candidate is hired from the applications.

   Very often, even though the required publication of the vacancy is satisfied, the management of the organization structures the requirements for the position in such a way to give a distinct advantage to a person who is identified within the organization for the position. This may include the years of experience, qualification and other prerequisites. This is not always so, since even though an external applicant may be better suited for the job, the organization may have already identified an internal candidate and was merely publishing the vacancy to satisfy a statutory requirement.

2. The internet has become a popular medium for publishing vacancies. Vacancies are usually advertised on the website of the organization. There are also several websites which specialize in making such vacancies available to persons who subscribe to

the organization or the list of vacancies is advertised as a free service. A popular website is www.devjobs.com. Increasingly, applicants are invited to email their applications for positions which have been advertised. The web page of some organizations has a blank application form which applicants are invited to fill and email to the organization. For some appointments the applicant may have to submit additional data such as a copy of academic and other certificates and recent testimonials, police clearance and other documents.

3. The referees report.
4. A person may have been informed of a vacancy by someone who is working in an organization,
5. Some persons send applications to a number of organizations which may have a specific position within the organization such as an economist in the Central Bank, Credit Officer in a commercial bank and medical doctor in a hospital. Enquiry can also be made about possible vacancies which may exist that are commensurate with one's qualification and work experience.
6. There are private and government employment agencies in several countries where persons can obtain information on vacancies, and suitably qualified persons may be able to secure an appointment with the prospective employers. There is often a cost involved, particularly with private job placement agencies. This may include a flat application fee or in some instances as much as ten percent or even more of the first year salary of the successful applicant. These contracts are usually binding and persons who attempt to contravene them may be fired by their employer or be confronted with a lawsuit from the job placement agency.

In some instances, persons find that contracting the services of legitimate job placement agencies secures a faster appointment than approaching a prospective employer independently. This is so because the job placement agency may have several years of experience of forging a relationship with prospective employers and employees in that particular geographic location. There are, however, several unscrupulous confidence tricksters who play on the gullibility and desperation of job seekers and do not genuinely offer a job placement service but swindle them of the fees demanded for a service which they fail to provide.

7. There are established companies, the military and other agencies in many countries who target prospective graduates of colleges, universities and other institutes and attempt to entice the best graduates to join their organizations. Forums such as job fairs, as well as the special relations between the job placement agencies and career guidance centers and other organizations facilitate this interaction. Some agencies also offer scholarships to outstanding students, with the objective of offering them employment under a contractual obligation which is commensurate with the number of years and the cost of the training program.

8. There are agencies which hire persons on a permanent or temporary basis and contract their services to other organizations. These include agencies which offer cleaning, security, medical and other services.

9. Some organizations offer students the opportunity of working on an attachment program where they are paid a stipend for their services. Outstanding persons may be offered permanent employment with the organization.

10. Some established organizations request that suitably qualified professionals submit their résumés, which are included on the Roster of Consultants of the organization for special projects on the data bank for possible permanent employment. The management of the organization would usually request that individual consultants and consulting firms submit bids for a specific project and/or program which they have to undertake. The bids for such contracts usually include the résumés of persons who are listed on their roster as resource personnel. This system is used extensively by professionals such as Accountants, Project Managers, Financial Consultants, Architects, System Analysts, Anthropologists, and other professionals who are seeking part-time or permanent employment.

Many professionals who have retired and are not desirous of continuing a full time appointment would seek to remain active in their profession by registering with a voluntary organization, and even established commercial and charitable organizations, and work as a consultant on selected projects. Many professionals, who enjoy traveling and living in other countries, would also take up such appointments. In many instances the professional earns far more working as a consultant on a small number of projects per year than if he were employed fulltime, since payments are often tax free. One may also enjoy benefits such as free accommodation, the payment of utility bills, free medical treatment and transportation facilities and also an allowance for one's spouse and children who accompany the consultant to the duty station.

11. There are also organizations which actively pursue persons who are distinguished in a specialized field and offer them an attractive package in an attempt to entice them to join the organization permanently or for a specific project or program. In such instances one is usually able to secure a salary and fringe benefits which would enable one to live as comfortable as one desire. These offers should not be taken lightly, for even if one is at the helm of the organization or in a strategic position and can dictate your terms and conditions of service, salary and other benefits, the new organization would obviously demand their 'pound of flesh.' One would have to perform at a level which is commensurate with one's earning or face the possibility of being fired. This practice is popular among professional sports personalities, actors, and senior executives of established companies. It is thus necessary that all contracts offered by prospective employer be thoroughly scrutinized, and it is often better to seek the advice of a legal practitioner.

The detailed format of the résumé submitted in response to a published advertisement is primarily dependent on the request of the prospective employer. Some organizations request a one-page résumé while others request a detailed résumé. The difference is that large organizations often receive so many applications that the administration department may not be staffed with enough persons to go through all the detailed résumés and select the best applicants to attend an interview. The result is that a summarized application, possibly on one to a maximum of three pages, is requested. There might then be a request for a detailed résumé from applicants who are short-listed, while some organizations would interview the short-listed candidates based on the summarized résumé. In the latter example much more is dependent on one's ability to orally convince the interviewing panel that one is the most suitable candidate for the job. This system is often used for positions such as Sales Representatives, Broadcasters and TV Presenters and other positions which demand that one has to be convincing and articulate in one's oral presentation.

*Managing the jitters of the job **interview***

"What are some of the 'do's and don'ts' of a job interview?"

Some of the important aspects of the preparation for a successful interview include:

1. ***Being conversant of what the organization or department does, who are some of the key managers of the organization, what your general function would be and how the organization would benefit from the specific skills which you have to offer.*** It may also be important to be aware of the salary scale of the position, for you may be able to negotiate for the highest possible salary scale for the position, without jeopardizing your possibility of being selected by requesting too much or undersell yourself by asking for too little. This may convey the impression that you may not be competent to fill the position, or may be a trouble maker, who merely wants to accept the job and would then demand a higher wage. In addition, some prospective employers attempt to have the applicant agree to enter the organization at the starting stage of the grade, where if one was better informed, one may have been able to negotiate a better employment package which may include wage and fringe benefits.

2. ***Attempt to anticipate some of the likely questions which may be asked at the interview and rehearse an impressive answer.*** However, though this may work in some instances, the important principle is to be as knowledgeable as possible of what the requirements of

the position are and ensure that one is well equipped to present appropriate responses with an air of confidence, rather than a negative trait such as nervousness and being unable to 'think on your feet.'

3. **Dressing appropriately for an interview cannot be over emphasized. In this regard, it is useful to know the dress code of the organization and dress accordingly.** It may be self-defeating to be overdressed and feel uncomfortable at the interview. It may be easy for persons on the interviewing panel to recognize that you are not comfortable and they may presume that you may be uncomfortable working in an environment to which you are unaccustomed. Similarly, if one is underdressed, it may convey the impression that one is rebellious and not the team player, or does not have the mental aptitude that the organization is looking for in their employees.

4. **Speak clearly and confidently, ensure that you are understood, and that you completely answer the specifics of each question.** Even if you do not know everything which is being asked, make an effort to provide the best possible answer. However, it may be necessary to say that one cannot answer a particular question rather than to give a stupid answer. It is important to realize that apart from attempting to assess the ability of the perspective employee to perform creditably at the position for which they are being interviewed, the interviewers may also be trying to assess your character traits such as honesty, friendliness and your ability to make competent decisions when you are working under undue pressure.

Managing Income Tax

INTRODUCTION

As the deadline for the submission of Income Tax returns approaches, many persons and institutions clamber to complete the form in an attempt to avoid paying the penalty for not complying with statutory requirement. Jesus set the example that as Christians, we should be law abiding citizens. It is true that we should not obey laws which conflict with the principles of the Bible, to the extent that we should be prepared to be martyrs, if necessary, for the sake of the gospel.

Christians and the payment of taxes

"Is it compulsory that Christians should pay taxes?"

The use of taxes by governments and other statutory bodies has been enforced in one form or another from the early period of civilization to present day. There are several types of taxes and other fiscal measures which are imposed by the government and other statutory bodies. They include:

1. *A way of recovering some of the wealth from persons or agencies which utilize the resources of the state for their own benefit and/or to make a profit,*

2. *Financing activities which other sectors of the country or community would not be willing, or are unable to undertake.* This includes the payment of the salaries of civil servants, the construction of public roads, the provision of health, educational and other public services.

3. *A method of redistribution of the wealth of the society.* Personal income, corporate income (taxation on businesses) and other activities are taxed and allocations from the proceeds are made for payment to old age pensioners, unemployment benefits and to other destitute groups,

4. *Used to assist in the management of economic aggregates such as inflation and devaluation of the local currency.* Where there is an excess liquidity, (that is, more cash, savings on the bank and other current assets), in the financial system, which can induce inflation, the government, through the Ministry of Finance or other monetary authority, may increase taxes with the intention of reducing the amount of money circulating in the economy. This method is often used in conjunction with monetary policies such as the

management of interest rates and the foreign exchange system of the country.

There are several types of taxes, including the following:

1. **Personal income taxes** where persons who earn above a statutory minimum income are required by law to pay a given amount of taxes on their salary to the government or state regulated tax authority. Employers usually make the necessary deduction from the gross income of their employees and send it to the tax authority. Persons who are self-employed are also required to pay their personal income tax monthly, quarterly or as stipulated by law. People and corporate entities usually have to submit annual income tax returns to the regulatory body for an assessment of whether or not they have paid the correct amount of taxes. A refund is usually made to persons who contributed more than they were required to contribute, while persons who have paid less than they were required to would have to pay the additional amount that was required.

   The importance of filing correct income tax returns cannot be overemphasized. Persons who attempt to defraud the system, once caught, may be prosecuted. If they are convicted, they may be fined and/or their assets confiscated by the state. It is often not easy to receive a prompt refund when one overpays one's income tax. In some countries before a person is allowed to leave the country or transfer the title of major assets such as a motor vehicle or house which is being sold or even being offered as a gift to another person, an income tax clearance certificate must be obtained to certify that no outstanding tax payment is owed.

2. **Property taxes** to the government, state or municipality are payable on land, houses, motor vehicles and other assets by the owner/s of the assets. These taxes are usually allocated to defray the cost of providing services which are directly related to the upkeep of these assets. These would include the provision and maintenance of drainage and irrigation facilities for farmland and the provision and maintenance of roads, schools, hospitals and other facilities.

3. **Corporate taxes** such as capital gains taxes, which commercial agencies are required to pay in some

countries, are usually leveled on the net income of businesses,

4. **Valued added tax (VAT)** is the tax leveled on all or a selection of goods and/or services by some governments, state or municipality expenditure. This is often a very effective method to ensure that adequate amounts of revenue are generated to finance capital and other national expenditure. This method seeks to ensure that wide cross sections of persons are contributing to the financing of the expenditure of the economy. VAT is usually charged to consumer, capital and other items which are sold and services offered to the public. The VAT, which is an addition to the markup of the seller, is usually collected by the seller and paid to the VAT office monthly or as otherwise directed. VAT is usually an unpopular form of taxation since it decreases the spending power of consumers and capital items are usually more expensive. Some Governments grant tax concessions to investors in order to promote investment.

The payment of taxes is frequently resisted by persons and institutions. There are several references in the Bible of the animosity which existed between the tax collectors and the tax payers. The tax collectors had often demanded more than the statutory amount and converted the difference for personal use. They also had the power to execute judgment such as imprisonment, confiscation of property, and enslavement of members of the defaulting family. Not-withstanding these defects Jesus admonished His disciples to adhere to the laws of taxation and other just laws.

Tax avoidance versus tax evasion

"What are some of the legitimate methods which we can use to avoid paying or at least reducing our income tax payment?"

There are several methods which tax payers use to avoid or reduce the amount of money which they pay in taxes. Persons and organizations employ the services of tax consultants, accountants, lawyers and other professionals who are versed in interpreting the income tax laws and would recommend that their client employ strategies to reduce their taxable income. Very often an accountant could use accounting principles where a company declares a loss for income tax purposes. The same accountant may produce a financial statement for the bank which shows the company generating a meager profit or meager loss. This may be in an attempt to justify the need for, or the continuation of increased bank financing. The true financial statement which is presented to the management of the company may declare a huge profit. This of course is an illegal act which could result in the imprisonment of the persons who supported this system. Christians are not expected to participate in such illegal practices.

Some organizations are also able to negotiate tax-free travel, housing, entertainment, clothing and other benefits for their staff. Where possible, employees often opt to receive a low percentage taxable income and a high non-taxable income.

Taxation Avoidance Verses Tax Evasion

- **Tax avoidance is the use of legitimate accounting and other methods to avoid or at least reduce the amount of money which one pays in taxation.**
- **Tax evasion is deliberately dogging, falsifying accounts and/or using other illegally methods to reduce the amount of taxes paid or refuse to pay taxes.**

Proportionately higher taxes for the poor versus the rich

"Is the principle of some governments to impose disproportionately high taxes and other penalties on the poor in favor of the rich necessarily wrong?"

A popular thrust of the tax policy of several countries is to impose a disproportionately higher level of income and other taxes on the poor who earn above the minimum wage and middle income persons. (The wages of persons whose earnings fall below the minimum wage are usually tax exempt). The low and middle income earners are usually the larger segments of most societies and they usually pay a higher proportional percentage of their income on income tax. Conversely, tax and other concessions are usually granted to the higher income earners and business sectors in an attempt to encourage them to save, and particularly to invest.

One of the primary reasons for this strategy is the fact that the poorer segment of most societies spends more money on consumption rather than on saving and investing. This is similar to the hierarchical Pyramid which has been popularized by Maslow, where the majority of the population who are poor, fall at the base of the pyramid. They are more focused on meeting their basic needs such as obtaining food, clothing and housing for themselves and family. As one progresses up the pyramid, the focus usually becomes more concentrated on saving and investment. However, *Maslow deviates from scriptural principles in concluding that the smaller percentage of the community at the apex of the pyramid would be more focused on self-actualization and on spiritual matters.* This is often contradictory in many societies in that the poor are often the ones to turn to the Lord since they come to realize that the Lord is their only true and lasting source. The rich on the other hand often place their confidence in their own entrepreneurial abilities, the 'security' of their material possessions and the influences which they have in the society. We are reminded that even though it is not impossibly for rich persons to become Christians, it is usually more challenging for a person who financially secured and can take care of most of his material and other needs to trust in the Lord. We are reminded of Matthew 19:24, Mark 10:25 and Luke 18:25 which state that it is difficult but not impossible for a camel to pass through the eye of a needle. It should be noted, however, that camels could have entered the literal 'Eye of a Needle' (the name given to the passage where camels entered into ancient Jerusalem), the camels which were dehydrated and their hump shrunken, were able to enter the passage. Similarly, a rich person who 'laid their burdens on the Lord,' can also become a Christian.

A high consumption pattern is good for the growth of the economy, particularly if they are consuming more locally produced commodities. Priority is usually granted to the productive sector since they would generate foreign exchange earnings by exporting their products and/or they save valuable foreign exchange, since they produce substitutes for imported commodities. In return for the high tax on the poor, economies such as the USA have established welfare systems which seek to assist the unemployed and other impoverished groups by granting social security, free, or at least subsidized medical, and other social benefits.

Correct completion of the Income Tax

"How can we manage the completion of the 'dreaded' Income Tax returns?"

The months of April or May in many countries are anxious months for most employees and business entities as they prepare to file their Income Tax returns. The forms are usually not very complex to complete and the income tax offices of many countries provide officers, as well as advertisements and conduct other educational programs to guide persons to correctly complete the income tax form. Many persons retain a copy of the forms which were filled for previous years for their personal record and this enables them to fill the forms for subsequent years consistent with previous applications.

Common features on most income tax forms include the name, address, date of birth, national registration and national insurance numbers. What make the filling of the forms complex for many persons is that they may not be conversant with an issue such as what constitutes income; since a person may receive income from rental of a property, the interest on savings account/s, dividends from shares and income from an estate which they may have inherited.

There are a number of expenditures from which one is allowed to derive a tax rebate. They may include a rebate on a stated amount on:

1. *The support of a spouse who is not working,*
2. *A maximum of two children under the age of eighteen years, or if they are over eighteen years, undertaking full time education and are being supported by the applicant,*
3. *Contribution made to charitable, religious or other organizations*. Usually the applicant has to produce evidence that this contribution was received by the recipient. It may be necessary that a **covenant** be presented by the applicant which is endorsed by the recipient that the contribution was indeed received. These may include a commitment made to contribute ten percent of his gross income to the church as his tithe. If he fails to fulfill this commitment but still claims for the amount of tax exemption which is allowed for the contribution, he has committed a fraud and thus a gross sin. The penalty for fraudulent disclosure is punishable by a huge fine and even imprisonment in some countries.
4. *Support made to dependant relatives or other persons directly under one's care*. This may include persons such as elderly relatives and one or several orphans under one's care.
5. *Interest paid on mortgage, life insurance policies, interest paid to a loan at a credit union and other acceptable claims,*

At the end of the computation, the calculation would identify whether insufficient taxes were deducted by one's employer or, for self employed persons, if they have underpaid taxes. The shortfall of the taxes due has to be paid. Where taxes were over paid, there is usually a tax rebate, once the person filing the returns is knowledgeable enough of the tax concessions which are due, the document is filled correctly and the claim is upheld by the tax authority. If the form is submitted after the official deadline for the submission by the applicant, there is usually a penalty fee even if the Inland Revenue office is to provide a tax refund to the applicant. If on the other hand an amount was payable by the applicant, a penalty fee is usually added on the amount due by the applicant unless there are extenuating circumstances such as the hospitalization of the applicant, which resulted in the delay.

Some Christians do not complete the section of the income tax form where they have to disclose how much tithes and offering they contributed, since they are of the opinion that their 'giving should be done in secret' and not disclosed to a public organization. Failure to do this would mean that they would forgo the tax rebate which they were entitled to. This amount could have been given back to the church, to a charitable organization or used for any other worthy cause, as one chooses. The disclosure of the amount contributed in tithes and offering to the Inland Revenue Department should not necessarily be viewed as a public disclosure since it is not likely to be made public unless there are extreme circumstances, such as the applicant being brought before the court, due to an allegation of false disclosure, for example

CONCLUSION

Just as it is important that we should love ourselves, it is equally important that we also invest in ourselves. This includes ensuring that we are adequately prepared to pursue the career path of our choice, attaining the positions in the organization and other factors which impact on our career and in other areas of our lives. The Lord has not only given His angels charge over us, but He also placed persons and opportunities at our disposal to assist us in the path to be a success at our station in life.

NOTES

****

Chapter 7
BUSINESS MANAGEMENT AND THE FAMILY

INTRODUCTION

This chapter reviews a sample of issues surrounding business management and the family. Increasingly, Christians are coming to the realization that apart from the professionals who are able to secure large salaries and live comfortably materially, most salary earners find it difficult to live on one source of income. As a result many persons have to secure two or more jobs, where they are available and they can be conducted without much undue difficulties and where it is economical to do so. Increasingly, persons are recognizing that it is prudent for them to engage in some business venture in order to supplement their income or as the sole source of their income. It should be noted that apart from Christians who enter business primarily for the financial returns, increasingly many Christians are entering the business arena since they view this as a ministry of witnessing to their internal and external customers, as a means of supporting their family and also to finance the spreading of the gospel.

Effective strategies of successful Christian entrepreneurs

"Are there any distinct advantages which Christians have over non-Christians which would enable Christians to be successful at business and other undertakings?"

Christians have a serious obligation to, as far as is possible, enjoy a higher standard of living than other members of society, not only in our spiritual lives, but in every area, for we are the salt of the earth and the light of the world (Matthew 5:13-16). It is recognized that salt heals, cures, irritates, flavors and preserves, among other attributes. Light also has characteristics such as dispelling darkness, hence, illuminating a given area as it exposes things that were previously hidden by darkness. Light exposes darkness and enables us to walk along the right path. These principles should be evident in the lives of believers. We have the extra impetus in the Person of the Holy Spirit, prayer, the Bible, and the church to guide us in every undertaking. In addition, we have the responsibility of being honest, hard working and displaying all the other positive attributes which are inherent in our new nature. So there is no reason why our businesses should fail because of factors such as poor management practices, lack of capital or improper use of the available resources.

Deuteronomy 28:1-4 relates some blessings which we inherit as we keep our side of the covenant to uphold the principles of the Bible. Hence, the onus is on us to secure competent financial advisors, accountants and other persons who can assist and represent us, where necessary, when negotiating with a financial institution to secure financial assistance.

Christian entrepreneurs have several advantages in their favor. These include:

1. We have the wisdom of God to direct us,
2. We have a right to enjoy the favor of the Lord, of course, when we are obedient to Him,
3. We have the backing of a family and/or the congregation in prayer,
4. A peaceful home in which to pray, relax and plan effectively for the advancement of the business venture,

In the 'body-ministry' which churches are increasingly inculcating, many congregations are endowed with believers with a wide range of academic and vocational skills who should be encouraged to share their knowledge and experiences with others. This is tantamount to the principles of the early church, where believers shared their resources. One can also receive prophetic guidance, the guidance of the word of wisdom and other spiritual gifts which have been received by various members of the congregation. Some Christian entrepreneurs could solicit a special person or group of believers who would be dedicated to consistently 'intercede' for the business. It would be beneficial if the management of such businesses provide some form of material contribution for their intercessors, even though some of them may reject such an offer but instead recommend that it be given to the church or to a charitable organization. The Board of Directors is made up of competent Christians who have the gifts of the Spirit such as 'Word of Wisdom' operating in their lives who can offer direction both in spiritual and business aspect of the company.

The time is well overdue for churches to use the talents and assets at their disposal and assist members and others in areas such as business management. It is commendable when symposiums, seminars and training programs are held for believers in areas such as financial management and the development of entrepreneurial skills. The body of Christ is also the best forum to forge allegiance with established business personnel who can assist budding businessmen and women. If we are to experience the overthrow of power base of secret societies such as lodges and the world of the occult in a greater measure, we must establish better systems of aiding each other to develop and expand in every area of our lives, which will be beneficial to the Kingdom of God.

| Is honesty really the best policy? |

"It is a common view that honesty does not lend itself to attaining and maintaining success in business. Is this true?"

There is often a debate about whether it is easier to become wealthy by being honest or dishonest. The argument that is often used to support the latter claim is that persons who indulge in drug trafficking, smuggling of commodities, prostitution, gambling, and other illicit activities, once they are not caught by law enforcement agencies or killed by rival gangs, for example, would usually become materially rich in a very short time. This reality sometimes acts as a disincentive to persons pursuing legitimate careers or businesses, when they see the wealth and affluence of their peers mushrooming overnight; where they are driving the latest model of luxury motor vehicles and living a lavish lifestyle which often characterizes persons who do not earn money legitimately.

Christians should be aware that dishonest gain lasts only for a season. Even while on earth, persons who are involved in illicit transactions would have the discomfort of living with the knowledge that their activities are destroying the lives of others, unless of course, their 'conscience is smeared.' There is also the possibility of being caught one day and disgraced in public and imprisoned for their activities. Such activities also disrupt the unity of the family, since the presence of the Lord cannot dwell where unrighteousness abounds. After death every person also has to give an account to God of our activities while we were on earth.

Several principles are necessary for the success of any business operation. They include:

1. The business must have a well-defined mission statement and vision of the organization which all staff should be committed to achieving,
2. A strong management team which is prepared as far as possible to keep abreast with the latest developments in areas that affect their operating,
3. Prudent business decision-makers who can secure the necessary capital at the best terms to manage their operations,
4. Workers who are committed to executing their tasks with maximum efficiency and where possible, surpassing their production, customer service and other targets,
5. Producing goods and/or services which are in high demand,
6. The implementation of an aggressive marketing strategy in order to surpass the sales target that is budgeted,
7.

Many of these principles are applicable to a family business and also for a large organization.

The management of a business may be engaging in dishonest practices such as robbing consumers by overpricing their products, underpaying staff, deducting personal income tax from the salary of employees and not paying it to the relevant government office, and excessively polluting the atmosphere by their waste products. Many legitimate businesses engage in practices which are dishonest but may not be indicted by law enforcement agencies since they are not caught. There are also businesses which are involved in illegal activities but are managed using many noble principles. As a result, the Bible emphasizes on the necessity for every person to have a personal relationship with the 'Second Adam' so that their minds can be renewed and they serve Him in spirit and in truth. Such a person would endeavor to ensure that all of their activities are in conformity with the principles of the Bible.

It is true that many persons who engage in sinful activities would see their business mushroom 'over night' to highly profitable entities. However, even if they were to 'gain the whole world and loose their souls, it would profit them nothing.' Even if a business where management and staff are flouting the law and engaging in other sinful practices and achieves a faster and higher rate of profitability than one practicing Biblical principles, the level of sustainability of the former business has a better history of longevity and sustainability than the former. It is only a matter of time before the Emrons and other companies where management and/or staff engage is unfair and illegal business practices, are disgraced publicly or fail because of other circumstances.

> *Christians unequally yoked in business relationship/s*

"Is the Biblical principle that Christians should not be unequally yoked applicable to our involvement in business activities and/or business partners?"

Many Christians extend the principle that Christians should not be unequally yoked to unbelievers not only in a marriage relationship but also to business and other activities. The foundation of a business owned and managed by Christians must be governed by Biblical principles such as honesty, dedication and foresight. Even though there are many non-Christians who practice these and other noble principles, a large percentage of non-Christians would more readily compromise on these principles in order to realize a higher level of profit. For these reasons, Christians cannot function efficiently in an environment where fundamental Biblical principles are consistently being flouted. It is difficult to conceive a company that produces alcoholic beverages or manufactures cigarettes, for example, being owned and/or managed by a born again believer. This is because such a company will be perpetuating the destruction of the body, soul and spirit by marketing such items. Persons who contravene such principles will contribute to a negative impact on the lives of individuals, their families and Christendom.

Some Christians correctly extend the principle that we should not be 'unequally yoked' to not purchasing shares and other securities of companies which manufacture commodities or engage in activities which are inconsistent with their faith. The outcry during the latter part of the 1980's and early 1990's regarding the boycott on purchasing shares or conducting business or purchasing commodities produced by companies which invest in South Africa, for example, was supported by many Christians who felt that these institutions were perpetuating apartheid.

In the same way, some Christian entrepreneurs do not enter a partnership, or have a minor share over a business transaction or operation, with unbelievers. This is usually in an attempt to avoid unnecessary conflicts that would arise when the unsaved partner may want to engage in unscriptural practices, such as bribing officials in an attempt to secure a contract or duty waiver and deliberately understating the profit on income tax returns, for example. This is not always an ideal situation, since it is sometimes difficult to obtain Christian partners for specific ventures. There may be some consolation where a Christian is a major shareholder, then the business can be managed consistently with the principles of one's faith.

There are several examples of the way God-fearing men in the Bible conducted business activities. A prominent example is the way Joseph conducted his business activities when he was in Egypt. As a result of the ability which God gave him to interpret Pharaoh's dream, Pharaoh appointed Joseph as his deputy, as governor over Egypt. Joseph's prudent management of the grains and other food items during the years of abundance, enabled Pharaoh to amass much wealth during the extended famine. This was because the Egyptians and surrounding nations were forced to sell and subsequently barter their cattle, and eventually their labor power in exchange for food. (It should be noted that satan often uses the calamities and even the 'elements' in his attempt to deceive man that it is wrath of Jehovah which is being poured out on man and we often referred to as an 'act of god.') It can be recalled that during that era, the Egyptians and the surrounding nations were primarily idolatrous. At the same time, the fact that God sent Joseph to Egypt and allowed the Egyptians to survive the famine is an indication that Jehovah's sovereign will is not always reflective of what we consider as fair and right, but it is unchangeable. Joseph's brothers also had to be punished for dealing unfairly with him by threatening to kill him and eventually selling him to slave traders. In addition, God used this period to show His people that He can protect them, in that Joseph was deliberately sent to Egypt to preserve the lives of the Israelites.

There are many examples in the Old Testament where believers were involved in business ventures such as cattle rearing, farming, carpentry, trading, weaving and selling of cloth. God grants a special favor that enables His people to progress in business activity, providing that they are glorifying Him in this and other areas of their lives. In Genesis Chapter 30, we read about Jacob, who used a 'scientific' method that produced an increase in the number of speckled and spotted sheep and goats and black lambs. Laban had agreed to give these animals to Jacob as final settlement of his wages.

Old Testament believers were expected to fulfill several requirements before they received God's favor. They included:

1. Produce from the first harvest of the crops and flock, were to be given to the high priest as a first fruit offering or tithe to the Lord.

2. When harvesting crops, farmers were instructed to leave a remnant for the poor, widows and orphans to glean for their own use. Boaz demonstrated this principle when Ruth, who was a widowed daughter-in-law of Naomi, gleaned in his field. This benevolent act caused Boaz to expand his wealth when he married Ruth since he inherited the land that belonged to her deceased husband. Boaz and Ruth were also blessed spiritually in that Jesus was their descendant.

3. During the year of the Jubilee, debts were forgiven. During this year, there was also provision to free persons held as slaves because of unpaid debt.

The only blessing which is given to a person in spite of identity is salvation. The ability to 'harvest' blessings is dependent on our lifestyles. God does not 'throw pearls to swine (pigs)', that is, He would not bless us if we are not mature enough to manage that blessing in a way which would glorify Him since we are immature and cannot use it efficiently and effectively. Every blessing is linked to identity. Deuteronomy 8 illustrates that certain actions have to be done to reap certain blessings. This principle is also supported by the Beatitudes. Unmerited favor or grace is the power to become the person or to perform the act God requires.

Effective business strategies

"What are some important strategies which should be applied when managing a business?"

Irrespective of how small or large a business undertaking is, the basic principle of effective budgeting requires that a realistic projection be made of the effect of the activities that are likely to occur during the year and beyond on the performance of the business. Management must be able to ascertain in the short, medium and long term, what we are aiming to achieve. Factors which have to be considered before establishing a business include:

1. **Selecting the best product to be manufactured, process to be conducted, crop to be planted and/or**

service to be provided; where cheap raw materials and other resources which are needed for the successful operation of the business are available in abundance.

2. **Employing the best possible technology** which is within the financial capability of the business is essential. Important factors to consider in this area include efficiency in the production process, operating with the lowest possible cost of production and yet consistently produce the desired quality and quantity output.

3. **Recruiting and maintaining suitable qualified staff;** it is essential that the necessary skills to man the operation of the business are readily available at a realistic cost to ensure the continual profitability of the business.

Many Christians omit the important principle of recording a **vision statement** for their business. In the same way as a vision is essential in our personal lives and that of the church, it is also important in business undertakings. The modus operandi of the business may change over time, but very often the vision remains the same or it may be expanded. For this reason, when starting a business, entrepreneurs must ensure that their Memorandum and Articles of Association are not restrictive, but will allow them latitude to conduct the business activities that are within their vision without the need to incur additional legal and other expenses to register a new business.

Managing the family business

"What are some of the challenges which are common in managing a family business?"

Business activities such as commercial farming, the sale of groceries, hardware and other products, the manufacturing of items and the provision of services have been the primary source of income for many families. These businesses may be wholly managed by members of the family or they occupy the key positions or at least are the major shareholders of such entities. As alluded to earlier, business entities operated by Christian families will prosper, once they are giving their tithes and offerings, and obeying the other commands of the Bible, such as being prudent, strategizing and making wise business decisions, they will prosper. However, there is a tendency for such businesses to lose the autonomy which the family had as they expand. This often occurs since as the business expands, the need arises for the injection of additional equity which the family may not have, even to qualify for a large loan. They may be forced to accept one or several partners. Secondly, a business may become so large that management feel that it would be more economical to sell shares than to secure additional credit. The other partners/shareholders are the additional owners of the business.

In many traditional societies it is advantageous when there are many children in a family. The more persons there are in the family, the more pairs of hands are available to provide cheap labor for the family business. The advantages of using family members in a business include the fact that it enable them to retain the profit and assets of the business in the family. In addition, trade secrets and the confidentiality of unique business practices are also protected, while they are assured of a place of employment.

There are extreme instances in countries such as India, Brazil, and in several African countries, where child labor is still exploited. Children are often used as major sources of providing income to their families by working as laborers on farms, factories and other activities. There are also instances where children are forced to beg and even engage in stealing and prostitution to support their parents who may or may not be disabled, sick and/or very old. Children are also used as herders for cattle, to sell in shops and engage in other income generating activities for their parents and in some instances for themselves, as occurs with street children.

In farming communities in LDCs, boys above a given age may have to accompany elders to the farm to learn basic techniques such as clearing the land and planting crops, while adults perform the more strenuous tasks such as plowing the land. As the child matures, he will be given more strenuous tasks and may eventually be given his own plot to manage.

In some traditionally societies the ownership of land, animals reared by the family and other major assets are handed down from the father to the eldest son when the father dies or is unable to continue his role as breadwinner of the family due to sickness. The inheritance of such properties is usually saddled with the responsibility of caring for the members of the family. Provision is usually made for the brother of the deceased to inherit such properties in circumstances such as when the deceased did not have a son. In some polygamous societies, such properties are given to the brother of the deceased who may have to marry the widow of the deceased and continue his lineage. This practice has resulted in disastrous consequences when the deceased died from AIDS, for example.

Chapter 4 of the Book of Ruth relates where the most eligible relative of Naomi's late husband, Elimelech, was willing to secure the land which belonged to her deceased husband, but he was unwilling to marry her widowed daughter-in-law. (In this instance marriage was necessary for the transfer of land and her husband's inheritance). Therefore, Boaz, who was mentioned in the line of relationship of Elimelech, was free to redeem the land and marry Ruth.

Family businesses are often inherited from ancestors. In many instances older relatives are reluctant to release the reigns of control of such entities to younger relatives. The rationale very often is that they are fearful that the younger generation would not appreciate the amount of sacrifice, planning, energy and resources which will injected in establishing the business entity to its present status. Such assets may be depleted or abandoned in a very callous manner because of the new owners:

1. Could not appreciate the potential which is in the business. In such examples persons who are aware of its full value may deceive the new owner into disposing of it cheaply, as illustrated in the maxim 'easy come, easy go.' The fear is often that the person inheriting the business, which the founder and subsequent generations may have labored extensively for, often will not appreciate its value.
2. Might be unable to manage it and are reluctant or unable to secure competent personnel to do so; or
3. May be interested in financing another business venture or to engage in other economic activities, hence, the interest to carry on the family tradition may not be very appealing or even financially viable.

Abandoning a family business which may have been successfully operated by previous generations is a sad event. In some instances it is necessary to change several of the methods used by one's predecessors in order to increase production and productivity or the output of the service. This becomes necessary because of factors such as the introduction of new technology and increasing competition due to globalization. This process of modernization may include the construction of a new building or the renovation of the existing one, the establishing of new plant and equipment, changes in the management structure and the recruitment of more academically and professionally qualified staff. This decision may cause a rift in the family, with elders clambering for family loyalty, while the younger generation may be supporting the necessity for modernization. The youths may advocate that the change is the only, or at least the most feasible, way of surviving in an increasingly competitive business environment. Once the necessity for modernization is marketed properly, the elders in the family may eventually be convinced of the wisdom of adopting the new strategy. In fact, the primary concern of the elders of the family may be to ensure that the family retains the ownership of the business and that the business continues to generate substantial returns for the family. Sometimes as is seen in generational gaps, it is the unwillingness of the older family members to change traditions which are outmoded.

There are examples where a privately owned business is forced to go public because of the need to secure a large amount of capital for necessary investment, needed to make the company profitable and remaining competitive. In many such instances the company goes public by selling ordinary shares. The family may be able to retain a significant percentage of the capital and ownership of the company in the form of preferential shares and a large amount of ordinary shares. There may also be clauses in the Articles of Association of the company which entitles preferential shareholders to receive some form of financial remuneration regardless of whether or not the company realizes a profit in a given year. Unpaid dividends for the years of loss may have to be paid with an agreed interest during the year of profitability. It is noted that companies which have a large percentage of preferential shares are usually not as attractive to private investors. This is because preferential shareholders usually receive a disproportionately higher percentage of dividends of the company relative to ordinary shareholders.

The management of a family business is prone to several additional problems than those encountered by non-family owned businesses. They include:

1. Suggestions of younger members of the family may be overruled by the elderly members of the family not necessarily on the basis of the flaw of the recommendation. The objection may be primarily on the basis of elders of the family believing that younger family members are not likely to be as knowledgeable as the elderly. This situation may occur when elders maintain an autocratic management style which demonstrates that being older is synonymous to being

wiser since they have a large number of years of experience of working with the institution and they are the ones controlling the finances of the business. In such instances younger members of the family may not be given senior appointments in the business even though they may be qualified to do so. This sad occurrence is evident in several instances where the family may have invested much in educating a family member in a specialized strategic area of the business. This is usually in order to maintain the control of the business in the family and to provide a lucrative career opportunity for their offspring. After being qualified, the young person may take advantage of more lucrative job opportunities which are available in other agencies which offer more attractive benefits. This may be an attractive alternative, particularly if the elders in the family business are not very receptive to accepting sound business proposals from younger relatives.

2. Introducing changes or hiring more experienced non-family members in strategic positions, may result in the displacement of family members and may result in major family disputes since there are emotional implications and family loyalty considerations which may take precedence over purely business decisions.

3. Family members may be underpaid and promotion may be based on chronological order of seniority and years of service rather than one's competence and qualification.

4. Serious disagreements on the worksite may interfere with their personal lives. The effect could be that they live in an environment where there is much tension at home as well as on the job.

5. Younger members of the family, after seeing the success or failure of their elders, may decide to embark on their own line of business which may even be in competition with the family business.

The more established family businesses have been maintained primarily because there is a conscious effort on the part of the management of the business to promote excellence in the mode of operation of the entity, with less importance given to family loyalty. This process may be facilitated by maintaining the services of only the most competent family members on the work force and emphasizing that each member of the family who are involved in the business should be highly trained in vital areas of the operations of the business.

In some instances, much effort is placed on maintaining family control on the Board of Directors of the company and in very senior and strategic positions in the business. The family may also employ the services of renowned lawyers and financial and other advisors in an attempt to be assured that the interest of the family is well protected.

The Christian family business has the potential to become a very profitable entity once they allow the Spirit of the Lord to lead it. There are examples of such families having morning devotion at home and/or on the work site to start the workday in the correct way. As expected, all transactions of the Christian business have to be conducted in a manner which reflects the practice of high Christian values. The management of some of these businesses tithe from the net income of the business. This practice will be more difficult once the business goes public and the laws of the country may not facilitate such practices, yet companies have sought to circumvent barriers of this nature by making contributions to charitable and other organizations as well as to other worthy causes. In addition, individual shareholders can also tithe from their dividend and other returns from the business and employees can tithe from their salaries. These practices will attract the blessings of the Lord in the personal lives of the employees, owners of the business and also lead to the expansion and greater profitability and viability of the business.

A distinct advantage of a family business is that a progressive member of the family may be given the unique opportunity to advance rapidly up the management channel. With the correct attitude and willingness to learn, one can receive rapid promotion since he already has the 'right contacts,' in the persons of other family members who are willing to see the business progress. This is not always a straightforward maneuver since there can also be vicious fights among siblings to get to the top.

Starting the new business on a solid foundation

"What are some of the principles which can be adopted to push start a new business in the right direction?"

Many Christians are desirous of starting their own business or expanding on a small-scale operation. It is so sad that many such persons do not know the essential things which they should do to ensure that the business succeeds and generates the high level of financial returns which they envisage. It is a fact that there is a high rate of business failure particularly in their first five years of operations. After the first few critical years, as the management becomes versed in managing the business, once they remain proactive in their business decisions, their chances of survival are usually increased. However, exogenous factors (which are beyond the normal control of management) such as the level of interest rates, inflation, exchange rates, the stability of the economy and other factors which are beyond their control must be taken into account when planning such undertakings.

There are several factors which influence persons who decide to embark on a business activity and which also influence the type of business they undertake. They include:

1. *The vision or some other form of revelation from the Lord of a specific direction in this area.* This may include the type of business activity which one should be involved in, the method of raising finance, the location of the business and the staff to be hired. Businesses are also formed when someone recognizes a demand for a particular product or service which is in short supply or which has the potential to offer lucrative profits. The organization's vision, objective, mission statement and other management framework must be formulated to ensure that the direction of management is maintained and developed as required.

2. *A thorough feasibility study should be conducted to ensure that the business venture is feasible, taking cognizance of the cost/benefit analysis of the business to ensure that it is not merely a dream.* If it is, one may awake one day to realize that a large amount of money was wasted and there is much frustration when persons have to be laid off because of a failed business venture.

3. *Know who one's major competitors will be,* even for a product for which one will have a monopoly, or be able to capture a niche market, account must be taken of what competitors are doing and how one would be able to capture the required percentage of the market to ensure that the business is profitable.

4. *The entrepreneur/s will have to decide on the method they will use to raise capital.* This may include using their personal savings, borrowing from friends and other business associates and/or the church,

borrowing from a financial institution such as a commercial bank or issuing shares to the public.

5. *Be aware of the cost of securing the level of technology which is required to make the business competitive.* Some types of businesses require that the company keeps abreast with current levels of technology which might require that a Research and Development department is established to ensure that the company stays one step ahead of, or at least abreast with competitors.

6. *Identifying and securing the best possible location of the business is very important.* Considerations such as the cost of transporting the raw materials to the business and the cost of transporting the finished product to the market or directly to customers are also important.

7. *Depending on the magnitude of the business, it may be necessary to at least register the business as a sole proprietorship or as a company.* For a company, their Article and Memorandum of Association may have to be formulated. These documents outline features such as who are the shareholders, the scope of the business, the amount of share capital injected by each partner and the method of distribution of profits.

8. *It is important that competent contractors are hired to construct the building for the factory, or the best possible building is purchase or rented to house the business.* In addition, machinery purchased must be of the correct type and quality to ensure that the production process is at the required standard, quantity and other specifications which have to be met.

9. *The best possible staff must be recruited and any relevant training provided to ensure that the required product and/or service targets are met with as little disruptions as possible.* The larger businesses would have to recruit specialists in areas such as marketing, financial analysts, accountants, personnel officers and other specialists and junior staff to manage the daily operations of the business. For smaller businesses, it would be necessary that the persons managing the business at least be familiar with basic book keeping principles, marketing and other practices which will enhance their success. It is important to maintain an excellent working relationship between management

and other staff to foster minimal disruptions due to industrial actions and also that employees would maximize production. This is so since they are confident that management has their best interest at heart and that every effort is being made to cater for their wellbeing, including the provision of adequate medical insurance, pension and other benefits where possible.

10. *Efficient marketing of product and/or service is absolutely necessary since it would be futile to produce a product or offer a service which is not in demand by customers at the required level to make the operations profitable.* The packaging of the product also has a very significant effect on attracting and maintaining customer loyalty.

11. *It would be necessary to secure ISO certification or at least the certification of the local competent authority that the product meets national standard specifications particularly for larger businesses, primarily those which are involved in export.* This is absolutely important since it gives consumers from foreign countries the confidence that the product is not one of questionable character.

It is a fact that a large percentage of businesses, and in particular small businesses, fail in their first year of operation. A primary reason is that the lofty ideas which the entrepreneurs had when the business was conceptualized, were not as easy to realize in the real world. The owner of a business which failed, classified the business climate as a '*dog-eat-dog world*' since his experience was that the atmosphere was not conducive for the successful operations of new businesses. Of course this is not a general view since each year many new businesses strive and become major operations. Other reasons why new businesses fail include:

1. *The entrepreneur/manager may not be very educated* and is unwilling to take advice from, or surround himself with experts who would be able to take the business to the level where it is needed to be competitive.

2. *Essential features such as formulating and adhering to a strategic or long-term plan is lacking in many of these businesses.*

3. *Management is unable to secure the additional capital* needed to purchase the working capital requirements and fixed assets needed for their

expansion of the business.

4. **The inappropriate use of finance**, where, for example, management diverts the funds from an overdraft to finance long term investment. The result may be that when the management of the bank recognizes this, they may cancel the overdraft limit and/or foreclose on any security held as surety for the overdraft.

5. **The cost of capital was too expensive**; for example, this factor is illustrated where the projected return is over-ambitious and management is unable to adequately service the credit facility.

6. **Difficulties experienced with managing employees** including industrial actions which results in contracts being cancelled and embezzlement by dishonest employees.

As advocated in the Bible, a person has to count the cost of establishing the business and keeping it in operation before embarking on such a course. If it is not working out as expected, it may be necessary to abandon the operation rather than consistently operating it at a loss over a number of years. It is true that at the initial stage of the operation of a business it may be necessary to operate at breakeven point (where the cost of production is equal to the sale) in the short run. However, it is expected that the profitability of the business will increase, as its product becomes popular on the market and as the company is operated more efficiently and management attains other positive attributes.

Accounting and the small business

"What are some of the important accounting principles which even a small business owner should become familiar with?"

There are several financial terms with which one should be familiar when starting a business. They include the balance sheet, income statement and cash flow statement. The balance sheet identifies the value of the assets, liabilities and the shareholder's equity (the input and/or ownership by the owners of the business). The income statement relates the amount of sales and/or other sources of income which was generated by the business and how it was spent and allocated. Many large businesses do not sell and purchase only on a cash basis. Therefore, accounting categories such as Accounts Receivable and Accounts Payable and other non-cash transactions are shown in the Balance Sheet and Income

Statements. The cash flow statement presents a more concise picture of the source and uses of cash transactions in the business. The nature and details of these financial statements is dependant on the type and size of the business.

Some of important areas for the **Balance Sheet** are:

1. **The assets of the business**; these usually include:
   a. Current assets such as the amount of cash which the owner/s of the business has on its premises and in the bank.
   b. Receivable, that is payments for goods and/or services supplied on credit and
   c. Working capital items such as stocks which would be used for future production and/or items to be sold. There may also be fixed assets such as building, furniture and fixtures, plant and machinery. There may also be other assets such as motor vehicles.

2. The **Liability** identifies the sources and uses of funds from external sources such as loans from a bank which were used to finance the operations of the business.

3. The **Shareholder's Equity** on the other hand, identifies items such as the amount of cash injected by the shareholders, and the amount of the net profit which has been retained by the business for future investment.

The Income Statement identifies the amount of revenue earned by the business and the amount of expenditure which was incurred in order to generate the level of net income of the business. A typical income statement would have the following features:

Income Statement
Phoenix Small Business Inc.
Year Ending December 2014

Total Sales Revenue		**$5,550.65**
Cost of goods sold:		
Salaries	$398.85	
Purchases	$328.61	
Utilities, rent and other general expenses	$425.76	**$1,153.22**
Gross Income		**$4,397.43**
Interest expense	$620.72	
Net Income After Interest Expenses		**$3,776.71**
Less corporate tax (at 40%)		$1,510.68
Net Income After Interest & Taxation		$2,266.03

Table 7.1 Hypothetical Income Statement of the Phoenix Small Business Inc.

Even though the Net Income or Net Profit After Interest and Tax of $2,266.03 represents the amount of profit which was earned for the year, the company may not have all of this as cash since the company may have outstanding payments due from its customers and may still have to pay suppliers for items supplied during the 2013 financial year. The actual cash which the company has at the end of the financial year is shown in the Cash Flow Statement.

CONCLUSION

The Bible has numerous examples of followers of Jehovah who were very successful materially and otherwise. However, apart from the same level of success which Christians can achieve from engaging in many of the activities mentioned above, there is also the fact that we receive divine intervention from the Lord to enable us to succeed above the level which non-Christians achieve. Unfortunately, most Christians do not attain our full potential since we do not seek, knock and/or wait on the Lord for the 'doors' to be opened and/or we do not consistently abide under His anointing, so that His blessings can continuously abide with us. It is true that as Christians, the spiritual aspect of our lives should be the primary focus of our lives, of course, without neglecting the sole and body. Nevertheless, we have to ensure that whatever income generating activity we engage in to sustain our family, we have to dedicate adequate time, energy and other resources to be classified as good stewards of the material and other assets of our family.

It is true that as Christians, we will be tempted by satan in every area of our lives. Thankfully not many of us experience the extreme as Job did, where we lose children, just about every aspect of our material possession and are also afflicted with extreme sickness. Nevertheless, we should be prepared, even for the extreme of accepting to be killed for the gospel. However, as conquerors in Christ, not every day of our lives will be a 'bed of roses,' for we will experience trials and tribulations. The difference is that we do not have to go through these experiences alone, for Jehovah promised the Children of Israel in in Deuteronomy 32:8, is also applicable all Believers: "[8]It is Lord who goes before you. He will be with you: He will not fail you or forsake you. Do not fear or be dismayed." Our responsibility is to 'abide under His anointing and stay under His control.'

In an effort to ensure that we are not pursuing a path which is inconsistent to His will and do not accept unwanted suffering or follow a path which is not in keeping with his perfect will for us. We also have to ensure that we 'stay connected to Christ – the True Vine, Who is our source of our sustenance.

NOTES

****

SELECTED REFERENCES

Burkett, Larry,   **Money Matters**, Thomas Nelson Publishers, USA, 2001.

Kiyosaki, Robert T. and
Lechter, Sharon L.   **Cash Flow Quadrant**, TechPress Inc., USA, 1999.

New Revised Standard Version, **The Holy Bible**, World Bible Publisher, Inc., USA, 1989.

Orman, Suze.   **The Road to Wealth**, Penguin Putnam Inc., USA, 2001.

World Bible Publishers Inc.   **The Holy Bible, New Revised Standard Version** USA, 1989.

Williams, Gladwin B.   **Financial Matters & the Family**, Create Space, USA, 2014.

ABOUT THE AUTHOR

Gladwin B. Williams is a Christian Counselor who specialized in Pre-Marital and Financial Management Counseling. He has fellowshipped with the Full Gospel Fellowship in Guyana. He has also been associated with the Assembles of God in Bangor, Wales, UK; in Maryland, USA; and in Guyana, the Abiding Word Ministries, The Gambia, West Africa and the People's Cathedral Ministries, Barbados, West Indies and a graduate of the Banjul Bible School. He recently held a position of lecturer at the University of Guyana, South America, and currently is the CEO of Island Castle Inc., an international financial consultant company. He has functioned in the noble office of an elder of the Stanleytown Full Gospel Fellowship, Guyana, where he was the Pre-Marital Counselors for the Fellowship. He also served in this capacity with the Abiding Word Ministries in The Gambia, West Africa. He is currently fellowshipping with the People's Cathedral in Barbados, West Indies.

Other books by Gladwin B. Williams include:
1. *A Prelude to Marital Bliss*
2. *What Does Sex Have to Do with it?*
3. *Financial Matters and the Family*
4. *From Genesis to Destiny*

For further information, the author can be contacted by email at: gladwilliams@yahoo.com

www.ingramcontent.com/pod-product-compliance
Lightning Source LLC
Chambersburg PA
CBHW051851170526
45168CB00001B/60